# CENTERING PRAYER
*and the Healing of the Unconscious*

# CENTERING PRAYER
## and the Healing of the Unconscious

## MURCHADH Ó MADAGÁIN

Lantern Books • New York
A Division of Booklight, Inc.

2007

Lantern Books

One Union Square West, Suite 201

New York, NY 10003

LIBRARY OF CONGRESS CATALOGING-IN-PUBLICATION DATA

O'Madagain, Murchadh.
Centering prayer and the healing of the unconscious /
Murchadh O'Madagain.
p. cm.
Includes bibliographical references.
ISBN-13: 978-1-59056-107-2 (alk. paper)
ISBN-10: 1-59056-107-4 (alk. paper)
1. Contemplation. 2. Subconsciousness. 3. Psychology,
Religious. I. Title.
BV5091.C7O66 2007
248.3—dc22

2007013615

*To my parents*

# Acknowledgments

THIS BOOK WAS ORIGINALLY a thesis to which I gave much time and energy and thoroughly enjoyed. However, no work like this is done merely by the author. I want to acknowledge all the help and encouragement that I got from so many people, which enabled me to keep going and eventually finish. I want to thank Fr. Thomas Keating, whose writings have inspired me and helped me so much in my own spiritual journey. I want to thank Fr. Fabio Giardini who guided me through my initial studies in this whole area during my time in Rome. I also want to thank my family, without whose help and ongoing support I would not have had the strength to persevere. I would like to remember and thank the many friends who have helped me along the way, in the Irish College in Rome, the Poor Clares in Galway, the Fraternity of Mary Immaculate Queen in Galway and so many other individual people who are too numerous to mention. Above all, I want to praise and thank God for giving me the gift of faith and the chance to explore this great adventure that is the spiritual life.

# TABLE OF CONTENTS

# ABBREVIATIONS

ASCENT   Ascent of Mount Carmel, from *The Collected Works of St. John of the Cross*, translated by Kieran Kavanaugh and Otilio Rodriguez, copyright © 1964, 1979, 1991 by Washington Province of Discalced Carmelites, ICS Publications, 2131 Lincoln Road N.E., Washington, DC 20002-1199 U.S.A., www.icspublications.org.

BWL   *Jesus Christ the Bearer of the Water of Life: A Christian Reflection on the "New Age,"* Pontifical Council for Culture, Pontifical Council for Inter-religious Dialogue.

C   *Conferences*, The Classics of Western Spirituality, John Cassian, Colm Luibheid (trans.), New York: Paulist Press, 1985.

CCC   *Catechism of the Catholic Church*, Dublin: Veritas, 1994.

CL   *Consecrated Life in the Third Millennium: Starting Afresh from Christ*, Congregation for Institutes of Consecrated Life and Societies of Apostolic Life, London: CTS, 2002.

CLOUD   *The Cloud of Unknowing and The Book of Privy Counselling*, William Johnston, (ed.), New York: Doubleday, 1996.

IC   Interior Castle, *The Collected Works of St. Teresa of Avila, Volume One*, translated by Kieran Kavanaugh and Otilio Rodriguez, copyright © 1976 by Washington Province of Discalced Carmelites, ICS Publications, 2131 Lincoln Road

           N.E., Washington, DC 20002-1199 U.S.A.,
           www.icspublications.org.

IWG        *Intimacy with God*, Thomas Keating, New York:
           Crossroad, 2002.

ITL        *Invitation to Love: The Way of Christian
           Contemplation*, Thomas Keating, New York:
           Continuum, 2000. Reprinted with the permission
           of the publisher, The Continuum International
           Publishing Group.

LIFE       Life, *The Collected Works of St. Teresa of Avila,
           Volume One*, translated by Kieran Kavanaugh
           and Otilio Rodriguez, copyright © 1976 by
           Washington Province of Discalced Carmelites,
           ICS Publications, 2131 Lincoln Road N.E.,
           Washington, DC 20002-1199 U.S.A.,
           www.icspublications.org.

LD         *The Ladder of Divine Ascent*, John Climacus,
           Colm Luibheid and Norman Russell (trans.), The
           Classics of Western Spirituality, Mahwah, NJ:
           Paulist Press, 1982.

LF         The Living Flame of Love, from *The Collected
           Works of St. John of the Cross*, Kieran Kavanaugh
           and Otilio Rodriguez (trans.), Revised Edition,
           Washington DC: ICS, 1991.

LG         Lumen Gentium, Austin Flannery (ed.), *Vatican
           Council II, The Conciliar and Postconciliar
           Documents*, Vol. I, Revised Edition, Dublin:
           Dominican Publications, 1975.

NIGHT      Dark Night, from *The Collected Works of St.
           John of the Cross*, Kieran Kavanaugh and Otilio
           Rodriguez (trans.), Revised Edition, Washington
           DC: ICS, 1991.

NMI        *Apostolic Letter, Novo Millennio Ineunte*, John
           Paul II, Rome: Libreria Editrice Vaticana, 2001.

OF      *Orationis Formas: On Some Aspects of Christian Meditation*, Congregation for the Doctrine of the Faith, Boston: Pauline, 1998

OM      *Open Mind Open Heart: The Contemplative Dimension of the Gospel*, Thomas Keating, New York: Continuum, 2000. Reprinted with the permission of the publisher, The Continuum International Publishing Group.

PR      *Praktikos*, from *Evagrius Ponticus: Praktikos and Chapters on Prayer*, translated by John Eudes Bamberger OSCO, Cistercian Studies Series Number 4. Kalamazoo, Michigan: Cistercian Publications, 1981. All rights reserved.

PDV      *Pastores Dabo Vobis: Post-Synodal Apostolic Exhortation on the Formation of Priests in the Circumstances of the Present Day*, John Paul II, London: CTS, 1992.

ST      *Summa Theologica*, Vol. I, St. Thomas Aquinas, Fathers of the English Dominican Province (trans.), New York: Benziger Brothers, 1947.

VC      *Vita Consecrata: Post-Synodal Apostolic Exhortation of the Holy Father: Consecrated Life, John Paul II*, Boston: Pauline, 1996.

WP      Way of Perfection, *The Collected Works of St. Teresa of Avila, Volume Two,* translated by Kieran Kavanaugh and Otilio Rodriguez, copyright © 1980 by Washington Province of Discalced Carmelites, ICS Publications, 2131 Lincoln Road N.E., Washington, DC 20002-1199 U.S.A., www.icspublications.org.

All biblical references in this work are taken from *The New Jerusalem Bible*, London: Darton, Longman & Todd, 1985, unless otherwise stated.

# INTRODUCTION

IN HIS BEST-SELLING BOOK, *Man's Search for Meaning*, the psychiatrist Viktor E. Frankl, gives a stark account of how he survived one of the Nazi concentration camps of the Second World War and what went on there. During his ordeal in this abyss of the most unimaginable human misery, Frankl observed the people around him, their behavior, the many who died, but perhaps more interestingly those who survived. What was curious was that those who survived the most horrendous conditions were not necessarily the strongest physically. Instead, it was often those who seemed to be motivated "spiritually." Those who were determined to survive because of their desire to see a loved one again, or because of their faith, had an ability to keep going even when many others could not take it anymore. The inner motivation that they had gave them an almost superhuman ability to keep going. Frankl realized the importance of what could generally be called the "spiritual life." When it came to extreme conditions of human suffering, having a deeper sense of purpose, or a broader vision than the immediate world provided, made all the difference. Here before his eyes was a powerful witness to humanity's need for meaning. Humanity continues to search for meaning and to try to make sense of a world that can sometimes seem incredibly cruel.

Today in the West there is a deep hunger for the spiritual, which can be seen from the enormous interest that is being shown in just about everything that comes under the heading of "spiritual." In bookshops, the biggest selling area is often the occult section. Many feel spiritually starved and are searching for something to satisfy this hunger. The Catholic Church has always had a very rich spiritual tradition, but in more recent years the contemplative dimension of the Gospel has experienced a certain neglect. While it should be the means to feed those who are spiritually starved, it is not. This has come about from a combination of factors that we will look at later on.

My first introduction to centering prayer was several years ago, through a friend of mine—an enclosed religious sister—who gave me a set of audiocassettes by Fr. Thomas Keating on centering prayer and the spiritual journey. I had previously read quite a number of books on the subject of contemplation, as it was an area of interest to me for some time. However, these tapes were the first presentation of a practice to help one in the direction of contemplative prayer, or prayer of silence, in a way that made complete sense to me. I was impressed. Unlike most books I had read on the subject, Keating's work uses modern terminology and generally avoids the more traditional terms applied to such matters. I later learned that he did this quite deliberately, as he realized that so many people were prejudiced against contemplative prayer through mis-education, and that the mere mention of the usual terminology tended to switch people off before they had a chance to be taken further.

In this book we will explore what has become known as "centering prayer." We will see that it is in fact a centuries-old form of prayer. We will also look at the claim that one of the fruits of this kind of prayer is the healing of the unconscious.

Since Thomas Keating is probably the best-known writer on centering prayer, we will also refer to his works quite a bit and compare what he says to some of the more tried and trusted writers, such as Teresa of Avila and John of the Cross.

## TERMINOLOGY

Before we begin, we should make a few points about the terminology that will be used. One of the difficulties that we meet in current writings to do with meditation and contemplation is a confusion of terminology. In the Eastern religious traditions, the words "meditation" and "contemplation" mean the exact opposite to what they have traditionally meant in the West. In the religions of the East, the word "meditation" is understood to mean an exercise that is completely silent, going beyond thoughts, words, and images. In the West, however, meditation—often more clearly distinguished as "discursive meditation" (going from one idea to another)—means reflecting on something, such as a passage from the scriptures or a mystery of the rosary. The term "contemplation," on the other hand, in the East has usually meant reflecting over an idea, or mystery, while in the West it has traditionally meant the prayer of silence, which is a gift from God that we can only dispose ourselves to receive. To add to the confusion, because of a more recent interest in meditation as taught by Eastern gurus, the terms are now often intermixed without people realizing that they can have completely different interpretations. Thus two people might tell you to "make a meditation on your own," while meaning two completely opposite practices. Because of this confusion we need to be clear as to what expressions mean what.

Centering prayer—while it is not, strictly speaking, contemplation in the Western sense—is very much a stepping-stone to contemplation. In this work the term "contemplative prayer" refers to the Theresian understanding of contemplative prayer, that is, a prayer of silence, or resting in God, that usually follows discursive meditation. It is something that is given by God and sustained by God. We can neither initiate it, nor sustain it, only be disposed to it. Keating defines it as:

> The development of one's relationship with Christ to the point of communing beyond words, thoughts, and feelings; a process of moving from the simplified activity of waiting upon God to the ever increasing predominance of the gifts of the Spirit as the source of one's prayer.[1]

It can also be understood—unless otherwise stated—that centering prayer is leading one to contemplative prayer. Apart from this, the term "meditation" on its own will refer to the same kind of prayer that involves disregarding the usual flow of thoughts, while "discursive meditation" will refer to the Western understanding of the term, that is, a reflecting on, or mulling over, a thought, idea, or mystery, etc. I hope that the use of each term will be clear as we come to it.

## Chapter 1

# THE BEGINNINGS
# OF CENTERING PRAYER

FR. THOMAS KEATING, O.C.S.O. (Trappist), is an
American Cistercian priest, monk, and abbot, currently living in St. Benedict's monastery, Snowmass,
Colorado. Born in Rhode Island on March 7, 1923
to a wealthy although not particularly religious family, he experienced an awakening of his faith while
studying at Yale. He found his religious worldview
deeply challenged by a philosophy class, which got
him thinking about his faith. Anne Simpkinson, in an
interview with Keating, describes the initial experience that he shared with her and about what first got
him interested in the contemplative side of his faith:

> While in the library reading Thomas Aquinas'
> *Catena Aurea*, a line-by-line exposition of the
> four Gospels by the great Church fathers, he
> experienced a profound conversion: He deeply
> grasped the fact that Christianity was a contem-
> plative religion. He realized that the spiritual
> sense of the Scripture was much more important
> than the literal and that union with the Divine

was not only possible but available to all. "That insight," says the seventy-four-year-old Trappist monk, "was the seed that has continued to grow all through my life. What I am doing now is trying to share that insight."[1]

After he graduated from Fordham University in 1943, Keating entered the Cistercians in Valley Falls, Rhode Island. Later he became novice master and then abbot, and has spent most of his life both practicing and studying contemplative prayer. Because of a fire in their monastery, the monks later moved to St. Joseph's Abbey in Spencer, Massachusetts. In 1971, Keating attended a meeting of Trappist superiors in Rome, where Pope Paul VI addressed them and asked them to try to help the Church rediscover the contemplative dimension of the Gospel. Throughout the 1970s, as the monks of St. Joseph's watched many thousands of people going to the East each Summer in search of "enlightenment" and to experience something of the Eastern traditions of meditation, they felt a great desire to set up some way of introducing people to the rich tradition of contemplative prayer that the Church has to offer—a tradition that so many were unaware of. As a result, in 1975, Fr. William Meninger developed the contemplative practice that became known as Centering Prayer, based on the fourteenth century classic *The Cloud of Unknowing*. This was then offered at retreats for priests, although it was mostly lay people who took the practice up with great enthusiasm. Fr. Basil Pennington also joined in the work, and retreats and workshops began to be offered to an ever-widening circle of interested people. In 1981, Thomas Keating resigned as abbot of St. Joseph's and moved to St. Benedict's Monastery in Snowmass, Colorado. He then began to explore the possibility of intensive centering prayer retreats. In 1983, the first intensive retreat was held at the Lama Foundation, San Cristobal, New Mexico. Since then, these retreats have become increasingly popular. They are now in great demand in the United States and are slowly beginning to acquire interest in Europe.

Thomas Keating is a founder of the Centering Prayer movement and of Contemplative Outreach. He has written extensively on the subject of contemplative prayer, and especially on centering prayer as a doorway to contemplative prayer.

Keating holds that it is important to present contemplative prayer and the method of centering prayer in a modern form, using psychological language, since so many people have a prejudiced idea of the spiritual life and are easily turned off by using the more traditional terminology:

> It is my conviction that the language of psychology is an essential vehicle in our time to explain the healing of the unconscious effected during the dark nights which Saint John of the Cross describes. For one thing, it is a language that is better understood than the traditional language of spiritual theology, at least in the western world. It also provides a more comprehensive understanding of the psychological dynamics which grace has to contend with in the healing and transforming process.[2]

## WHAT IS "SILENT PRAYER"?

Before we go any further we need to address one important question: What do we mean by silent prayer, or contemplative prayer, and why should we bother with it anyway? When we begin to take our spiritual life seriously at all, when we open the door to the Holy Spirit and allow the Spirit to lead us forward in our relationship with God, the Spirit takes us through various different stages of growth, bringing us ever deeper and "closer" to God. This may take various forms. It may be that someone suddenly decides that they want to learn a bit more about their faith, or it may take the form of a conversion experience, as it did with me. Whatever form it takes is not really important. What is important is that we respond to this invitation from the Holy Spirit to begin or deepen our relationship with God. After an initial awakening of our faith we may experience great joy and enthusiasm. Perhaps we might become interested again in the mass as never before, or begin reading scripture for the first time. We may find that we have a new interest in our faith as never before. Either way, let us say that our faith has been rekindled to some degree and we want to take it more seriously. Most people find that devotional prayers such as the rosary or the chaplet of divine mercy are a great help. They help us to reflect on the mysteries of Christ and relate to him a little better. The scriptures of course are probably the best guide of all, as they are the inspired word of God, and the Holy Spirit speaks to us through them like nothing else. But after some time, which may be months or years, many people find themselves more attracted to spending time in silence. Here a dilemma arises for many. They begin to wonder: should I spend more time sitting in silence before the Lord, or should I give the time to my prayer as it has been up to now? Is this sitting in silence a waste of time? Would I not be better "doing" something? Am I wasting time that I could be using to pray for someone else? These are good questions, which we will try to answer.

St. John of the Cross says that at a certain stage when someone finds themselves drawn to spending more time in silence it can be an indication that the Lord is bringing them to a new stage of prayer. It usually comes with three signs, which we will come back to. St. John says that when people find themselves attracted to silence, it is important not to be afraid of it, but to go with it. It is as if our devotional prayers and reflections have given us as much benefit as they can, and now the Lord wants to do more of the work in us and only asks us to be quiet and to rest in this silence. This is where good spiritual direction is so important, although it is often sadly lacking. This attraction to silence does not mean that we should forget all our devotions, but it often does mean that we should go along with it, as it is more important than any other kind of prayer that *we* could do.

So when we talk about prayer of silence, we are really talking about being quiet and allowing God to do more of the work in us. We are required to "do" less and to "be present" more. This may sound easy, but in practice most of us are not very good at being still and we need some kind of method to help us do this, as well as a bit of understanding as to why we should be quiet and what happens.

## Healing and What Needs to be Healed

It is said that one of the fruits of the practice of any kind of prayer such as centering prayer, is the healing of the unconscious. If healing is needed in the unconscious, it would seem to imply that there is something wrong with it to begin with. But how can we know? Then, if it is unconscious, how do we know that "it" needs healing and whether it has been healed? Finally we must look at contemplative prayer, what it is, how it works, and why it might be a tool that will bring about healing in the unconscious.

Thomas Merton writes:

> Christianity is a religion for men who are aware that there is a deep wound, a fissure of sin that strikes down to the very heart of man's being. They have tasted the sickness that is present in the inmost heart of man estranged from his God by guilt, suspicion and covert hatred. If that sickness is an illusion, then there is no need for the Cross, the sacraments and the Church.[3]

One thing that everyone in the world has in common is the search for happiness. They may have very different ideas of what they consider happiness to be, but everyone wants to be happy. Why is it then that so many are not? What is it that prevents us from finding happiness and why does it seem to be so hidden from us? According to Thomas Keating this is because we come to full reflective self-consciousness without the sense of the presence of God. We feel alienated from God and so the world is a frightening place to be in. If we had the sense of union with God, we would not be afraid; but since we do not, we feel alone. So we search for happiness in all the wrong places, in power and symbols of security, or emotional supports of various kinds. We are living out of what he calls "the false self."

## THE FALSE SELF

When we come into the world as helpless infants, we have many needs. We need to be fed, kept warm, loved, touched, kept clean. We also have three very basic psychological needs, which could also be called "energy centers." They are the need for survival/security, affection/esteem, and power/control. As children, almost all of us experience a lack, or perceived lack, of at least one of these basic psychological needs to some degree. For example, when we were infants we may have been born into a family with only one parent or into a hostile environment where we got the sense that we were in danger a lot of the time. If one or both of our parents were going through a stressful time, perhaps under great economic pressure or with marital problems, we will have sensed the tension, the dis-ease, but we will have been too young to be able to reason that this was not our doing or fault. We may well have unconsciously concluded that the lack of love or security was our fault, or directly related to us. We then develop what could be termed "emotional programs"[4] to compensate for this perceived lack. In other words, we develop an unconscious way of behaving to help us make up for the perceived lack. We usually see it as a way to attain what we perceive as happiness, or what will make us happy. We therefore put huge investment into symbols of our perceived lack, such as symbols of security or love and affection, depending on which of these basic needs we feel most deprived of. Needless to say, all this is done quite unconsciously. It also goes without saying that these symbols in which we invest so much energy cannot possibly bring us happiness, because they are finite:

> The fulfillment we find in creatures belongs to the reality of the created being, a reality that is from God and belongs to God and reflects God. The anguish we find in them belongs to the disorder of our desire which looks for a greater reality in the object of our desire than is actually there: a greater fulfillment than any created thing is capable of giving.[5]

When baby John first comes into the world, his parents are completely enamored by him. They delight in his every move and do their best to attend to his every need. As he begins to grow and they start to teach him, they will usually use a certain amount of discipline to help him to learn. However, what can often happen is that the mother or father will begin to communicate messages that imply something like this: "Daddy only loves you if ... you eat your vegetables, be good, and succeed in school." Of course it is not said in words, more often in a silent language, but all the time we are picking up the messages that we are only lovable if we have something (success, achievements, prestige, wealth, etc.).

The false self is the self that we have grown up with. It is the understanding we have acquired that we are not lovable in ourselves, but rather for what we do and achieve. So we live and work to please others. Most of us when we grow up introduce ourselves by saying, "Hello, my name is John, I'm an accountant," or, "I'm a teacher." But of course "I" am not a teacher, or an accountant. If I quit my job as a teacher, "I" will still be here, so "I" must be much more than a teacher/accountant, or whatever.

The only thing I can definitely say "I" am is a center of consciousness. I may live out my life as a priest, accountant, teacher, or anything else, but this is not what "I" am. We tend to associate ourselves with what we do because we tend to equate what we do or do not do with how valuable or lovable we are. This is what we have learned growing up. Very few people will introduce themselves by just saying, "Hello, I'm John." And if they do, someone else will probably soon ask them, "What do you do?" This is living under the "false self." We have created a false self for ourselves and need to be set free from it. If we really perceived that we are totally loved by God just by virtue of the fact that we *are*, then we would be free from the need to present ourselves to others in a certain light, to show that we are worth something. However, most of us do not enjoy such freedom from the false self and live our lives trying to make up for this lack of "something" within us. We are deeply influenced by what people think and say about us. The fashion industry alone is a striking witness to this. We are dominated by the false self, made up of what Keating calls our "emotional programs for happiness." These programs are what cause us to put great investment into what we think will make us happy. But as long as we are living under the false self, this can never be.

The false self must die or be dismantled so that the true self can live in fullness: "Anyone who wants to save his life will lose it; but anyone who loses his life for my sake, and for the sake of the gospel, will save it" (Mk 8:35).

In his writings, Fr. M. Louis of Gethsemani—better known as Thomas Merton—describes his own journey to becoming "a new man," in other words the death of the false self and the new vision that comes with the freeing of the true self. He, in turn, drew his knowledge of the true and false self from the teachings of St. Bernard of Clairvaux. He describes the journey beautifully in many of his writings. In *Seeds of Contemplation*, he presents us with a picture of the false self, in these words:

> Every one of us is shadowed by an illusory person: a false self.... My false and private self is the one who wants to exist outside the radius of God's will and God's love—outside of reality and outside of life. And such a self cannot help but be an illusion.... For most people in the world, there is no greater subjective reality than this false self of theirs, which cannot exist. A life devoted to the cult of this shadow is what is called a life of sin.... Therefore there is only one problem on which all my existence, my peace and my happiness depend: to discover myself in discovering God. If I find Him, I will find myself; and if I find my true self, I will find Him.[6]

To say I was born in sin is to say I came into the world with a false self. I came into existence under a sign of contradiction, being someone that I was never intended to be and therefore a denial of what I am supposed to be.[7]

For me to be a saint means to be myself. Therefore the problem of sanctity and salvation is in fact the problem of finding out who I am and of discovering my true self.[8]

The false self is therefore, literally, a self that is not real, not really who we are at our core. It is a self we have created and spend our life trying to please and maintain, although in vain, since it can never be satisfied or pacified, as it is false. It is not made in the image of God. If we are to find peace, we must turn away from this false self, or rather allow it to die. This is something that we cannot do by our own efforts, but it is something that God can and will do, if we allow him. According to Keating, one of the ways that this will happen is through the regular practice of centering prayer. By continually being silent before the Lord, or *being to* God in the depths of our soul, we give no room for the false self, which will eventually die as it is no longer being nourished. It kind of starves to death.

As we grow older if we encounter a situation that seems to affect one of the emotional programs for happiness that we have developed, we react, because we feel that our happiness is being threatened in some way. This is because we have convinced ourselves, albeit unconsciously, that we must not be deprived of these symbols (whatever symbols in particular we have come to associate with our lack of security or esteem, etc.), or we cannot be happy.

Since all this happened at an age when we were too young to reason what was going on, and that it probably was not our fault that we were deprived of these basic needs, we developed these unconscious programs at a very early stage, which then became firmly embedded in our unconscious[9]. From then on, it influenced how we see the world and how we act. Through centering prayer we take the road that will help us return to the true self and gradually dismantle the false self. This takes time. The true self that we are trying to get in touch with or set free is our deepest self, created in God's image. In order to reach our true self, we must unblock it of all the emotional wounds that we have accumulated throughout our life.

In *The New Man*, Thomas Merton describes the true self in these terms:

> Self-realization in this true religious sense is then less an awareness of ourselves than it is an awareness of the God to whom we are drawn in the depths of our own being. We become real, and experience our actuality, not when we pause to reflect upon our own self as an isolated individual entity, but rather when, transcending ourselves and passing beyond reflection, we center our whole soul upon the God who is our life. That is to say we fully "realize" ourselves when we cease to be conscious of ourselves in separateness and know nothing but the one God who is above all knowledge.... The image of God is brought to life in us when it breaks free from the shroud and the tomb in which our self-consciousness had kept it prisoner, and loses itself in a total consciousness of Him who is Holy.

This is one of the main ways in which "he that would save his life will lose it...."

The recovery of the divine image in our souls, insofar as it is experienced by us at all, is an experience of a totally new manner of being....

The recognition of our true self, in the divine image, is then a recognition of the fact that we are known and loved by God.[10]

Psychology recognizes that traumatic events in our early life (and later on as well) that are too difficult or painful to cope with can be buried or frozen in the unconscious as a means of coping with the pain. However, these feelings can and will affect our behavior unless properly attended to at some stage.

Keating uses the example of a wealthy businessman with millions of dollars in the bank. He already has more than he could ever spend, yet he is never satisfied. He always wants more and he continually tries to make more, to the point that he is willing to obtain it even through fraud. What is driving him to act this way? Unknown to himself he is acting out of an emotional program that is trying to help him find happiness in a way that can never succeed. This may be a lack of security from his early childhood that unknown to himself is still influencing how he works and behaves. Perhaps because he lacked security when he was small, he then began to place huge emphasis on symbols of security or power (such as money) to try to make up for this real or perceived lack. Now, no matter what he does, even if he has a conversion and joins a monastery, he will continue to act out of these false programs for happiness until he faces these issues in himself. In a different situation it would simply come out in a different way, unless he faces the underlying problem: "At some point we have to face the fundamental problem, which is the unconscious motivation that is still in place, even after we have chosen the values of the Gospel."[11]

Often when people experience a conversion of some kind, they joyfully begin to live the Gospel message (if they happen to be Christian) and may initially feel that they have left their old habits and life behind. However, after some time the dust settles and then the old patterns of behavior resurface, often to the dismay of the individual, who may now begin to wonder whether their trying to live the Gospel was a foolish idea, as they do not seem to be able to do it after all. As nothing really seems to have changed, they may feel cheated or foolish, and see the Christian life as being impossible for them. To themselves they appear to be just as bad as before, if not worse. However, all that is happening is that they are beginning to see the false self, something that they may never have been aware of before. This is a normal part of growth and with good direction they will be encouraged to go on, as now the real spiritual journey is getting under way.

This fundamental need that we experience, or lack of "something" that causes us to act this way, Keating calls "the human condition": "The human condition is my term for the doctrine Christian tradition has referred to since St. Augustine of Hippo first proposed it as original sin and its consequences."[12] St. Augustine called it "original sin" and modern psychology is recognizing more and more that there is some kind of a universal "lack" or "flaw" common to all people.[13] Benedict Groeschel calls it "the original wound," since it is something that we are suffering from, rather than something that any one actually did.[14] Keating further explains it thus:

> The term *original sin* is a way of describing the universal experience of coming to full reflective self-consciousness without the certitude of personal union with God. This gives rise to our intimate sense of incompletion, dividedness, isolation, and guilt.[15]

As a result of this "human condition," we begin to develop the false self,[16] out of which we live and act. It becomes our way of thinking and seeing the world:

> Even though my natural acts are good they have a tendency, when they are only natural, to concentrate my faculties on the man that I am not, the one I cannot be, the false-self in me, the person that God does not know. This is because I am born in selfishness. I am born self-centered. And this is original sin.[17]

Since this is a misguided way of seeing the world, it will drive us in the direction of seeking happiness in all the wrong places.

In their book *Psychic Healing and Wholeness*, Anna Terruwe, M.D., and Conrad Baars, M.D., acknowledge that it is essential that our emotions be fully integrated with the whole person if we are to reach full maturity. Emotions that are suppressed at any stage are simply "buried alive" and will make themselves known at some stage in a person's life, one way or another:

> In each developmental phase, all emotions specific to that phase must be given the opportunity to be experienced and satisfied and not held back and repressed. This holds true for all age levels—infancy, childhood, puberty, and adolescence—but the earlier these emotions become repressed, the graver the consequences will be.[18]

Through the regular practice of centering prayer, or some other method of prayer that disposes us to contemplation, the false self is gradually dismantled and the Holy Spirit begins to re-integrate our emotions, helping us to re-assess values taken on as children and to become free and open to the presence of God within us since our baptism. Without the help of God, we cannot do this:

> The conscious resolution to change our values and behavior is not enough to alter the unconscious value systems of the false self and the behavior they engender. Only the passive purifications of contemplative prayer can effect this profound healing.[19]

Robert Assagioli affirms that a moral conversion is not enough by itself to help us become whole or integrated. There is a whole process that we must go through to reach this stage of fulfillment or self-realization:

In the past a moral conversion, a simple whole-hearted devotion to a teacher or savior, a loving surrender to God, were often sufficient to open the gates leading to a higher level of consciousness and a sense of inner union and fulfillment. Now, however, the more varied and conflicting aspects of modern man's personality are involved and need to be transmuted and harmonized with each other: his fundamental drives, his emotions and feelings, his creative imagination, his inquiring mind, his assertive will, and also his interpersonal and social relations.[20]

The human person is a complex reality and both growth and healing take time. So what need to be healed are the suppressed emotions, which are now causing us to look for fulfillment in the wrong places. This healing can and does come about through the regular practice of centering prayer. It also may require psychotherapy, depending on how much damage has been done.

One obvious difficulty is how to tell when someone is "healed." This is not really something you can measure. How can you tell if the unconscious has been healed and these false emotional programs have been dismantled? This is told more by the fruits of the person's life than anything else. There is no hard and fast measure for this, at least not in the spiritual life.

*Chapter 2*

# GROWING IN CONSCIOUSNESS

THERE ARE VARIOUS MODELS of the development
of consciousness, for example M. Basil Pennington,
another well known writer on centering prayer, speaks
of the Alpha, Beta, and Gamma stages culminating in
the Omega point of transformation in Christ. Thomas
Keating first mentions the developmental model of
consciousness, put forward by child psychologist Jean
Piaget. He then follows the evolutionary model of the
human person as developed by Ken Wilber, which he
calls "the Great Chain of Being":[1]

> The developmental model is actually a sub-
> set of an even more comprehensive model, the
> evolutionary. The infant experiences the same
> developmental pattern and value systems that
> the human family as a whole experienced. In
> other words, each human being is a microcosm
> of where the human race has been—and where
> it might be headed.[2]

Human consciousness is constantly evolving and
this is one theory that helps to explain that develop-

ment. According to this paradigm there are four different stages of development of consciousness in the human person, which correspond with the more universal level of development of the human race. One is a microcosm of the other. As the child develops, so the human race as a whole has also developed, and is still developing.

This theory suggests that about five million years ago the first differentiation between humans and animals took place, with the development of what is now termed "reptilian consciousness." It is also known as the "uroboric" stage.[3]

## REPTILIAN OR UROBORIC CONSCIOUSNESS

> The mythological symbol of this stage of consciousness is the serpent eating its tail, signifying the recurrence of natural processes: day and night, summer and winter, birth and death, desire and satisfaction. The most primitive humans were totally immersed in nature.[4]

Life at this stage was focused on survival, food, and shelter, and on the fulfillment of instinctual needs. Humans lived on a moment-to-moment basis. There was no sense of time or the future and, as a result, no fear of death. There was no consciousness of a separate self:

> Dawn Man, in other words, began his career *immersed* in the subconscious realms of nature and body, of vegetable and animal, and initially "experienced" himself as indistinguishable from the world that had already evolved to that point.

Man's *world*—nature, matter, vegetable life and animal (mammalian) body—and man's *self*—the newly evolving center of his experience—were basically *undifferentiated*, embedded, fused and confused. His self was his naturic world; his naturic world was his self; neither was clearly demarcated, and this, basically, in unconscious homage to his past.[5]

The infant in the first year of his or her life experiences this, being totally immersed in obtaining food and rest and depending totally on his or her parents for protection. Bonding with the mother is very important as it helps the baby accept the new life it has begun outside the womb. The baby doesn't experience him- or herself as a separate self for several months. The mother is like an extension of the baby.

## Typhonic Consciousness

The second stage of consciousness is known as "typhonic consciousness," which is thought to have evolved around 200,000 years ago. Humans began to distinguish themselves from the objects around them, although they were still deeply entrenched in animal instincts for survival, food, and shelter. The mythological symbol of this stage of consciousness is the Typhon, part human, part animal, signifying the first stages of recognizing the body as distinct from the world around it. At this stage the concept of magic played an important role. The world was a magical place to the people of that time and anything could happen. We have a similar experience today when we are dreaming. According to this theory, our dream world is how the humans of 200,000 years ago would have experienced their world. As a result, it could be quite a terrifying place at times. Death happened suddenly and out of the blue. There was no explanation for anything. The hunt was an important sign of the development of these people, because it is an indication that they had a sense of the future, even if only a very limited one. However, it was enough to plan a hunt to provide for food, which indicates a sense of time. In the uroboric period, the human was conscious *in* time but not *of* time. In the typhonic period he began to be conscious of time, but only of the present.

What is also important about this stage is that, as these early humans began to emerge from the state of subconsciousness and began to experience themselves as separate from nature, they also became aware of their mortality, which then brought fear of death and the concomitant desire to live longer. They feared death and longed for immortality, yet they experienced a sense of being separate from God— hence the search for God and later for higher states of consciousness, which in itself is a kind of search for God, a search for the transcendent. Therefore, coming to consciousness meant coming into a frightening world, where there was death, a sense of alone-ness and of being separated from God. This explains the need to prolong life and ward off death for as long as possible.

Between the ages of two and four the infant experiences him- or herself as being separate from the objects around them. The child now begins to explore the world around them and to try things out. His or her dreams are generally about animals, or animal images that personify people. This is expressed in the child's games where everything has a dream-like quality and any object can represent anything the imagination cares for. At this stage the child is also usually afraid of the dark, the unknown, and nature, just as the primitive people of the typhonic consciousness period were.

## MYTHIC MEMBERSHIP CONSCIOUSNESS

Around 12000 BCE, it is thought that people began to evolve to the stage of mythic membership consciousness. At this stage society became more structured, there was time for art, leisure, reflection, and politics. Farming is one of the most important developments of this time, giving us evidence of the change:

> If man cannot find true and eternal Life in timeless Spirit, he will farm for it exclusively in time, fussing about in the temporal realm in search of that which is timeless and piling up tokens of this correct but misplaced search.[6]

Farming was an indication of a huge change in evolutionary consciousness. Man was now aware of himself as a separate being and was aware of a future. So he needed to plan for it, in order to push death further away. We still have the farming consciousness today, in working and planning for the future: buying time, avoiding death, extending life:

> The origin of human drivenness is *religious* because man experiences creatureliness; the

amassing of surplus, then, goes to the very heart of human motivation, the urge to stand out as a hero, to transcend the limitations of the human condition and achieve victory over impotence and finitude.[7]

The people of this period began to associate with their society, area, and peers, which gave them a sense of belonging and protection. The struggle for land began, increasing in ever widening circles. As people became more self-conscious they began to fear death more and to try to hide their fear of it. It is believed that murder and eventually war also began to come into society during this period.

Between the ages of four and eight years, the child enters into this stage of consciousness, where she associates with her peer groups, family, and friends. She absorbs unquestioningly the values of parents, teachers, and peers and the predominant society in which she is growing up. Their values are her values. There is nothing wrong with identifying with such groups. The problem is when we over-identify with them. When we over-identify with a group, we give them unquestioning loyalty, whether or not their system of values is moral or not. Well-established groups often resist change because their members over-identify with the group and as a result they often stagnate or even become dangerous, since anyone who questions the group's principles can be accused of being a traitor. Many political parties behave in the same way, with misuse of the "party whip" to force conformity:

When authority functions on the mythic membership level, it easily moves from the exercise

of authority to authoritarianism.... Authority
in the Christian religion is designed to lead us
out of the swamp of self-centered motivation
into the freedom and accountability of full
personhood.[8]

As children, unable to reason things out properly
for ourselves, we unquestioningly accept the value
systems presented to us by our parents, teachers,
friends, and social group. However, once we get a bit
older we need to be able to re-assess the values we
have been taught, as they may not always be healthy
for us. The sometimes-erroneous values of others
must not stand in the way of true growth. Knowing
that something is wrong may call for withdrawing
from a group or from friends, but this is essential if
we are to grow. It is also essential in the Church that
decisions can be challenged using the right channels,
so that we can truly grow as a Christian community.
To live in fear of authority figures is very unhealthy
and will prevent true growth. However, because of
the false self, many people have not reached the kind
of maturity that will allow them to challenge those
in authority, even if they know they are wrong. This
is one reason why purification of the false emotional
programs is so important. We cannot live in a Church,
or any group, where authority cannot be challenged
simply because it is authority.

I would like to add a word on the superego,
which is "an emotional judgment of what is right or
wrong behavior."[9] As children we grow up with a lot
of instructions about what we can and cannot do.
These tend to turn into "shoulds" later on. We find
commentaries in our heads telling us that we really

"should" be acting differently. Keating says that this is not the conscience but the superego bringing in a guilty verdict on anything we do, once we begin to move away from some of the values we were taught, even if they were not the best values. Our conscience will remind us when we have done something wrong or gone against our principles, but the superego will continue telling us that we should have been better or that that action was not good enough:

> True guilt is the realization that you have acted against your conscience; that is to say, that you have done something against what you believe is right. The sense of guilt warns you, "Hey, you have gone against your principles." As soon as you regret your fault and say, "My God, forgive me," you should forget it. Guilt feelings that last longer than half a minute are neurotic. Pervasive, prolonged, and paralyzing guilt is the result of the superego at work. It is an emotional judgment about right and wrong, not a true judgment of conscience.[10]

A large part of our moral development will be reevaluating the many instructions that we were given as a child. As our reason develops, we have to re-evaluate these "rules" so that we can be free of the superego that turns many of the instructions we were given into "shoulds." Much of the spiritual journey consists of trying to overcome the effects of the superego. What we learned about God when we were young may continue to influence our vision of God for years, even into old age for some. For example, if we were presented with a God who is always watching us to see if we do wrong, we may spend many years, even our whole religious life, trying to placate this God. The spiritual journey helps us to re-evaluate the teachings we received and may change our outlook significantly. This is essential for real growth. Many adolescents rebel against their religion, especially if they have grown up in a very moralistic family. They need to re-assess their values and decide what it is they believe in. This is a necessary part of growing up and can be very healthy. However, if the family influence has been very moralistic, it may take years for the person to re-evaluate it and sometimes they may never do so, as they have come to associate their idea of God with the idea presented by their family. If the idea of God presented to them was that of a police officer or judge, naturally they will want to be free from the influence of such a tyrant, and so for some it can be a difficult journey to find God again. Fortunately for us, God also comes to our rescue in many different and unexpected ways.

We must also remember that at each stage of emergence into new consciousness, we both retain the previous stages and have the potential to move on to the next stage. A few people in each society usually do move onto the next stage of consciousness (the saints or mystics), but only to the beginnings of the next stage: "The human being, then, is a compound individual of all lower levels of reality, capped by its own particular and defining level."[11]

## MENTAL-EGOIC CONSCIOUSNESS

It is thought that around 3000 to 2500 BCE one of the most important developments took place: the emergence of the ego and reason. This is known as the "mental egoic consciousness" period. In mythology mental-egoic consciousness is symbolized by Zeus slaying the dragon. The dragon represents the primitive levels of consciousness and the domination of the emotions. Zeus represents reason. The emergence of the ego was represented in mythology by the sun gods and sun heroes. The sun, the symbol of light, was a symbol of enlightenment but not transcendence. It was the light of mental clarity. At this stage people began to look beyond their own immediate needs and to think of the future and the needs of those around them. They were becoming more responsible for themselves and others.

The child reaches the mental-egoic stage somewhere between the ages of twelve and fourteen years:

> The arrival at the mental egoic stage of consciousness is characterized by basic attitudinal changes. One graduates from mere self-concern and is motivated by the larger concerns of family, country, and the world.[12]

According to this theory, this is where the human race should now be. However, because of "the human condition" and the false programs for happiness that we have developed from early on, it seems that we have not yet reached this stage and instead have a sense of being alienated from God. If we emerged into full reflective self-consciousness with a growing sense of being in union with God, then we would continue to develop in the process of ever-higher levels of consciousness, because of the security that comes from our union with God. However, because of our sense of alienation from God, we are afraid and feel alien in the world. The world is experienced as a threatening place.

The purpose of the spiritual journey, which culminates in union with God, is to help us to be purified of the false self, to reach union with God and so develop to the greatest maturity that God has intended for us: "I came that you may have life and have it to the full" (Jn 10:10). As Thomas Keating writes:

> Human development depends on freeing ourselves from emotional fixations on these instinctual levels in order to grow to full reflective self-consciousness. The gospel calls for the full development of the human person and invites us to the further growth that God has in store for us: the intuitive and unitive levels of consciousness to which mature faith and love gradually raise us.[13]

The call of Jesus in the Gospel is a call to grow up, to leave behind false values, and to dissociate ourselves from the values of our cultural conditioning, insofar as they hinder our personal response to Christ. However, because of the values that are firmly entrenched in us from our early childhood, when we reach the normal stage of mental egoic consciousness, we are not properly free to re-evaluate what we were taught at an earlier stage. As a result, we tend to use our newfound intellectual powers to rationalize or justify our false programs for happiness and the values of our culture, instead of challenging and reassessing them. We try to control the world around us.

Our pathology is simply this: we have come to full reflective self-consciousness without the enjoyment of divine union—indeed, without any awareness of it at all. Because that crucial conviction, born of experience, is missing, our fragile egos seek every possible means to ward off the painful and at times agonizing sense of alienation from God and from everyone else.[14]

## Original Sin

Having looked at the development of consciousness, let us now return to the question of original sin. Keating uses the term "the human condition" for original sin:

The term *original sin* is a way of describing the universal experience of coming to full reflective self-consciousness without the certitude of personal union with God. This gives rise to our intimate sense of incompletion, dividedness, isolation and guilt."[15]

However, this explanation leaves some fundamental questions unanswered, at least from a Christian point of view.

Ken Wilber suggests that the Fall is not so much a *fall* from, as a *rising* from. The Fall was a question of the human race emerging (rising) into the stage of self-consciousness. Man began to realize that he was indeed separate from the world around him. However, this brought with it the further realization that he was mortal, that he would die. At this stage we are half way between the ego in the subconscious and the superconscious. This is where the ego has reached reflective self-consciousness, but not yet transcendence. As a result it is in a state of anguish. Wilber calls it "the time of the great reversal."[16]

According to Wilber, therefore, original sin is not a fall from an original state of heavenly bliss, but rather an emerging from the state of subconsciousness (and therefore ignorance) in the evolutionary process. Eve took the fruit from the tree of knowledge of good and evil. She chose to "know," to learn, thereby taking the step into consciousness, which brought with it the awareness that we are already separate from God, from our original source. This coming to knowledge of ourselves brought with it guilt and shame, as we felt alone and separate. We realized we would die. We felt we were separate from God, the source of eternal life. According to this theory then, the theological Fall means that by virtue of the fact of creation—in other words God creating apart from Godself, creating a universe separate from God—once we came to know this, we would acutely feel the pain of the lack of union. The very act of creation then was the Fall, the separation of things from God. The state of innocence in the Garden of Eden was not the enlightened state before a fall by choosing sin, but rather the state of ignorance before recognizing that we were separate from God. And all people are born into this state—the state of being separate from God—which is the state of original sin. This is Wilber's explanation.

This raises one problem: If this is so, then where does the idea of turning one's back on God come in and what about the need for a savior, because of the "sin" which separated us? If the Fall was just a matter of coming to the natural recognition that we are separate from God and in this state are mortal and will die, then why would we need a savior? Perhaps, it could be argued, we would need a *teacher* to point the way back to God, to enlightenment, but not a savior? Baptism then would be the re-uniting with God through Jesus, the Way to the Father. In other words, this theory denies the need for a savior, as there is no deliberate rejection of God at any stage. Instead, there is a sense of being separate from God and this is hardly something one can be blamed for. This is radically different from the Christian understanding of original sin, which involves a definite rejection of God at some stage at the beginning of our history.

The Catholic Church teaches us that there was a very definite turning away from God, so merely explaining that coming to consciousness involved a sense of being separate from God would seem inadequate. The *Catechism of the Catholic Church* addresses this very difficulty and the temptation to "explain away" original sin apart from the light of revelation:

> Only the light of divine Revelation clarifies the reality of sin and particularly of the sin committed at mankind's origins. Without the knowledge Revelation gives of God we cannot recognize sin clearly and are tempted to explain it as merely a developmental flaw, a psychological weakness, a mistake, or the necessary consequence of an inadequate social structure, etc. Only in the knowledge of God's plan for man can we grasp that sin is an abuse of the freedom that God gives to created persons so that they are capable of loving him and loving one another.[17]

Man tempted by the devil, let his trust in his
Creator die in his heart and, abusing his freedom, *disobeyed* God's command. This is what
man's first sin consisted of. All subsequent sin
would be disobedience toward God and lack of
trust in his goodness.[18]

From the teaching of the Church we understand from
divine Revelation that there was a very definite, conscious turning away from God in freedom by our first
ancestors.

Wilber's theory could still possibly make sense,
insofar as coming to self-consciousness was *part* of
what is called "the Fall," but it couldn't only be this.
It would also have to involve some kind of rejection
of God, or disobedience against God to fit in with
the Christian understanding. Perhaps it could also be
understood in this way: When the ego began to evolve,
Wilber says that in being "strong," it both rejected its
subconscious origin and its superconscious potential.
If by "superconscious potential" could be understood
its possibility of union with God, then perhaps this
would be one way to understand a rejection of God,
a deliberate turning one's back on God. From this
would come the need for a savior to repair the damage, and make union with God possible. If, however,
"superconscious potential" only means the possibility
of higher states of consciousness, then this would also
rule out the theory.

## Chapter 3

# CENTERING PRAYER
# AND CONTEMPLATIVE PRAYER

WE WILL NOW LOOK at the teaching of centering prayer itself and why it is considered such an effective way to help one be disposed to contemplative prayer. In fact, centering prayer cannot be totally separated from contemplative prayer as the two overlap. One of the problems here is that it is difficult to say exactly where centering prayer finishes and where contemplative prayer begins, but it is probably most accurate to say that centering prayer helps to dispose one for contemplative prayer. One cannot begin or sustain contemplative prayer[1] by one's own ability, since it is totally given to us from God. So here when we talk about the practice of contemplative prayer, it can be understood to mean, through a receptive method such as centering prayer. In other words, healing takes place through contemplative prayer, which we dispose ourselves to through the regular practice of centering prayer.

One of the first words of Jesus in his public ministry is "repent" (μετανοειτε, Mk 1:15), that is, "change the direction in which you are seeking happiness," according to Keating's interpretation.[2] It is a call to look at ourselves, to address the issues that we need to face. It is not just a matter of doing penance and self-mortification, but a change in our direction. The challenge of the Gospel is to be open and prepared to change. In other words, it is a call to grow up, to mature. As we begin to face the various issues and psychological baggage that we carry, we are faced with a darker side of ourselves that most of us would prefer not to know is there; the "false self" we looked at earlier.

For some of us, we may be faced with this shortly after we enter religious life, which is designed to help us grow in the spirit. If we are really open to growth, it is one of the first things that will happen. We may suddenly find ourselves noticing all kinds of patterns of behavior we never noticed before that are really quite selfish. The spiritual consolations that might have been part of our reason for entering the religious life begin to dry up and suddenly we seem to be in a desert. In fact we *are* in a kind of desert, and need to be there in order to discover and deal with the false self. For others, it may be after a certain period in their marriage, or through various crises at points in their lives, that bring addictions or other destructive patterns of behavior to the surface. How do we begin to tackle such issues? Is there anything that can be done about them?

According to Keating, centering prayer is one way that we can deal with such issues:

> [Centering prayer] brings us into the presence of God and thus fosters the contemplative attitudes of listening and receptivity. It is not contemplation in the strict sense, which in Catholic

tradition has always been regarded as a pure gift of the Spirit, but rather it is a preparation for contemplation by reducing the obstacles caused by the hyperactivity of our minds and of our lives.[3]

Later we will look in greater depth at the development of contemplative prayer and of centering prayer, which is not something new but rather a centuries-old practice of prayer based on the fourteenth century spiritual classic, *The Cloud of Unknowing*, and which can be traced back further to the Fathers of the Desert, such as Cassian and Evagrius. Here we will look at what the practice itself involves.

In centering prayer we begin to quieten the mind and learn to "let go" of the many thoughts that are perpetually flowing through it, so that we can be more open to God. As the mind gradually learns to be more detached from these thoughts, we start to enter into a deep rest or peace. Over time, this helps us to begin to let go of some of the emotional wounds that we are carrying deep in the unconscious. We begin to let down the guard of the unconscious, as it were, which thus allows the loosening up of some of the deep-rooted psychological issues we are carrying. In turn, this emotional baggage begins to come to the surface of our consciousness and be "processed" or released in the form of emotions or thoughts:

> Unarticulated emotional experiences that are traumatizing may be pushed into the unconscious where their energy remains. Emotions are energy. They can only be dissipated by acknowledging or articulating them.[4]

We may find ourselves suddenly having strong feelings of anger while we are praying, or crying without any explanation why or where these emotions are coming from. What is happening is that emotional wounds of the past are beginning to come up from deep within our own being. The Holy Spirit is healing us of wounds that we might not have been aware were there at all.

In his book *Centering Prayer*, Basil Pennington points out that dreams have a similar role in processing thoughts or ideas while we sleep. Various tests carried out on people while they were asleep showed that by continually disturbing their sleep just as they were about to enter the dream phase of sleep known as REM (Rapid Eye Movement), people were prevented from dreaming:

> These scientists have established in their experiments that if they consistently prevent a person from dreaming even for a relatively short period of time—a few nights—the person is very apt to undergo a psychotic episode.[5]

There is obviously a need for the body to dream, which seems to be a way of "clearing out" or "processing" thoughts or tension. What happens through centering prayer is very similar.

The memory behaves like a powerful computer that records all events, emotions, and feelings throughout our whole life. Some feelings or emotions, which may have been too strong for us to cope with, are suppressed into our unconscious, as a way of coping with them until we are ready to face them. Eventually when we are ready, they will come to the

surface. This may happen through some kind of psychotherapy or else through the regular practice of
centering prayer.

Nemeck and Coombs describe more or less the
same process where the mind is being filled with
thoughts or distractions during contemplative prayer.
They are speaking more about contemplative prayer
than centering prayer specifically, but since centering prayer generally leads to contemplative prayer it
applies the same way:

> When God is making the soul more receptive
> to his transforming love, he empties the intel-
> lect of all particular concepts. As this occurs,
> much in the soul's unconscious which it was
> previously too occupied to face comes gushing
> forth into consciousness. Thus a person given
> more to contemplation than to discursiveness is
> paradoxically more prone to barrages of distrac-
> tions, tangents and temptations during actual
> prayer.[6]

What is most important in this kind of prayer is
fidelity to the practice. Over a period (usually several
years for most people), the false self is gradually dismantled. Our false programs for happiness are being
taken apart and we are discovering a new freedom
inside. What is happening, in fact, is that the obstacles within us to divine union are being removed and
we are coming closer, in a manner of speaking, to
the presence of God within us. Since our baptism,
the Holy Trinity has been present within us through
grace. For us it is a matter of becoming more aware
of this presence through the gradual dismantling of

psychological baggage, which prevents us from being aware of the divine indwelling. In the deep rest that we experience through centering prayer, we are in the perfect environment of God's protective love and so able to let down our guard and begin to process some of these emotions. Let us now take a closer look at how centering prayer works in practice.

## The Practice of Centering Prayer

Centering prayer is one of the simplest and possibly most effective methods of meditative prayer that disposes one to contemplative prayer. The practice works as follows: We sit in a comfortable position, with our eyes closed, preferably somewhere very quiet.[7] When we sit down to pray and try to be quiet we are usually faced with a stream of thoughts flowing through our mind like a river. Every time we become *aware* of any thought,[8] emotion, image, feeling, or idea, we gently use a sacred word to let it go:

> Centering prayer as a discipline is designed to withdraw our attention from the ordinary flow of our thoughts.... [These thoughts] are resting on the inner stream of consciousness, which is our participation in God's being. That level is not immediately evident to ordinary consciousness. Since we are not in immediate contact with that level, we have to do something to develop our awareness of it. It is the level of our being that makes us most human. The values that we find there are more delightful than the values that float along the surface of the psyche.[9]

Keating uses the analogy of boats on a river, representing our thoughts floating on the inner stream of consciousness. Each different boat is a thought, feeling, or emotion. When we are praying in silence it is as if we are sitting on the bank looking on as these thoughts pass by. Often we see a boat of particular interest and we jump on board to see what it is. We go with the thought or begin to explore it. At this point we are becoming distracted and need to refocus on what we are doing, that is, trying to be quiet and open to God, *being to* God, resting in his presence. So we use a sacred word to "center" our minds or re-express our intention.

The sacred word should be short and should not have too many associations attached to it. We could use a word such as, Yahweh, Amen, Peace, Jeshuah, God, Love, Ruah, etc. The purpose of the sacred word is simply to express our *intention* as opposed to our attention. This is a subtle but important difference. In other forms of meditation a word is used as a focus of attention. Sometimes it is repeated continually as a mantra, the idea being that the continual repetition of the word will "block out" all other thoughts. In centering prayer, however, the sacred word is only used when necessary, that is, as soon as we become aware that our mind has become taken up with another thought. The purpose of the sacred word is to express our loving intention to be in God's presence, open and consenting to his presence and action within us. Each time we use the word, it is like a gentle reminder of our purpose. It is always used ever so lightly, so as not to be a form of distraction in itself. It is not meant to be used as a kind of mental bat to beat off the onslaught of thoughts.

This kind of prayer is in fact a very self-less and pure kind of prayer, since, if it is done properly, it is a complete giving of oneself to God. It does not seek anything for itself or involve judging how one is doing. Rather it calls for a total letting go of everything, including our thoughts, in order to be present to God. In this way it could be said to be a perfect response to the commandment, "You must love the Lord your God with all your heart, with all your soul and with all your strength" (Cf. Dt 6:5). It is a total giving of oneself to God without asking for anything back.

If you find yourself wondering "How can I be sure that I am actually praying and not just in some kind of silent void?" remember that each time you repeat the sacred word you are inviting God to work within you. But instead of continually saying something like, "Lord I give myself to you for this time and I invite you to bring me closer to you," we just say one word, the sacred word, which represents all of this. So it is very much prayer.

As the mind slowly begins to quieten down and we get better at letting go of the various thoughts that are streaming through our mind, the boats on the river gradually begin to spread out, leaving more and more space between them. Every so often we will find ourselves on another thought drifting along the river, exploring the thought, as it were, and then once again we gently use the sacred word to let it go. With practice this becomes easier. As more space begins to develop on the river and a sense of deep peace starts to develop, we may then find that strong emotions or memories begin to come to the surface. Sometimes what seems like a whole asteroid field of thoughts may come along and we have to just be patient and sit it out. This is often a point at which people are tempted to give up, as they feel they have gotten nowhere and are now going backwards. The temptation for most people is that when it becomes difficult, dry and seemingly impossible, they want to stop and go back to where they were experiencing some kind of consolation, as this made them "feel" that they were making progress. Another danger is that they can become engrossed in meditation, which is really no more than a kind of meditation on themselves, instead of just being open to God. What is important is that we always remain open to the action of the Holy Spirit, who may lead us in different directions or even ask us to let go of certain kinds of prayer for a while, in order to make us freer and perhaps bring us on to a different kind of prayer.

When we begin to experience times that seem almost impossible to be silent because of the amount of thoughts that are going through our head, it should not in any sense be taken as a "failure" on our part. Indeed it could be taken as a good sign more than anything else:

> Once you grasp the fact that thoughts are not only inevitable, but an integral part of the process of healing and growth initiated by God, you are able to take a positive view of them. Instead of looking upon them as painful distractions, you see them in a broader perspective that includes both interior silence and thoughts— thoughts that you do not want, but which are just as valuable for the purpose of purification, as moments of profound tranquility.[10]

These times of great distraction can be a sign of the unconscious unloading and some of the deep emotional hurts of the past coming to the surface, usually in the form of thoughts or felt emotions. The temptation is to try to judge whether we are making progress or not. However, individual times of prayer can never be an indication of progress, as what may appear to be a fruitful time of prayer may not be, and vice-versa. Eventually, if we persevere, we will again encounter a certain amount of peace, until the Holy Spirit decides that it is time to bring us to the next level and then the process starts all over again. What is especially important here is fidelity to the practice.

Centering prayer is a kind of "divine therapy," where we continually need to attend the sessions if we want to experience healing. If we bail out when the going gets tough, we aren't going to make much progress in the end. It is impossible for us to judge whether a prayer time is fruitful or not, since there is nothing by which we can measure any period of prayer. Rather it is by the fruits of a person's life that we can tell what is really happening.

The idea of centering prayer is to dispose us to contemplative prayer, where God takes over and does the work. All the healing that needs to take place deep within our unconscious is something that God can do most effectively, since He knows exactly what needs to be dealt with and when we are able to face it. Through the regular practice of centering prayer, or some other similar technique, we open ourselves up to this possibility. But the practice must be regular, or it won't be effective:

The regular practice of contemplative prayer initiates a healing process that might be called the
"divine therapy." The level of deep rest accessed
during the prayer periods loosens up the hard-
pan around the emotional weeds stored in the
unconscious, of which the body seems to be the
warehouse. The psyche begins to evacuate spontaneously the undigested emotional material of
a lifetime, opening up new space for self-knowledge, freedom of choice, and the discovery of
the divine presence within. As a consequence, a
growing trust in God, a bonding with the Divine
Therapist, enables us to endure the process.[11]

This opening up of the unconscious can also happen through the use of certain types of drugs. However,
one of the many dangers with the use of such drugs is
that they may release material from the unconscious
before we are able to deal with them. Then instead of
helping us, they may further our suffering and cause
a terrible emotional crisis.

Some people object to the idea of having to use
any kind of "technique." However, there are many
different kinds of techniques that are continually
used in Christian prayer, such as the rosary, the spiritual exercises of St. Ignatius, and the use of the Jesus
Prayer. Of course it is also possible to enter into contemplative prayer without the use of any particular
technique, but techniques have proved very useful over
the centuries, and the technique of centering prayer
has already proved itself. It is helping thousands of
people enter into contemplative prayer who previously
thought it was beyond them.

The "goal"[12] of centering prayer is really the practice itself. Fidelity to the practice will lead to deeper union with God, which in turn will enable us to live in the world at a deeper level and to be more effective in our work or ministry. Once the false self has been dismantled and a greater union with God is experienced, we are then better enabled to minister to people without the crippling and often damaging prejudices that we were carrying before. We are then living in reality, seeing things for what they really are. The purpose of bringing us through the dismantling of the false self is so that we can be more effective instruments in the hands of God. We are then freer to live life to the full as God has intended for us.[13] The regular practice of centering prayer is a very effective way to bring this about. Without the experience of union with God, it is very difficult to go through this process as it leaves us completely naked, as it were. To be exposed to so many emotional hurts or wounds of the past we need to be in a very loving and secure environment, or else we might not be able to cope with such pain. Centering prayer is the ideal environment to deal with the false self, since it is being dismantled with the assurance of the divine presence, our greatest security:

> Moments of contemplative prayer bring about deep rest and deep bonding with God. As a consequence of this bonding, we have the courage and trust to face our mixed motivation and the dark side of our personality. The purification of our mixed motivation and selfishness can now begin because we can acknowledge our deepest wounds only to someone whom we know loves us and whom we trust. Love is the only

way a human being can come into full being. If this has been withheld in a significant degree, then we have developed coping mechanisms and are driven to seek happiness in pleasure, affection and esteem symbols that are fantastic, and hence their inevitable frustration gets us tied up into emotional knots.[14]

Another obstacle that we face to growth in this kind of prayer is that we live in a world that measures the value of everything in terms of "success," that is, quantifiable achievement. This kind of prayer is not a matter of success but continual practice. Progress can only be seen in terms of its fruits. Apart from this it may appear to many as a waste of time, as there are no obvious and immediate effects.

There are some who will object to so much silence, saying that it is better to "do" something, such as reflecting on the mysteries of Christ or on scenes from the Bible. While this kind of prayer is of course important, there may come a point where the Spirit begins to draw us beyond this kind of prayer, since God is not to be found in words, images, or concepts. Ultimately we are called to simply *be* in him and present to him, without doing anything. God then prays in us and we just allow it to happen:

It's a risky thing to pray, and the danger is that our very prayers get between God and us. The great thing in prayer is not to pray, but to go directly to God. If saying your prayers is an obstacle to prayer, cut it out. Let Jesus pray. Thank God Jesus is praying. Let him pray in you.... The best way to pray is: stop. Let prayer pray within you, whether you know it or not. This means a deep awareness of our true inner identity.... But the point is that we need not justify ourselves. By grace we are Christ. Our relationship with God is that of Christ to the Father in the Holy Spirit.[15]

If the Spirit begins to prompt us to be silent, then not only will it be very difficult to continue practicing discursive meditation (reflecting on different ideas), but we may also find ourselves going against the guidance of the Holy Spirit. Sadly this is a point where many, often through lack of good direction, get stuck, believing that they cannot go on. They then either give up completely or else try to forcefully continue to practice discursive meditation, even though the Spirit may have caused this kind of prayer to dry up. This is where good spiritual direction is essential.

## THE AFFLICTIVE EMOTIONS

We will now look at the "afflictive emotions," which play a major part in helping us to identify what is going on under the surface. These emotions are the key to identifying the false programs for happiness within us:

> We can learn to recognize our emotional programs for happiness by the afflictive emotions they set off. Basically, these emotions might be reduced to anger, grief, fear, pride, greed, envy, lust, and apathy. If we have an emotional investment in the instinctual needs for survival/security, affection/esteem, or power/control, the events

that frustrate these desires will inevitably set off one or another of the afflictive emotions.[16]

The imagination and the emotions work together, interlinked, so to speak. One always affects the other. Along with every emotional frustration we experience, we also find various commentaries arising from our individual temperament or history. Because of this interaction, the process becomes more intense and more violent. It is very difficult to stop, even though we know it is not helping us and often want to stop. This may even happen at times when we feel renewed spiritually and physically and are ready to begin again. The very fact that we can lose control so quickly is an indication that there is something going on under the surface that needs to be addressed.

Take a man just back from a very refreshing retreat or holiday.[17] He is full of good intentions to get on with the people at work and those he lives with. However, it only takes one person who is able to "push his buttons" to quickly send him into a rage once more. There happens to be a colleague at work that he can't stand. Everything she does annoys him, and no matter how patient he tries to be with her she seems to have an ability to enrage him continually. So he has just arrived back and is full of good intentions to treat this lady better, but in no time she manages to do just about everything to frustrate him, even though she is unaware of it. Within a short time he is in a rage again, and the people at work and at home are thinking, "So much for his retreat!" What went wrong, since he began with such good intentions?

Each frustration was tapping into one of his emotional programs for happiness. As each false program for happiness became frustrated, more commentaries began to flow in his head. He begins to remember all the unreasonable things that this woman seems to have done to him. Then he begins to think of all the unreasonable things that everyone has ever done to him. The commentaries he hears in his head feed the emotions of anger and jealousy that are building up in his system until eventually he can no longer stop himself and he finds himself in an uncontrollable rage.

The point is that these afflictive emotions that are ruining his day are the key to what is really wrong with his value system. They are an indication of a false program for happiness, perhaps for control, in his unconscious. So each time the false program is frustrated he unconsciously believes that this will take from his happiness in some way and so the reactions of anger and frustration begin to mount. The problem is not the woman who seems difficult, but with himself and the unconscious value system in place. He finds himself saying, "If only I could get rid of this woman, everything would be all right." This is the same kind of sentence that millions of people say to themselves every day: "If only I could change someone else, then I would be okay." Objectively it seems laughable, and yet almost everyone does it continually. We think we need to change the world around us and then we will be happy. In fact, the world around us is all right; we are the ones with the problems that need to be resolved.

Let us now take a closer look at some of the afflictive emotions, which point us to the values of the false self. Anger responds to something that we feel is difficult to obtain, or an evil that is hard to avoid.

Apathy is the emotion that comes from recurrent frustration, resulting in bitterness or pervasive boredom. It is "the licking of one's own wounds." Lust in this context, is the overwhelming desire for satisfaction and it can be physical, mental, or spiritual. It is a way of trying to cope with what we perceive as people being cruel to us, by not living up to our unreasonable demands. Our demands are not being met and so we feel sorry for ourselves and take refuge in some pleasure or escape. This is typically how addictions work, but at a much more intense level. Pride, as an emotional reaction, can be experienced in two ways. It can result in self-rejection or self-inflation. Self-rejection is a way of believing that you are not living up to your own self-imposed standards. Instead of reacting to others who may have hurt you, the person turns in on him- or herself, condemning themselves for not being better.

We should remember that anytime we experience an upsetting emotion, it is pointing to something deeper that is not right. If we find ourselves upset, it is because some emotional program has just been frustrated. The only way to resolve this ongoing problem is to face the issue within us, instead of trying to tackle the millions of issues that will trigger off this reaction from the outside, which obviously is impossible. Until these false programs for happiness are undone, we will go on reacting and being miserable, blaming the rest of the world for our own unhappiness.

The call of the Gospel is the call to face these issues and change. Jesus continually challenged his listeners to think about their hidden motivation for doing things and to focus on their own shortcomings, instead of those of others. "Why do you observe the splinter in your brother's eye and never notice the great log in your own?" (Mt 7:3).

The practice of centering prayer is the doorway to resolving these problems. It may also require some psychotherapy, especially if there has been very serious hurt. Once we begin the spiritual journey we start to wake up to the fact that our emotional programs for happiness are preventing us from reacting positively to others and their needs. We are caught up in our own merry-go-round of emotions and false programs. Only when these programs are dismantled can we begin to see others and their needs in reality: "The clarity with which we see other people's needs and respond to them is in direct proportion to our interior freedom."[18]

The development of psychology has been particularly helpful for understanding the human condition and the spiritual life, especially with the discovery of the unconscious. Literature on dysfunctionality and codependency gives us more specific insights into the consequences of original sin, or the human condition, than catechesis did up until recently:

> Each of us needs to be reassured and affirmed
> in his or her own personhood and self-identity.
> If this assurance is withheld because of lack of
> concern or commitment on the part of parents,
> these painful privations will require defensive
> or compensatory measures. As a consequence,
> our emotional life ceases to grow in relation to
> the unfolding values of human development and
> becomes fixated at the level of the perceived depri-
> vation. The emotional fixation fossilizes into a

program for happiness. When fully formed it develops into a center of gravity, which attracts to itself more and more of our psychological resources: thoughts, feelings, images, reactions, and behavior. Later experiences and events in life are all sucked into its gravitational field and interpreted as helpful or harmful in terms of our basic drive for happiness. These centers, as we shall see, are reinforced by the culture in which we live and the particular group with which we identify, or rather, overidentify.[19]

In her book *When Society Becomes an Addict*, Anne Wilson Schaef claims that the whole of society behaves just like someone with an addiction. It is manipulative, controlling, deceitful, full of fear, and refuses to acknowledge that there is a problem with the system (the system being "the addictive system"). According to Schaef up to ninety-six percent of the population is codependent, a codependent being "a person who is currently involved in a love or marriage relationship with an addict, had at least one alcoholic parent or grandparent, and/or grew up in an emotionally repressive family."[20] If this is true, then most of the population is carrying a lot of psychological baggage, which needs to be dealt with if we are to begin to experience healing and growth toward God:

> What happens is that the Addictive System creates God in its own image to suit its own purposes. This is an integral part of the delusionary nature of the system. That distortion further separates us from our spirituality and our awareness of ourselves as spiritual beings.[21]

As long as we are in denial of the problem, we cannot begin the healing process. As soon as we begin the spiritual journey we are faced with the fact that there is something wrong. Only then can the healing begin. The spiritual life is not some kind of an escape into God, rather it calls us to own up to the very things that we need to face if we are to grow.

According to the hugely successful movement of AA (Alcoholics Anonymous), the first step for an addict in recovery is to admit that they have a problem with the addiction and that they are powerless over it. Once they have admitted that they are powerless over alcohol, drugs, sex, or whatever happens to be their addiction, only then can they begin to do something about it. When we begin the spiritual journey, we also soon begin to see that there are many problems with our inner world. The spiritual journey challenges us to deal with these issues. Through contemplative prayer, this is exactly what begins to happen.

## Consent and Growing Up[22]

"The spiritual journey is a training in consent to God's presence and to all reality."[23] Throughout our life there are several "consents," or times of letting go. Each of these is a consent to God's goodness and to grow a little more in the direction in which God is leading us. The first occurs in childhood when God asks us to consent to the basic goodness of our being. This does not refer to particular talents or skills, but to our very being itself, before we do anything. If at this stage we have had some bad experience of our basic goodness because of our environment or family situation, we may not have fully accepted the basic goodness of our being, and we may then carry this ambivalence with us to the next stage of development.

As young adolescents we come to the second stage of consent. Now we begin to experience new talents and abilities. We also begin to experience sexual energy for the first time and the potential to enter into relationships with people in a deeper way. However, if our sexual energies have been awakened before we are ready for them emotionally, we may develop a fear of our sexuality that will in turn affect the way we relate to others. We may not even give proper consent to the goodness of our sexuality:

> When any emotion is felt to be dangerous, fear may repress that emotion into the unconscious, where it continues to express itself surreptitiously in physical illness or unhealthy forms of behavior.[24]

As we grow in the spiritual journey and God begins to dismantle the false self, various fears and suppressed emotions begin to come to the surface. God helps us to integrate them into our being in a healthy way, and to realize that some of our perceptions of what were not good were mistaken. God is giving us another chance to decide for certain things that we may have rejected earlier in life, and to help us become more fully integrated so that we may enjoy the fullness of life that God intended for us.

People who have repressed their sexual feelings are often further affected in the general development of their emotions. When sexual repression has taken place, people often have difficulty in relating to others in an intimate or truly caring way. This can be a serious impediment to our work or ministry and in a marriage relationship. Since sexual energy is so powerful it is very important that it is properly integrated, or it may emerge in mid-life with twice as much force as it did in adolescence, with obviously dangerous consequences.

The third consent comes in early adulthood when we begin to experience having to let go of people and situations, and probably also when we begin to encounter more of death. We experience the reality of our own frailty and that we too will die. Now we are asked to make the consent of accepting this part of our existence and our own limitedness. Throughout our life we will be asked to continually let go of friends, family, possessions, and finally of life itself. This consent is directed toward accepting the fact that we must ultimately let go of everything. If in early childhood we lost a parent or had some other major loss in our life, we may find it difficult to make this consent. Equally if we have not properly made the other consents before this one, we may also find it hard to consent to the idea of our vulnerability, or even of our non-being.

The fourth kind of consent is the consent to be transformed. While this might sound appealing, many people are in great fear of it, as they do not know what it involves and do not want to rush into it: "The transforming union requires consent to the death of the false self, and the false self is the only self we know."[25] People can be more afraid of this than of physical death.

These four consents are all ways of acknowledging and surrendering to God's world, the gift of life and all that God offers us. We can enjoy them and then we are asked to let go and move on to something else. However, our consents are only supposed to be directed to the good things in life as stepping-stones to God:

> The emotional programs for happiness seek symbols of survival/security, affection/esteem, and power/control for the sake of the symbols themselves. Because of our fixations on particular programs for happiness we treat survival/ security, affection/esteem, and power/control symbols as absolutes, that is, as substitutes for God.[26]

As a result we find ourselves frustrated, since these symbols cannot give us the amount of happiness that we unreasonably demand of them. The various consents that God continually asks us to make are consents to his goodness, present in all things. At each period of life we are asked to make a different consent. This does not mean that we reject that part of our life, but rather leave its limitations behind:

> True asceticism is not the rejection of the world, but the acceptance of everything that is good, beautiful, and true. It is learning how to use our faculties and the good things of this world as God's gifts rather than expressions of selfishness.[27]

Through all these periods of change and letting go, God is inviting us to grow up, to go deeper into the spiritual journey so that we may be transformed. By consenting to God's goodness at ever deepening levels, we are agreeing to leave behind what is no longer appropriate for us as adults, and we are becoming more integrated as people. This is the dying of the false self and the emergence of the true self:

> By consenting to God's creation, to our basic goodness as human beings and to the letting go of what we love in this world, we are brought to the final surrender, which is to allow the false self to die and the true self to emerge. The true self might be described as our participation in the divine life manifesting in our uniqueness.[28]

*Chapter 4*

# THE NIGHT OF SENSE AND SPIRIT

THE WHOLE OF ONE'S life is really the spiritual journey. Strictly speaking it would be a mistake to say
that we only begin at some particular stage. However,
at some point in a person's life it often happens that
they will more consciously begin the spiritual journey, that is to say they become conscious of the fact
that they are on a journey toward/into God and have
more of an input. As individuals, we are continually
moving in the direction of transformation in Christ.
Our whole life and the whole of creation, too, is being
transformed in Christ. Since our ultimate destiny is
to be transformed in God, who is Spirit, therefore the
whole process could be called "spiritualization." The
journey is therefore more of a spiritual one than anything else:

> Spiritual, therefore, designates that towards
> which we are all being moved. It is that into
> which we are being transformed. The agent of
> this process is God himself: the Holy Spirit. We
> are already becoming spiritual. But we are not
> yet completely spiritual (Rm 8:24–25), for this

side of death we are still fleshy and we are still
in our *soma psychikon*. However, God is inexo-
rably bringing to completion what he has begun
(Ph 1:6).[1]

Here we speak of the spiritual journey in terms of
the healing of the unconscious motivations and the
removing of obstacles within us to divine union.

As we "begin" the spiritual journey, following
what might be called a personal conversion,[2] it is not
long before we are faced with various temptations,
to try to dissuade us from continuing with the new
life we have begun. This can take many forms, but
classically it is usually in the form of reminders of
the "easier" way of life that we may have left behind.
How much sweeter things could be for us if we were
to give up these new "difficult" ideas and reminders
of all that we could have become in the future. As
the false self is being confronted, it rebels against the
new way of life. Having undertaken a new way of life
walking in the footsteps of Christ, we may soon be
tempted by Satan who will try to dissuade us, and get
us to go back to the older ways that may now seem
more appealing. Combat with the false self, facing
one's various personal issues and weaknesses, can be
understood as fighting one's demons. That is not to
say that combat with the demonic itself is not also
real, but in this case the demons can be understood to
mean combat with the false self.

Next follow the more subtle temptations, where
we are offered the greater good. We may be reminded
of all the good we could have done if we had stayed in
the world. We are reminded of those we left behind,
families, needy parents, and lovers. If only we would

give up this way of life, we could prevent their suffering, or help others in a much more "useful" way. For example, a man who studied with me for the priesthood was the only child in his family. His parents had a business that he was to inherit. But since he opted to become a priest they eventually had to sell the business as it was becoming too much for them on their own. No doubt on difficult days of doubt he must have been tempted to think of all the hardship he was putting his parents through, and how he could have made them so happy if only he had kept on the family business. The reality was that they were extremely proud that he became a priest. These kinds of temptations are much more subtle and often more successful in getting people to give up the spiritual life, as they come under the guise of "the greater good."

Why do we experience these temptations of both aversion to our new life in Christ and attraction to return to the world? The devil will tap into some of our emotional programs for happiness, which are still in place at the unconscious level. Until these programs are dealt with, we continue to be dissatisfied with the things around us and have to struggle to persevere. It is usually not long after we begin the journey that we will enter into the "night of sense":

> The night of sense is that aspect of the dark night which corresponds to God's loving transformation of us in himself at the threshold and well into the stage of emergence. The immediate cause of the night is transforming union. The principal cause of the darkness (or pain) of the night at this point is our weakness, our resistance, our vacillation, our inner poverty.[3]

St. John of the Cross says there are three signs that indicate that we are entering into the night of sense.[4] The first sign is that we find both prayer and daily life begin to lose their general appeal. Prayer dries up and becomes uninteresting and difficult. The initial consolations that began with our new-found love for God seem to disappear. It is no longer easy to pray and takes a real effort even to give time to prayer. The second sign is that we feel we may have done something wrong or committed some personal sin that has offended God. Since there is no consolation at this time either, this seems to confirm our thinking that we have offended God in some way. This can cause great suffering to the soul. The third sign of the night of sense is that we are no longer able to use discursive meditation. Discursive meditation now becomes virtually impossible. St. John says that if all three of these signs are present, then we are probably beginning the night of sense. Now we are beginning to face the false self, which we would rather avoid. However, if we really want to grow, which our consciously beginning the spiritual journey would suggest, then we cannot avoid this process. We are beginning to face up to what we are really like: "Centering prayer, as it becomes contemplative in the strict sense, gently but relentlessly invites us to face up to issues that we are not acknowledging in our lives."[5]

During the night of sense there are three trials in particular that we may undergo. Not all three will necessarily affect each person, sometimes only one. The first trial is that of sexual temptation, also called "the spirit of fornication." People can find themselves bombarded with strong sexual thoughts accompanied by sexual feelings. This may happen during prayer as well as apart from prayer. This can be a terrible trial, especially for someone who is now trying to live a chaste life, as they may feel they are letting God down and it is not always easy to judge if, or how much, one is giving in to these temptations. However, the very presence of worry and sorrow at the thought that one may be offending God is often an indication that one is still resolved to be faithful to him, in spite of the temptations. Along with this we may be tempted to think that we really are losing the battle as we seem to be getting worse, and so perhaps we should give up. When we finally come through this trial, we may also be tempted to think that *we* have just won this battle. Again this is the false self in action, wanting to control and dominate everything. We must recognize that it is pure grace that enables us to overcome these difficulties. The spirit of fornication helps us be purified of the need for immediate and often selfish pleasure.

The second kind of temptation is the temptation to blaspheme God, also known as "the spirit of blasphemy":

> At other times a blasphemous spirit is added; it commingles intolerable blasphemies with all one's thoughts and ideas. Sometimes these blasphemies are so strongly suggested to the imagination that the soul is almost made to pronounce them, which is a grave torment to it.[6]

These kind of blasphemies can happen surprisingly easily. For example, a young man who joined a lay school of evangelization in Rome had been used to fasting twice a week. However, once he joined, he was told by those in charge of the school that they did not allow fasting for the students while they were in the school. Suddenly he found his "holy" ideas being challenged. He had been inspired through his interest in Medjugorje to fast and he felt he was doing a holy thing in responding to this call. Yet now he was being told not to by another Catholic group. No doubt he was tempted to say "Lord, why are you allowing this to happen? I am doing this good work for you and yet now you stop me?"

With the spirit of blasphemy, people may find themselves in this kind of dilemma. If they are not allowed to act as they think they should, they may find themselves complaining against their superiors, or even against God that He has made their life so difficult, when they were previously living such a virtuous life. In fact, what they are being faced with is the letting go of their own selfish desires and submitting to the Lord's will through their superiors. However, with the emotional programs in place, this can cause quite a reaction. This is another indication of how much work needs to be done:

> The night of sense reveals the full extent of the selfishness of which we are capable. Humility is the fruit of the bittersweet experiences of this intimate kind of self-knowledge. It is the peaceful acknowledgement of our faults without the reactions of blame, shame, anger, or discouragement. Self-incriminations are neurotic.[7]

The temptation with any of these trials is to think that the spiritual life, or religious life, is not for you: "You're not able to live this life (the perfect kind of life that you expect of yourself), so maybe you should leave it to those who can." This temptation is one of pride, as we are still depending on what we can do ourselves.

A third trial in the night of sense consists in a terrible uncertainty that comes over the soul, leaving it in turmoil and unsure of what to do, and unsure if it has done wrong. This is known as "the spirit of dizziness":

> Sometimes another loathsome spirit, which Isaiah calls *spiritus vertiginis* [Is. 19.14], is sent to these souls, not for their downfall but to try them. This spirit so darkens the senses that such souls are filled with a thousand scruples and perplexities, so intricate that such persons can never be content with anything, nor can their judgment receive the support of any counsel or idea. This is one of the most burdensome goads and horrors of this night—very similar to what occurs in the spiritual night.[8]

The soul is left in a state of terrible confusion with regard to some matter, which could be of conscience or of some important decision in life such as a vocation. There seems to be no let up, even when spiritual guidance is sought. The individual may feel quite abandoned by God. This trial helps to purify the soul of the desire to know everything, which again is a form of being in control.

The purpose behind each of these three trials is to help us see that at the heart of our various emotional programs for happiness lies selfishness. During the night of sense, all sensible satisfactions dry up. As a result we are left craving some kind of satisfaction: "The spirit of fornication reveals the intensity of desire that fuels our instinctual need for pleasure, affection and esteem."[9] We begin to see that our motivations are not as pure as we might have liked to think. Sexual activity is one of the most intense pleasures that humans have and so the person going through this dryness can easily be led to this kind of temptation. It may also manifest itself in other forms of over-indulgence, such as eating, drinking, or escapist entertainment.

The spirit of blasphemy focuses on our need to control things. In the night of sense, God will deliberately take things out of our control, which we are not used to and so we resist intensely. All our plans, even those that may appear to be very good plans, come to nothing and everything may seem to go wrong. This can lead to great frustration until we begin to accept it and let go of the need to control everything ourselves. We like to think that we are in control in the spiritual journey, but God shows us that if we want to progress we must let go completely and allow him to take the driving seat.

The spirit of dizziness focuses on the need for certitude. This comes from our need for security. In this trial we become uncertain of almost everything and we may feel quite adrift. God is calling us into the unknown. God knows where He is bringing us, but will not reveal it to us until the right time, and this is for our own good. This was the call that Abraham received: to leave everything familiar and go to a land that God would show him.[10] It is one thing to leave everything dear to you and set out for something that you know is better, but to head off for an unknown destination is much more difficult. The Spirit asks us to put our trust in his providence rather than in our own plans: "The desire or demand for certitude is an obstacle to launching full sail on the ocean of trust."[11] God is calling us and helping us to grow up and leave childish ways behind. His call to us is to let these programs die, and to do this we must consent to let them die, since we cannot do this directly ourselves:

> By letting go of our desires for satisfaction in these areas, we move toward a permanent disposition of peace. Upsetting thoughts and emotions arise, but they no longer build up into emotional binges. The immense energy that we required to bear the afflictive emotions that flared up when our programs for happiness were frustrated is now available for more useful things, such as loving the people with whom we live and whom we are trying to serve.[12]

As we are going through the night of sense, the unconscious also begins to release its energies:

> The night of sense is doing more than dismantling the false self. In relaxing our compulsions and habitual ways of over-reacting, it also releases the energies of the unconscious. This is particularly true if our journey is grounded in the regular practice of contemplative prayer

by a receptive method such as Centering Prayer. Through the process of resting in God, beyond thoughts, feeling, associations, and commentaries, we are moving from the level of our physical faculties and their perceptions to the level of the spiritual faculties and their intuitions, and opening to the divine presence at a deeper level still. This brings even greater rest. And this rest, in turn, loosens up the material in the unconscious that the defense mechanisms of early childhood have previously kept out of our awareness.[13]

This energy from the unconscious can come in a positive or negative form. If positive, it may take the form of psychic abilities, spiritual consolation, or charismatic gifts. If we have not already begun to experience humility through self-knowledge, then these new gifts may cause pride. If the energies are negative and we experience more of the darker side of our personalities, then without humility we may find ourselves going into the depths of despair or discouragement. This is why God allows us to be humiliated first. Pride must be dealt with for our own good.

Another positive benefit coming from the release of these energies is the development of the intuitive level of consciousness. This level transcends the mental egoic level of consciousness and opens us up to a new perspective on reality. According to the mystics, the present level of human consciousness that we experience is a doorway to higher levels of consciousness.[14] We are only beginning to experience our full potential as human beings, but it seems that first we have to clear out all the emotional baggage that we are carrying.

## THE STRUGGLE WITH CULTURAL CONDITIONING

Every time we come through a time of struggle we move to a new level of integration. To ourselves we may not appear to be getting anywhere, except having to struggle all the time, but we are constantly being led to a higher level, which is then followed by "level ground," a period where we learn to integrate into our lives and relationships all that we have learned from the last struggle. This cycle repeats itself, bringing us ever higher. After each plateau there seems to be a time of ease, until the spiritual food that we enjoy at that level no longer nourishes us sufficiently and then it is time to begin the next struggle. When we are ready, the Spirit entices us to make the next step in the journey, which usually involves overcoming the cultural conditioning that we have been brought up with and are probably quite unaware of.

Our cultural conditioning is much stronger than we may realize. We probably accept all kinds of unwritten "laws," which are purely from our culture. Much of what is considered acceptable, or unacceptable behavior, is from the culture that we have grown up in. We are conditioned with ideas about how we should dress, what we can say, how and what we should eat. As we are purified in the spiritual journey, the Spirit enables us to step out of this conditioning, which we have grown so accustomed to. This may involve going against our spiritual director's advice, perhaps even leaving the religious life, having recognized that our motivations for entering were the wrong ones and that we are not really suited to it. For a separated man or woman it might mean having the courage to look for an annulment, so that either partner can move on in their life. At the time it may be a huge trial, as we are likely to feel very alone in our decision. But if we are faithful to the promptings of the Spirit, the Lord will see us through.

Mother Teresa of Calcutta's work with the poorest of the poor is another example of this. In Indian culture, many of the people she worked with are known as the "untouchables," and for her even to begin working with and caring for them would have been quite shocking to many. However, because of her response to God's call, the fruits of God's grace proved the greater in the end and people's thinking began to change. She had the freedom to do this kind of work, in spite of what people thought:

> To become free—that is, to move from mythic membership to mental egoic consciousness—requires a journey away from cultural expectations, stereotypes, and mindsets into an increasing trust in the goodness and power of God.[15]

To go against what we have been taught for thirty, forty, or fifty years is no mean feat. It takes the purifying work of the Spirit to enable us to do this.

One of the difficulties that we face in any of these trials is the fact that it may go on for quite a long time. We are tempted to ask, "Why is God allowing this to happen for so long?" However, God knows exactly how long the trial needs to last for each individual for the proper fruits to be produced: "If the divine help comes too soon, before the work of purification and healing has been accomplished, it may frustrate our ultimate ability to live the divine life."[16] Every trial and struggle that we go through, God can use for our growth and transformation. In his providence everything works for the good: "We are well aware that God works with those who love him, those who have been called in accordance with his purpose, and turns everything to their good" (Rm 8:28).

## THE NIGHT OF SPIRIT

Even though much of the false self is dismantled in the night of sense, some of it still remains at a deeper level in our spiritual faculties. This is dealt with in the night of the spirit.

In the night of the spirit (also known as the dark night of the soul) all "felt" mystical experiences cease and we are left in the darkness of faith, meaning that we feel and sense nothing but persevere because we believe it is the right thing to do, in spite of the fact that there is no consolation and it may even feel as if we have been abandoned by God. This can be especially hard for someone who may have experienced mystical or charismatic gifts at an earlier stage. However, without this purification we will not be able to reach divine union. We may be secretly satisfied with the spiritual gifts God has given us or we may have an inflated ego over the fact that we are considered a spiritual teacher, leader, or guide. We may be inclined to over-identify with the gifts that God has given us. There is still a lot of selfishness and pride under the surface.

The night of the spirit deals with these hidden motivations so that we are reduced to nothing, as it were. God shows us what we are really like and that we are capable of every kind of evil. God is really giving us a greater freedom in him, while at the time it may feel like we are being annihilated.

One of the difficulties in the night of spirit is that all the work is taking place within and we are not aware of it. We have been used to using our faculties of memory, imagination, and reason, but in contemplative prayer these are put to rest and God works from within, in silence. The language of God is silence, and God speaks to us through this silence. The desire to be silent can in itself be a sign of the work of God within us. Initially, when we are not used to praying in silence, we may find it hard to believe that there is much happening. However, God is continually at work. To us, the prayer may just seem like dryness. One indication that something is happening is the fruit we experience: humility and trust in God. Humility helps us not to be so judgmental, as God gives us greater insight into ourselves. As a result we see how mixed our own motivations are. This in turn helps us not to judge others. We may also begin to find a deep sense of gratitude for many things, as we begin to recognize that everything is a gift from God. Saint Thomas Aquinas says that the only thing we can really take credit for is our sins!

It is always difficult to describe these experiences, as they do not amount to concepts or ideas but rather a deep sense of the presence of God. Different people experience it in different ways. It may seem to come from above or below, from within, or from outside. It can happen gradually or suddenly. There are no hard and fast rules:

When [the memory and imagination] are completely still and the will is totally absorbed in

God, there is no self-reflection. This is the experience of the "prayer of full union" in which all  the faculties are motionless and rest in God.[17]

The whole purpose of this purification is to lead us to a deeper union with God, that is, to remove the obstacles that prevent us from experiencing union with the Holy Trinity, already present at the core of our being from baptism:

> Transforming union is a restructuring of consciousness, not an experience or set of experiences. In the course of this restructuring, as we shall see ... the presence of God becomes a kind of fourth dimension to the three-dimensional world in which we have been living. In the light of transforming union, therefore, the most important element in contemplative prayer is the practice itself, not its psychological content. If we fully grasped this truth, it would make the spiritual journey much easier.[18]

John of the Cross also describes this journey, but in a different way. He says that there is also another way, which he calls the path of pure faith. He calls this the "hidden ladder" and it seems that more people experience the journey this way than any other. With the hidden ladder, as the name suggests, the soul is not aware of the progress it is making and may have little or no felt experiences at all, but it is progressing just the same toward transforming union, "which is the abiding sense of rootedness in the divine presence within."[19] The soul may only experience dryness and appear to be going nowhere most of the time.

Again this is where commitment to the journey is so important. The journey can take the form of the way of light, which involves more "felt" experiences but which only a few people enjoy, or the way of darkness, which seems to be the more common experience. However, both ways lead to God who can only be experienced in the darkness of pure faith.

Even as we progress in the journey of prayer, the false self is still at work in subtle ways. The worldly desires for satisfaction may now be transferred to prayer, and we need to be purified of these as well if we want to be completely transformed in God. God is aware of exactly what each one needs and as a result some may experience more spiritual gifts or consolations than others:

> Some people need [the consolations of contemplative prayer], especially those who have been severely hurt in childhood. God bends over, caresses, and virtually makes love to people who have been deeply hurt, in order to convince them that it is all right to enjoy pleasures that they thought they should not enjoy, or were taught that they should not enjoy. God invites them to review the emotional judgments of childhood and to accept the good things of life with grateful hearts. Gratitude is an essential disposition in the spiritual journey.[20]

Since all the gifts that God gives are to help us serve his Church, we must learn to see this clearly, to understand that they are not just for the individual and that we cannot take any credit for them. Jesus himself continually reminded his disciples that he had come to serve and that they must do the same: "For the Son of man himself came not to be served but to serve, and to give his life as a ransom for many" (Mk 10:45). Jesus' own ministry met with rejection, persecution, misunderstanding, and eventually death. We may be called in the same way. God continually reminds us that He is asking us to follow him on His and not on our own terms. While we may be convinced that we are doing God's will, we may be quite surprised to find how much we resist a change that involves letting go of some of the respect and prestige that perhaps our work or ministry has given us. The false self is still at work, but we cannot see it. God asks us to let go of what we cling to: "The spiritual journey is not a success story but a series of diminutions of self."[21] It is, however, important to understand humility properly. Humility does not mean putting oneself down for no particular reason, rather it is "the experiential awareness, born of the divine light, that without God's protection we are capable of every sin."[22]

There are five fruits in particular that come from the night of the spirit: The first is the freedom from the temptation to think that we are especially important because of some gift or charism that we have received. God shows us that we are just the same as everyone else and should be treated the same way too, in spite of any gifts we may possess.

The second fruit is that we are no longer dominated by any emotion. We tend to be dominated by our emotions in spite of our best efforts to be free. The night of the spirit frees us of this and helps the emotions be properly integrated into the whole person where they can then serve us as they were so intended by God: "The integration of our emotional life with reason and faith and the subjection of our whole being to God constitute Saint Thomas Aquinas' definition of human happiness."[23] The last of our emotional programs for happiness are laid to rest in the night of spirit, so that we can begin to enjoy the harmony that was intended for us.

A third fruit is the purification of our idea of God. Depending on what we were taught about God as children, as young adults, and on the idea of our peers or social group, we will have been left with a particular idea or understanding of God. In the night of the spirit, this idea is purified and we begin to experience God in a completely different way. God will also purify us of the idea we may have developed of him in any mystical experiences we may have had:

> God reveals himself in the night of spirit in a vastly superior way—as infinite, incomprehensible and ineffable—the way that he appeared to Moses on Mount Sinai and to Elijah on Mount Horeb.[24]

Another fruit of the night of spirit is the purification of the theological virtues of faith, hope, and love. As our faith is purified we may find ourselves being misunderstood, or even rejected by our family or friends in circles of faith. We may suddenly find that we can no longer relate to our spiritual director. We are being asked to accept God on God's terms and let go of whatever may be an obstacle to that union. We may find that our own idea of Church, God, faith, vocation, and life itself changes dramatically. We can observe this from many of the characters that we meet in the scriptures. Mary, the mother of Jesus, is a particularly good example. Her ideas of her vocation were turned on their head at the annunciation. Her faith in the promises of the angel must have reached crisis point at the time of the crucifixion. All through Jesus' public ministry she had to watch him being continually rejected and misunderstood, even though she had been told that he would be the Messiah whose reign would never end.

Through the night of the spirit God brings us through some extraordinary experiences of darkness, but only to emerge with greater faith, trust, hope, and love in him:

> The greatest fruit of the night of spirit is the disposition that is willing to accept God on his own terms. As a result, one allows God to be God without knowing who or what that is.[25]

If we can allow God to be God, in a way that seems completely foreign to us, then we begin to trust God in a new and deeper way. God's action no longer depends on our idea of what that action should be or how it should work, according to our very limited idea of God. What can be very disconcerting about the night of the spirit is that we do not see this happening, as we are left completely in the dark and God seems to be hidden from us.

A fifth fruit of the night of spirit is a longing for divine union and to be free of all selfishness that may hinder that from happening. The self is becoming ever smaller and God's presence in us is being given more space, as it were: "Thus, the divine plan is to transform human nature into the divine, not by giving it some special role or exceptional powers, but by enabling it to live ordinary life with extraordinary love."[26]

## The Transforming Union

The dismantling of the false self, the night of sense with its various trials, and finally the night of the spirit all have one goal: the transforming union. When the false self is completely dead or dismantled, there is no longer any obstacle to divine union and that is exactly what happens. We are transformed by being fully united to God. The purpose of this is so we can live more fully in the world, but without being dominated as before by our emotions and false programs for happiness. Now our emotions have been fully integrated and will better serve the whole person. The emotions will still be there, but they will not have the lingering and damaging effects as before. They will now serve their purpose at the right time, by responding to various situations we encounter and without dominating us. Jesus getting angry in the temple is a good example of this.[27] Jesus was enraged at what he saw happening in the temple and drove out the moneychangers and traders. But when it was over Jesus was calm again. The emotion of anger had served its purpose and was totally integrated in his whole person. On the other hand, if someone still dominated by the false self got angry in this situation they might easily have remained so for days and completely overreacted or perhaps directed their anger at the wrong people.

Once we have reached the transforming union—which should be considered the norm for all Christians, although the experience of it seems limited enough—we can then act with greater clarity, love, and compassion in the world, because we see reality for what it is. We are no longer looking through the colored lenses of prejudice or emotional domination, as these have all been put to rest in the nights of sense and spirit. We can now more perfectly reflect the love and the compassion of God, and this is what other people experience in us. We are now totally given to service without seeking anything for ourselves, because we are completely filled with God, as it were. We also have much greater energy than before for serving other people, since we are no longer drained of energy through the false programs for happiness. This can be seen in some of those holy people of our world who have an extraordinary ability to keep serving others, often in very difficult conditions. The false self is now gone and so the true self, united to God, can act much more effectively, unhindered by the emotional programs. The disciple is called to serve and once we are united to God in the transforming union we are enabled to serve with greater intensity. The transforming union enables us truly to follow Christ as we are called:

> The tendency of the transforming union as an abiding state is rather to be without extraordinary experiences and to lead ordinary daily life in an unobtrusive way. If one has special gifts, these are exercised in dependence on God. One is completely free of the results and does not draw one's identity from any glamorous role, but is simply, like God, the servant of creation.[28]

We can see that the interior journey to which God invites us, is quite an adventure. There is far more going on than we might have imagined. In the light of the spiritual journey the many trials we go through in daily life begin to make more sense, though of course not usually at the time! I would like to conclude this chapter with the following quotation, which I believe is a good summary of what we have been talking about:

Contemplative prayer is addressed to the human situation just as it is. It is designed to heal the consequences of the human condition, which is basically the privation of the divine presence. Everyone suffers from this disease. If we accept the fact that we are suffering from a serious pathology, we possess a point of departure for the spiritual journey. The pathology is simply this: we have come to full reflective self-consciousness without the experience of intimacy with God. Because that crucial reassurance is missing, our fragile egos desperately seek other means of shoring up our weaknesses and defending ourselves from the pain of alienation from God and other people. Contemplative prayer is the divine remedy for this illness.[29]

## Chapter 5

# THE INFLUENCE OF THE DESERT

THE ABBAS AND AMMAS (or Fathers and Mothers) of the desert have had a great influence on Western spirituality and particularly on the development of monasticism. These men and women intent on giving their whole lives to Christ sought a way of life whereby everything they did would be conducive to their growing in holiness. So they left "the world" and took refuge in the desert. Anthony of Egypt was one of the first to do this. In the desert they lived in extreme poverty and simplicity making daily war on the "demons" or the passions, hoping to grow continually closer to Christ in every way. Several became known for their wisdom and later many of the sayings of the desert were written down, leaving us a rich heritage from which to draw.

Until the Edict of Milan in 313 CE[1] many Christians had to face the daily possibility of martyrdom, which was considered (and still is) the greatest witness to one's faith in Christ. However, after this edict was passed, martyrdom was no longer as likely and people began to wonder how they could now hope to give such a great witness to their faith. The asceticism of the desert began to be compared to the sacrifice of martyrdom and St. Athanasius, the author of the life of Anthony of Egypt, even dared to say that the two were equal. It became known as "white martyrdom." As a result hundreds of men and women fled to the desert seeking direction from the desert Abbas and Ammas, hoping to grow in holiness by this way of life.

Laura Swan, O.S.B., points out that while many considered the retreat into the desert to face the false self and all the spiritual battles that it entails the greatest sacrifice, it is in many ways more difficult to remain in the world in the various communities in which we find ourselves and put up with the trying weaknesses and eccentricities of others. This may not be quite as exciting, but the reality is that it is at least as difficult and certainly just as much a path to holiness:

> Desert ascetics remind us that life hands us authentic asceticism: meetings, deadlines, "smallness" of income in the midst of aging, the ministrations that frail members call for, authority and obedience in tension in our individualistic culture, and difficult community members. Families have difficulty building and sustaining relationships in a culture that undermines those values and commitments. Desert ascetics sought to disappear, taking their wisdom with them. We know that the greater challenge is to build healthy communities and a healthy church. To us it seems the easier thing to disappear, to seek hiddenness.[2]

Since the majority of people do in fact live this way today, perhaps it should be given more attention. The contemplative journey is meant for everyone. You do not just have to be in a monastery to live this way. Since many lay people feel that the spiritual journey is only for priests and religious, they often exclude themselves from some of these great treasures that are meant for everyone. Indeed, many lay people have to struggle through greater difficulties than religious, financially and otherwise. To help more lay people realize that they are already just as much on the journey as many religious would be a great source of encouragement and support in our effort to live the Gospel:

> Contemplative prayer, in some form or other, really is for everyone. Instead of speaking of the "extraordinary" grace of contemplative prayer (the beginnings of which, at least, we are here equating with Centering Prayer), we should speak of the extraordinary grace of prayer itself. Given the great miracle of prayer itself, contemplative prayer, as well as every other degree or intensity of prayer, ought to follow naturally, as it were.[3]

The spirituality of the desert is today often seen in a very critical light, as being extremely negative and anti-body. The desert mystics saw the body as positively evil, something to be subdued at all costs if the soul was to make any progress in the spiritual journey. In spite of the negative side of the spirituality, which should be seen in the context and understanding of the time, we still can learn much from their ideas today, though some of them obviously need to be interpreted to fit the context of our time. Kenneth C. Russell makes the point that John Cassian was one of the strong exceptions to this point. He was very practical and quite a psychologist, as can be seen from his writings. He speaks of the ascetical life as a means to treat the "sickness" of the whole person not just the soul. He has what is perhaps the advantage over our modern culture, of treating the subject in a more holistic way than we generally do:

> As the list [of passions] Cassian received from Evagrius Ponticus passed through time, it became a list of vices or capital sins. But we must bear in mind that for Cassian it is a list of *diseases*, which call for healing. Sickness, not guilt, is the primary reality, and the issue is not how we got this way but what we are going to do about it.[4]

> ... Cassian's conception of asceticism is broader than our own. Cassian is dealing with the complex psychospiritual and social elements which press an individual in one direction or another. Asceticism, therefore, is as much about psychology as it is about spirituality. Cassian, in fact, has a holistic view of human nature. He is trying to solve human problems, and, since he does not share our piecemeal view that *this* is a psychological problem while *that* is a spiritual problem, his asceticism aspires to cure the whole person.[5]

Cassian also gives several examples of how many of the Desert Fathers with whom people spoke were very welcoming, how they would often cut short their talks in order for their guests to get some sleep, or even present them with exquisite meals (by desert standards, that is!).

All through his writings Cassian is presenting us with a balance: not too much of anything but at the same time enough for the needs of the person. It should also be remembered that these people had a different understanding of the needs of the body than we do today. Cassian, at least, presented quite a balanced view of the needs of the body, as understood in that time. So while generally we may have a negative picture of desert spirituality, we can still learn a lot from it today. It is largely a question of interpretation.

Here we will mention three of the Christian writers from the desert: Evagrius Ponticus, John Cassian, and John Climacus. We can see how the development of centering prayer has been very much influenced by their thinking and how it is continuing the same ancient tradition, although with new insights. We will begin with Evagrius of Pontus.

## EVAGRIUS PONTICUS (346–399)

Evagrius was the first important writer among the monks of the desert. For his time, he had some extraordinary insights into psychology. His teachings are very similar to what is being taught today. Evagrius organized into a coherent system the teachings of the Desert Fathers on prayer. He gave his own definition of the ascetic life as "the spiritual method whose aim it is to purify the part of the soul that is the seat of the passions."[6] Evagrius spoke of *apatheia*[7] as the health of the soul. But alone it is not enough for a complete return to health:

> The effects of keeping the commandments
> (that is to say, *apatheia*) do not suffice to heal
> the powers of the soul completely. They must
> be complemented by a contemplative activity
> which is appropriate to these faculties and this
> activity must penetrate the spirit.[8]

Contemplation in his view, is not merely a luxury for a few specially favored souls, rather it is an essential part of the spiritual journey for any Christian who wants to become perfect in prayer. For Evagrius the most important aspect of the Christian life is prayer: "Go, sell your possessions and give to the poor, and take up your cross so that you can pray without distraction."[9] Instead of "come follow me," as found in the Gospels, we find, "so that you can pray without distraction." In other words, for Evagrius, to pray is to follow Christ, to live the Gospel. For Origen, martyrdom was the greatest way for the Christian to imitate Christ, but Evagrius took this further and said that contemplation was the equivalent of martyrdom.[10] Prayer involves purification, since the highest form of contemplation, which is union with God, cannot take place without this purification. For Evagrius, it was unthinkable that this union could take place without the purification of the passions, and this takes time and dedication to the life of prayer. Perhaps this is why he was prepared to compare it to martyrdom, as he knew well how much suffering it could involve.

This brings up the question that is often asked, as to whether one can or should practice centering prayer that leads to contemplation without first having gone through this purification. In other words, is it wise for people to begin with this kind of prayer, when they haven't already been practicing a life of prayer for a long time? Keating answers this by saying that this purification takes place in and through centering prayer, over time. Centering prayer usually leads to contemplation, which in turn can lead to union. Just because one is practicing centering prayer does not necessarily imply that one is experiencing full union with God. This purification does take place and the most effective way to bring it about is through a practice such as centering prayer.

While Cassian, Climacus, and Evagrius are all in agreement that one must undergo a purification before one can reach union, this does not go against what Keating teaches. It is simply a question of how and when you understand this to happen. Indeed these writers do not specify that you should not practice the prayer of silence until you have purified the passions, rather that the purification must take place for pure union to come about. Anyone can practice centering prayer, but this will begin a process of inner purification. When this process has been completed, there are no longer any obstacles to divine union.

Earlier we mentioned how distracted we can become by the many different thoughts that flow through our minds when we try to pray. If we allow ourselves to get caught up with these thoughts, we will find ourselves drawn away from the inner peace. The idea is to let these thoughts go continually. Interestingly, Evagrius mentions virtually all the same kind of thoughts, starting with the very ordinary:

> When the devils see that you are really fervent in your prayer they suggest certain matters to your mind, giving you the impression that there are

pressing concerns demanding attention. In a little while they stir up your memory of these matters and move your mind to search into them. Then when it meets with failure it becomes saddened and loses heart.[11]

There are eight general and basic categories of thought in which are included every thought. First is that of gluttony, then impurity, avarice, sadness, anger, *acedia*, vainlglory, and last of all, pride. It is not in our power to determine whether we are disturbed by these thoughts, but it is up to us to decide if they are to linger within us or not and whether or not they are to stir up our passions.[12]

The devil so passionately envies the man who prays that he employs every device to frustrate that purpose. Thus he does not cease to stir up thoughts of various affairs by means of the memory. He stirs up all the passions by means of the flesh. In this way he hopes to offer some obstacle to that excellent course pursued in prayer on the journey toward God.[13]

In the second passage quoted above Evagrius says that "it is up to us to decide if [these thoughts] are to linger within us or not." This is the same as the practice of "letting go" of thoughts, which centering prayer recommends.

Now Evagrius also mentions the kind of disturbing (or emotionally charged) thoughts that well up within us. We remember a situation where we were perhaps unjustly treated and, as soon as this thought comes

into our consciousness, we find ourselves welling up
with emotions. Then the various commentaries from
the past begin to play and we get caught up in a whole
cycle. If we are unable to let these thoughts go early
on (through use of the sacred word), we are likely to
get completely caught up and distracted from that
place of peace. These emotionally charged thoughts
are being released from the unconscious and we experience them in the form of thoughts. All we have to
do is let them go:

> Those memories, colored by passion that we
> find in ourselves, come from former experiences
> we underwent while subject to some passion.
> Whatever experience we now undergo while
> under the influence of passion will in the future
> persist in us in the form of passionate memo-
> ries. And so the conqueror of the demons, who
> are the ones who cause this sort of thing in us,
> despises not only the demon he conquers, but
> also these kinds of thoughts he causes in us.
> For, be sure of it, the immaterial enemy is more
> fierce than the material one (that is, the passion-
> ate thought).[14]

Evagrius says that we must learn to be free of these
thoughts.[15] What we are aiming at is to have our mind
completely free of thoughts or concepts, or at least
not to be distracted by them. This is what he calls
"pure prayer":

> When your spirit withdraws, as it were, little by
> little from the flesh because of your ardent long-
> ing for God, and turns away from every thought

that derives from sensibility or memory or temperament and is filled with reverence and joy at
the same time, then you can be sure that you
are drawing near that country whose name is
prayer.[16]

You will not be able to pray purely if you are all
involved with material affairs and agitated with
unremitting concerns. For prayer is the rejection
of concepts.[17]

This is also the idea of reducing as much outside sensible interference as possible. So we pray in a comfortable position, with eyes closed, somewhere quiet and
if possible without moving. In this way we reduce the
intake of information through the senses, being left
only to deal with the world of thoughts.

Evagrius also mentions the possibility of being
deceived by images or apparent visions. This is a trap,
as the only thing that is important during the time
of prayer is to remain in silence and to let go of all
thoughts. God is beyond our images or ideas, and we
must be aware of the temptation to reduce Him to a
vision, idea, or concept, "for prayer is the rejection of
concepts":

Beware of the traps your adversaries lay for you.
For suddenly it may happen when you are praying purely, free from all disturbance, that some
unusual and strange form appears so as to lead
you into the presumptuous thought that God is
actually situated there as in a place. This is cal-
culated to persuade you, through the very sud-
denness of the revelation, that God is something

qualitative. But God is without quantity and without all outward form.[18]

Evagrius goes on to warn about the various types of images that the demons will try to produce, simply to distract you from your prayer. What may appear to the inexperienced to be progress in the form of a vision or image, even if it appears to be a heavenly one, is in fact only a distraction. Since God is beyond images and ideas, we must not seek Him in these. Evagrius gives several chapters (consisting only of one line each) to his idea of what the monk is trying to attain. It is to be stripped of all, to be unconscious of self during prayer, to be completely free of the awareness of material things. "Happy is the spirit that attains to complete unconsciousness of all sensible experience at the time of prayer."[19] The more modern presentation contains all the same basic elements:

The importance of prayer, especially prayer of silence.

That the most important kind of prayer is non-conceptual.

The need to reduce outside sensible experience during prayer.

The continual letting go of thoughts.

Not allowing oneself to be distracted by apparent visions, or profound thoughts, even of God.

I will finish discussing Evagrius' teaching with one more point of interest. Often the spirituality of the desert is criticized for being very egocentric. The same is sometimes said of contemplative prayer by those who do not understand it. Nevertheless, Evagrius points out that in fact this deep prayer helps one to be more in harmony with the rest of humanity than anything else. The deeper we go into God, and the greater the union with God we experience, the more this unites us with all of humanity as it gives us an ever increasing awareness of the dignity of our fellow human beings. This is founded on the idea of the person being made in the image of God:

> Happy is the monk who considers all men as
>     god—after God.
> A monk is a man who is separated from all
>     and who is in harmony with all.
> A monk is a man who considers himself one
>     with all men because he seems constantly
>     to see himself in every man.[20]

Keating also reminds us that this kind of prayer is in no way self-centered, but very much ecclesial. Far from separating us from others, it actually brings us closer to them:

> Any practice moving towards contemplation is ecclesial in its effects. It bonds the people who are doing it with everybody else who is doing a similar practice, and indeed with everyone else in the human family. It creates a community. As we sit in silence, we realize our oneness with others, not only with those with whom we pray, but with everyone on earth—past, present, and to come. What is deepest in them, their oneness with the divine presence, resonates with what is deepest in us. Hence, their joys, their trials, and

their openness to God are part of us. In this way we share each other's burdens, as Paul says.[21]

## JOHN CASSIAN (365–435)

Cassian speaks of the necessity of a "pure heart" for those who hope to progress in the spiritual life. The idea of joining a monastery is to live in an atmosphere of prayer, with others of a similar mindset. The fewer worldly distractions there are, the easier it is to dedicate one's life to the spiritual. Yet very few are strong enough to live this properly on their own, without the help of a structured way of life and a definite pattern of prayer. Hence the need for regular prayer times, where the monks chant the psalms. The whole day is designed to keep one immersed in the atmosphere of the scriptures. All this is to lead to a pure heart, so that in turn we come closer to God. In many of his *Conferences* Cassian put his writings directly on the lips of some of the Desert Fathers. Cassian and his close friend Germanus journeyed to various Desert Fathers, seeking their counsel. On the subject of a pure heart, Cassian reports the words of Abba Moses:

> Seeing our amazement at all this, the old man resumed: "As we have said, the aim of our profession is the kingdom of God or the kingdom of heaven. But our point of reference, our objective, is a clean heart, without which it is impossible for anyone to reach our target. If we keep to this point of reference we will proceed with all assurance, as though along a carefully drawn line."[22]

Everything we do, our every objective, must be undertaken for the sake of this purity of heart. This is why we take on loneliness, fasting, vigils, work, nakedness. For this we must practice the reading of the Scripture, together with all the other virtuous activities, and we do so to trap and to hold our hearts free of the harm of every dangerous passion and in order to rise step by step to the high point of love.[23]

Now one of the things that comes about as a result of the regular practice of centering prayer is a purity of heart, in the sense that we are continually being purified through this kind of prayer. We are gradually being freed from much of what clutters our lives on an interior level. This only happens with time. The dual period of meditation in the morning and evening is meant to help us remain in the peace of God's presence throughout the day. However, another practice that is also to help us stay immersed in God's presence during the day is mentioned here by Abba Isaac. It is the use of a particular phrase from scripture that we continually repeat in our mind, during our work and through many of the mundane things that fill our days, when nothing else in particular is happening. This is also recommended by those who teach centering prayer.

In Conferences 9 and 10, Cassian writes about his journey with Germanus to the dwelling of Abba Isaac, who spoke to them at some length about prayer. On their first visit, the old man spoke about the importance of the kind of prayer that can raise the mind to God and help the soul be freed from the continual distractions of the world, enabling it to stay focused on the things of God. Cassian and Germanus were greatly impressed by this, but on their way home realized that they still did not know *how* to do this in practice. The second day they visited Abba Isaac, he shared this secret of using a phrase from scripture.

First of all Abba Isaac mentions that the monk's life must be set on the life of virtue, for without this there will be no progress in prayer:

> This endless, unstirring calm of prayer that I have mentioned can neither be achieved nor consummated without these virtues. And likewise virtues are the prerequisite foundation of prayer and cannot be effected without it.

> First, there must be a complete removal of all concern for bodily things. Then not just the worry but even the memory of any business or worldly affair must be banished from within ourselves.

> Having completely expelled and sliced away these and similar vices ... we have then to lay the indestructible foundations of deep humility, foundations which can support that tower rising upward to the skies. Next comes the spiritual edifice of virtue. After that, the soul must be restrained from all meandering, from all slippery wanderings, so that it may rise bit by bit to the contemplation of God and to the gazing upon the realms of the spirit.[24]

Abba Isaac goes on to speak of the necessity of living a simple life and not having more than one needs. So the life of a monk should be basic, but sufficient.

The temptation is always to have "more than enough." It is difficult to apply this directly to those who have to live in the world, but obviously each must judge for themselves what is necessary for their way of life. The rule is not to make one's life more cluttered than necessary, as the clutter itself is a distraction.

On the second visit the blessed Isaac continued his discourse on prayer and was more specific as to what exactly one had to do. The problem, which Climacus and Germanus had mentioned, is that of the continual wandering of the mind when one is trying to pray or reflect on scripture. This is where Isaac suggested the use of a set phrase from scripture:

> This is something which has been handed on to us by some of the oldest of the Fathers and it is something which we hand on to only a very small number of the souls eager to know it:

> To keep the thought of God always in your mind you must cling totally to this formula for piety: "Come to my help, O God; Lord, hurry to my rescue" (Ps 69:2).[25]

Abba Isaac continues at length to give examples of the many ordinary things that happen during the day, where one can use this phrase to keep one's mind on God rather than getting too wrapped up in the world. As long as the monk keeps returning to this line of scripture, he is both recognizing his need for God and asking the Lord for help. This, according to Abba Isaac, is the key to pure prayer. Keating speaks about this phrase completely apart from the "sacred word," which he suggests using for the practice of centering prayer. This phrase, which Keating calls "an active prayer sentence" (and in fact various other phrases were also used by the Desert Fathers), is meant to help you keep your mind turned toward God, while getting through the many different aspects of the daily grind—even for the life of a monk, which is already meant to be quite God-centered. Just because one lives in a monastery and may have a better setting for a God-centered life, it does not mean that it will necessarily be so. It is good to use a phrase like the one mentioned, and continually repeat it in our mind while doing ordinary tasks such as waiting for a bus, sitting in traffic, getting a meal ready, etc. Once we have been repeating this over and over for some time, it will begin to repeat itself in the subconscious, thereby helping us to remain more at peace. It can be used especially if we are suddenly disturbed by something, or when one of the emotional programs is triggered:

> Once worked into the subconscious memory, this new "tape" tends to erase the prerecorded tapes already in place. Whenever one of the emotional programs is frustrated, a painful emotion promptly records the fact, and an appropriate commentary arises from our store of prerecorded tapes: "How can this happen to me? ... How cruel everybody is to me! ... I'm no good." If we have worked a sentence into our subconscious memory that is about the same length as our normal commentaries, it erases the former tapes and thus reduces the force of the upsetting emotions.[26]

This phrase is simply another tool to help us to remain in God's presence, or at least to be more aware that we are in God's presence, since we can never in fact be out of it. Cassian quotes Abba Isaac:

> But with an ever more perfect life and by perfect virtue we especially must be carried along toward the types of prayer which are rooted in the contemplation of eternal goodness and in fervor of love.... In no way can our spirit attain those more exalted modes of prayer of which I have been speaking except by the step-by-step journey upward through all those pleas we pour forth.[27]

> This endless, unstirring calm of prayer that I have mentioned can neither be achieved nor consummated without these virtues.[28]

This is one point on which several modern writers differ from the teaching of the Desert Fathers. It concerns the idea that one must practice prayer for many years before one can hope to reach those "more exalted modes of prayer." The reasons for not agreeing with this are several. First, many people who went to the East and learned various forms of meditation were soon showing the same signs of deep prayer, or what seemed to be contemplative prayer, as those who had walked this path for decades. Keating and his confreres began to realize that obviously it wasn't necessary to pray and live the "virtuous life" for years before one could hope to have any experience of contemplative prayer. This is one of the reasons why they decided to offer this kind of prayer to people in general, and not just to contemplatives or people who had been praying for years. Thelma Hall in her book, *Too Deep for Words,* also agrees with this:

> Most of us seem to assume that union with God is attained by laboriously ascending a ladder of virtues, which finally fashion our holiness and make us fit for him. In truth, the reverse is far more accurate: the great saints and mystics have been those who fully accepted *God's* love for *them*. It is this which makes everything else possible.[29]

This has also generally been the experience of people who have taken up this kind of prayer. Many begin to experience this deep prayer after a relatively short time.

## JOHN CLIMACUS (C. 597–649)

John Climacus is best known for his work, *The Ladder of Divine Ascent.* In the book he speaks at length on the need for simplicity in prayer. He mentions the parables of the Pharisee and the publican and that of the prodigal son. Both the publican and the prodigal son prayed with great simplicity:

> Pray in all simplicity. The publican and the prodigal son were reconciled to God by a single utterance....

> In your prayers there is no need for high-flown words, for it is the simple and unsophisticated babblings of children that have often won the heart of the Father in heaven.

Try not to talk excessively in your prayer, in
case your mind is distracted by the search for
words. One word from the publican sufficed to
placate God, and a single utterance saved the
thief. Talkative prayer frequently distracts the
mind and deludes it, whereas brevity makes for
concentration.

If it happens that, as you pray, some word
evokes delight or remorse within you, linger
over it.[30]

John recommended keeping prayer as simple and
uncomplicated as possible. As in the last line quoted
above, he recommends keeping to one word or phrase,
if you find it particularly useful. He also recommends
the use of phrases from scripture, as did other Desert
Fathers in fourth century Egypt: "Cry out to God,
Who has the strength to save you. Do not bother with
elegant and clever words. Just speak humbly, beginning with, 'Have mercy on me, for I am weak'" (Ps
6:3).[31]

John also refers to one type of prayer to which
he gives particular importance, the "Jesus Prayer."
By this he means not just the later and better-known
Orthodox prayer, "Lord Jesus Christ, Son of God,
have mercy on me a sinner," but any short prayer
with the name of Jesus. In fact, John only mentions
the Jesus Prayer three times in the whole *Ladder*, and
yet it has been a great influence on many writers who
have come after him.

The first mention of this prayer is in step fifteen,
when John is speaking of the monk preparing to go
to sleep and having to fight the temptations of impure

thoughts presented by the demons. Here John says, "Let the remembrance of death and the concise Jesus Prayer go to sleep with you and get up with you, for nothing helps you as these do when you are asleep."[32] John is one of the first authors to refer to the "Jesus Prayer" and he recommends it as a monosyllabic prayer, the strength being in its simplicity and in the name of Jesus. John doesn't actually give a specific formula for this prayer, only that we use the Jesus Prayer in whatever form appeals.

The second mention of the Jesus Prayer is in step twenty-one, on unmanly fears, when the monk experiences the childish fear of the dark. Here again, John says, the solution is the name of Jesus: " ... when you reach the spot, stretch out your hands and flog your enemies with the name of Jesus, since there is no stronger weapon in heaven or on earth."[33] In this case he seems to mean only the name of Jesus.

The third and most important passage is in step twenty-seven: "Stillness (*hesychia*) is worshipping God unceasingly and waiting on Him. Let the remembrance of Jesus be present with your every breath. Then indeed you will appreciate the value of stillness."[34] Here John does not specifically mention the Jesus Prayer itself, rather the *remembrance* of Jesus. According to different commentators this could mean various things. It could just be keeping Jesus "in mind" in a general sense, but it could also refer to a Jesus Prayer, and this seems to be how most readers have interpreted the text. It is interesting that John mentions in this passage, that the prayer should be unceasing and not just for a particular time or situation, as he mentions in the other two references. The prayer is meant to be continuous, something that keeps the monk in an unbroken state of prayer, through use of this word or phrase. This is very similar to the effect of the "sacred word" and of the "prayer phrase," which as we saw earlier can be traced back to Abba Isaac (Isaac in turn claimed that he had learned it from other ancient Fathers). The idea is that the constant repetition of these words or phrases helps to keep one in a ceaseless state of prayer.

In his introduction to *The Ladder*, Kallistos Ware also says that this remembrance of Jesus, which is to "be present with your every breath," can also and more literally be translated as "be united with your breathing." Some interpreters see in this the idea that John intended an actual physical technique, where the Jesus Prayer is linked to one's physical breathing. This is something that has later been used in various meditation techniques, where the mantra or sacred word is linked with the person's breathing. Some people find this helpful with centering prayer as well.

In the passage of John's that we have quoted, there is also a link between the use of the Jesus Prayer and inner stillness. Ware observes:

> Constantly to keep Jesus in remembrance is a way of attaining inner quiet: the Jesus Prayer helps to make the monk into a "hesychast," one who possesses silence of heart. *Hesychia* is a key word in John's doctrine of prayer, and the step which he devotes to it has proved, with the possible exception of Step 7 on the gift of tears, the most influential in the whole of *The Ladder*. By "stillness" he means both an outward manner of life—that of the hermit or solitary, living

in a cell on his own—and also an inner disposition of continual prayer, as in the passage
under discussion: "stillness is worshipping God
unceasingly."[35]

In step twenty-seven, on stillness, John is primarily concerned with the interior silence of the monk
rather than just the eremitical life. It is not just physical isolation that counts but the silence within:

> Strange as it may seem, the hesychast is a man
> who fights to keep his incorporeal self shut up in
> the house of the body.... The cell of a hesychast
> is the body that surrounds him, and within him
> is the dwelling place of knowledge.[36]

The point here is that the true hesychast is not just
one who lives in physical isolation, but is the one who
has learned to be silent at the deepest level. In this way,
he or she can be living in the midst of noise and yet
not be disturbed inside. The center of his or her heart
is focused on God. This is the contemplative dimension of the Gospel, from which we draw our energy.
This is the "better part" for which Jesus commended
Mary.[37] There is a great need for us to rediscover this
practice today.

Where is all this leading? The point of being able
to cultivate an inner disposition of silence is so that
we may remain in the presence of God, and ultimately
to experience union with God, which is the culmination of the spiritual journey. From what we have been
saying we can see that the contemplative dimension
of the Gospel has never disappeared, but that there is
perhaps a greater need to rediscover it at this time.

*Chapter 6*

# THE CLOUD OF UNKNOWING

WE WILL NOW LOOK at *The Cloud of Unknowing*, an anonymous fourteenth century spiritual classic, on which the teaching of centering prayer is largely based. Because of its older style, *The Cloud* can be a little tedious to read, but with careful examination we can see that almost all the elements of the practice of centering prayer can be found there.

## CONTEMPLATION AS A WORK OF LOVE

The author begins by saying that this book is not for everyone, as it will neither be appreciated nor understood by many. Throughout the centuries contemplative prayer has frequently been misunderstood and sharply criticized. The same holds true today, even within the Church. The author of *The Cloud* takes a few chapters to discuss this problem using the story of Martha and Mary,[1] which has always been understood by the Church as an analogy of the active and contemplative life. Not everyone appreciates the contemplative, but it is in fact the more important of the two, as it is a purer giving of the self through love. Contemplative prayer is a work of love, a giving of oneself to God in love in one of the most complete ways that is humanly possible. Nothing is held back as everything, even one's thoughts, is given to the Lord through the silence.

In *The Cloud of Unknowing* the author speaks about Mary of Bethany resting at Jesus' feet in contemplation. What he points to is her giving of herself to Jesus in love. Mary rested at the feet of Jesus in loving contemplation, undisturbed even when Martha complained. He also mentions the incident where this same Mary came into the room where Jesus was dining and wept on the feet of Jesus, drying his feet with her hair and then anointing his feet with costly ointment.[2] The writer points out that this was another indication of her enormous love for the Lord, which was confirmed by Jesus himself, who indicated to the Pharisee who had invited him that she showed great sorrow because "she loved much." This is a key element in this kind of prayer, that it is primarily a work of love. If the healing of the unconscious also takes place, it is a desirable fruit of the practice, although it is not the most important thing. Loving God for God's sake is the most important aspect of this prayer.

## THE METHOD OF PRAYER

*The Cloud* is structured as a set of instructions from one individual to someone who is open to learn about the contemplative form of prayer. In order to explain himself properly, the author first begins to point out that while active or mental prayer is good in itself, it cannot compare to the pure gift of self that is required by contemplative prayer. While our thoughts of God, heaven, the angels and saints, can be a wonderful thing, he says, they are not God, but merely thoughts about God, and so we need to move beyond them if we want to come "closer" to God. God can only be known by pure faith and so this is the path that we must take. In order to enter into this cloud, we must, the author states, also have underneath us what he calls, "a cloud of forgetting." In other words, we must be able to let go of all our thoughts and ideas, no matter how good they may seem to be:

> Center all your attention and desire on him and let this be the sole concern of your mind and heart. Do all in your power to forget everything else, keeping your thoughts and desires free from involvement with any of God's creatures or their affairs whether in general or in particular.[3]

> Think only of God, the God who created you, redeemed you, and guided you to this work. Allow no other ideas about God to enter your mind. Yet even this is too much. A naked intent toward God, the desire for him alone, is enough.[4]

Here the author mentions the need only for one's "naked intent" toward God. This is enough. In the same way with centering prayer, what is important is one's intention, indicated by the use of the sacred word. It is not an exercise of attention but *intention*; each time the sacred word is used, it repeats this intention. The author of *The Cloud* goes on to say that the best way to reduce the mind's activity is to choose one word, preferably short and one syllable, such as "God," or "love," and to use this as a way of expressing your desire to give yourself to God:

> This word will be your defense in conflict and in peace. Use it to beat upon the cloud of darkness above you and to subdue all distractions, consigning them to the *cloud of forgetting* beneath you. Should some thought go on annoying you demanding to know what you are doing, answer with this one word alone. If your mind begins to intellectualize over the meaning and connotations of this little word, remind yourself that its value lies in its simplicity.[5]

Although it is preferable for this word (the "sacred word" in centering prayer) to be short, even one syllable, there are no fixed rules, as some may be inspired to use a longer word. The word is not important in itself; rather it is an expression of one's intention during the prayer. The writer of *The Cloud* also goes on to mention another point of interest. He asks:

> Then why is this work so toilsome? The labor, of course, is in the unrelenting struggle to banish the countless distracting thoughts that plague our minds and to restrain them beneath that *cloud of forgetting* which I spoke of earlier.[6]

This is one place where Keating diverts a little from the teaching of *The Cloud of Unknowing*, something he mentions himself. While the author of *The Cloud* describes the labor in trying to "banish" the many thoughts that continue to flow through one's mind, Keating says that this should not be a task, since centering prayer is not meant to be a great effort. Rather than having to struggle or fight to get rid of the continuous flow of thoughts, one simply lets them go. The practice is helping one to be more and more detached from these thoughts. The thoughts will continue to flow through the mind, but we become less disturbed by them. Centering prayer is not an exercise in trying to make one's mind go "blank," which is extremely difficult if not impossible. There should be no struggle in the practice, rather a continual letting go. The sacred word is always used with gentleness. As Keating says:

> I have drawn from St. Francis DeSales and St. Jane de Chantal the idea of the gentleness with which to return to the sacred word. This emphasis is missing in the *Cloud*.[7]

## A Contradiction?

In chapter thirty-four of *The Cloud* an interesting point is made. Here the author says that we must be very careful not to approach contemplation with methods, as contemplation is a pure gift from God and not something that we can merit in any way:

> I am trying to make clear with words what experience teaches more convincingly, that techniques and methods are ultimately useless for awakening contemplative love. It is futile to come to this work armed with them. For all good methods and means depend on it, while it alone depends on nothing.[8]

Now some who object to the practice of centering prayer refer to this passage in *The Cloud* and argue in the same way that since indeed contemplation is a gift from God we must simply wait for it. However, here we must remember the distinction between acquired and infused contemplation. Acquired contemplation is something that we can indeed work toward, through some practice such as centering prayer. But in it we simply dispose ourselves to the gift of God. Ultimately we must wait on the goodness of God to grant us this gift, if God so desires. However, to argue against any kind of method or discipline seems contradictory, since the author of *The Cloud* has already gone to some length to explain the use of a single word repeated to help one be free of thoughts, as well as the importance of being faithful to the practice, etc. If this is not a method, what is? M. Basil Pennington also comments on this point:

> It is precisely here that we find an important difference between Christian prayer and methods of meditation passed on by some other traditions. Natural methods depend on the procedure. And so there are *rules*—spelling out exactly what must be done in order to obtain the desired effect. Christian prayer simply does not work that way.
>
> ... This is a concern some have had about using a method. Are we trying to force God to give us contemplation? No. But since he respects our freedom, we are using this freedom to open the space so that he can, if he wills, give us the gift of himself in contemplative prayer. In a sense, it might be said we are

putting "pressure" on God. God is faithful. And he has said, "seek and you shall find."[9]

So what exactly does the author of *The Cloud* mean when he says that one should not come to contemplation armed with any kind of techniques or methods? I believe he is trying to help us to understand that infused contemplation is in no way something we can achieve ourselves, by our own strength or perseverance, rather it is something that we can dispose ourselves to, using the practice that he has outlined. However, to argue that because the author of *The Cloud* says that we should avoid methods, and then to point to Keating and say he is going against the teaching of this book, is to misunderstand completely the teaching. Virtually every kind of prayer involves some kind of "technique," even though it may not be specifically defined in this way. If it did not involve any kind of method, it would mean that prayer would have to be completely different every time we approached it. At the same time it is important not to be too rigid, since the Spirit will move people in different ways and we should be flexible enough to respond to the promptings of the Spirit, rather than being caught up in rules.

## THE QUESTION OF HEALING

Now let us return again to the question of the healing of the unconscious. As we mentioned earlier, through the regular practice of centering prayer or another such method that leads to contemplation, the unconscious is gradually healed of all the emotional wounds going back to the beginning of our life. The practice of contemplation is one of love, and the work of love—especially divine love—brings about healing. Now while *The Cloud of Unknowing* doesn't mention the healing of the unconscious in the way Keating does (no one would expect a fourteenth century writer to!), it certainly does mention healing several times:

> You would have taken to [this work of love] naturally had man not sinned, for man was created to love and everything else was created to make love possible. Nevertheless, by the work of contemplative love man will be healed. Failing in this work he sinks deeper into sin further and further from God, but by persevering in it he gradually rises from sin and grows in divine intimacy.[10]

The whole process is an ongoing interior purification, indeed a kind of purgatory. First when one begins to practice this kind of prayer regularly it may seem peaceful, but after a while, as the unconscious begins to unload, one is bombarded with thoughts to such an extent that one may think the practice is a complete failure and definitely not meant for you. This is where it is tempting to give up and revert to more "meaningful" kinds of prayer. The following passage from *The Cloud* sounds a lot like this interior work of purification, although it is not couched in such direct terms:

> How wonderfully is a man's love transformed by the interior experience of this nothingness

and this nowhere. The first time he looks upon it, the sins of his whole life rise up before him.

At times the sight is as terrible as a glimpse of hell and he is tempted to despair of ever being healed and relieved of his sore burden. Many arrive at this juncture in the interior life but the terrible, comfortless agony they experience facing themselves drives them back to thoughts of worldly pleasures.

He who patiently abides in this darkness will be comforted and feel again a confidence about his destiny, for gradually he will see his past sins healed by grace.... Slowly he begins to realize that the suffering he endures is really not hell at all, but his purgatory.[11]

And finally there will come a moment when he experiences such peace and repose in that darkness that he thinks surely it must be God himself.[12]

The problem, of course, is trying to get people not to give up too soon, when the going gets really tough. When our imagination seems to have so much going on in it and the very use of the sacred word seems completely futile, we may feel we couldn't possibly be praying. This could indeed be the "hell" that the author of *The Cloud* describes above. For those who are able to persevere, however, the reward is the healing of so many of these pains. Nevertheless, it certainly does take commitment to the journey.

*Chapter 7*

# LECTIO DIVINA

LECTIO DIVINA IS A practice of prayerfully reflecting on the scriptures. Today it has once again become popular in many parts of the Church—at least in Europe—as a means of helping people to enter the scriptures at a deeper level. However, some of the modern approaches to Lectio may still not be terribly faithful to the original idea.

Originally Lectio Divina developed largely in the monastic tradition and out of the spirituality of the desert. The monastic environment is meant to be a scriptural one, in other words where the whole life-style is designed to help the monk live in such a way that he is constantly listening to the scriptures. And so there is much time given to the chanting of the liturgy, silence, and prayerful reading of the scriptures. The understanding is that the scriptures are constantly leading one to a deeper level of faith and of prayer. For instance, chapter forty-eight of the Rule of St. Benedict begins with the instruction: "Idleness is the enemy of the soul. Therefore, the brothers should have specified periods for manual labor as well as for prayerful reading (*lectio divina*)."

There were traditionally four "levels" or "senses" of scripture. The first level was the literal level, which is often the one most focused on by scholars today. This is the literal meaning of the text, the philological study of the words and culture, in order to understand the text better. The second was the moral level. It is said that when one begins to live the Gospel message and not just read it, one is then at the moral level. In other words it refers to how it applies to your life. The third is the allegorical level. This is where one begins to see one's own life reflected in the scriptures, for example, the people of Israel escaping from Egypt and wandering through the desert for years. A person may recognize his or her own struggle with sin as being the same kind of journey. This is the allegorical level. The allegorical level of scripture also involves an inner purification. Our trust in the scriptures helps us to trust in God and in God's word, enabling it to work in us. We begin to encounter the biblical desert and the inner purification starts to take place:

> Deep prayer increases our trust in God so that we can acknowledge anything and are not blown away by it. Without that trust, we maintain our defense mechanisms.... By our acknowledging [our dark side], God takes it away. The process of contemplative prayer is a way of releasing what is in the unconscious. The psyche has a need for evacuation the same as the body, and it does this as a result of the deep rest of contemplative prayer.[1]

The fourth level of scripture is the unitive or ana-gogical level. This is where one seems to be possessed by the scriptures. They radiate through you and through your life. John Cassian says that when you find yourself praying the psalms as if you were com-posing them, you have reached this level.

Now the practice of Lectio Divina involved a kind of "savoring" of the scriptures. Traditionally there were the four stages of *lectio*, *meditatio*, *oratio*, and *contemplatio*. One began with *lectio*, slowly and prayerfully reading over the scriptures. If at some point you were struck by something you read, you simply stopped and rested with it. You may only have managed to read one line, or even one word, but the amount read was not important. This led to *meditatio*, where one just rested with the word and pondered over it as long as was necessary, allowing God to speak to one through the word. *Meditatio* in turn brought the reader to the stage of *oratio*, where prayer was spon-taneous and the reader might be inspired to pray in thanks or for a particular need. Finally, the reader was led to the stage of *contemplatio*. Here the reader sim-ply rested in silence, savoring the divine presence.

The first three stages were all meant to bring the reader to this stage of *contemplatio*. In a way, it is misleading to speak about "stages" in this practice, as there was not meant to be a definite and conscious "moving onto the next stage," rather this all happened spontaneously without really working it out. Only after the Reformation and with the great tendency for analysis that came with the Scholastic Middle Ages, was *lectio* more concretely categorized:

While leading to contemplative prayer as its fruition, Lectio incorporates within a unified unfolding movement those forms of prayer which only as late as the sixteenth century were separated into distinct categories—namely, discursive prayer (or meditation), affective prayer (or "prayer of the heart"), and contemplation (or "mystical" prayer). In Lectio, these are spontaneous and integrated, in an orientation toward progressively greater simplicity and depth, the realm of contemplation. We have evidence here again that the tradition of centuries assumed contemplation was not an exclusive privilege of an elect few, but was the normal fulfilment of prayer, available to all genuine Christians willing to dedicate themselves to a serious following of Jesus.[2]

Because of the tendency to analyze everything at this period of history, the problem was that the fourth stage of *contemplatio* was generally omitted. The one praying was encouraged to stay with the first three more analytical stages, while *contemplatio* became to be considered something that might happen at the end of your life, but generally after a lot of hard work. It was usually believed to be for those in the cloisters and even in a limited way at that:

> this area of transition from *Oratio* to *Contemplatio* was the abortive "cutting-off place" in the spirituality of prayer that was taught beginning around the sixteenth century.... Its result was to isolate contemplation from what was considered normal prayer, and

to set it apart in a category for rare "chosen souls" only.[3]

Since the original idea was to bring the person praying the scriptures to the stage of *contemplatio*, this was a serious omission. Today the need to return to this final stage of *contemplatio* is great, and gradually this seems to be happening. The practice of Lectio Divina was meant to be spontaneous and this needs to be restored. Today the difficulty is that we still tend to be of a categorizing mentality and not many people are that comfortable with the more spontaneous side of Lectio. Another problem with our hyperactive world is that few people believe you can be praying without *doing* something. Most people feel it is necessary to be saying prayers or meditating on something. The idea that just *being* in the presence of God is more powerful is quite foreign.

What is the connection between Lectio and centering prayer? Since Lectio was intended to help bring one to contemplative prayer, it still has a very important role to play for those who wish to grow in prayer. What is crucial is that the right understanding of Lectio is developed once again and, in particular, that people properly understand what the purpose of it was initially. It was not meant to be simply a mental exercise. Lectio is therefore an integral part of this kind of deep prayer, although many may feel that it can be left aside:

I am often asked to clarify the relationship between Centering Prayer and Lectio Divina. Centering Prayer is not a part of the method of Lectio Divina. It is rather a distinct method of

prayer that emerges out of the same tradition.
It is closely related to Lectio Divina, but not
so much in its method as in the developing
relationship with Christ that Lectio Divina
implies and fosters.[4]

Keating points out that the problem today is
getting from the third stage of Lectio Divina to the
fourth. He suggests that this is one place where centering prayer has an important role to play, as it is one
tool that can help people make this transition from
mental prayer, to resting in God in silence:

> Centering Prayer relates to Lectio Divina as a
> discipline designed to correct what hinders or
> prevents us from moving from simplified affec-
> tive prayer into contemplation. This does not
> mean that if we practice Centering Prayer, we
> never do anything else. We simply do Lectio and
> other forms of prayer at another time.[5]

Keating goes on to address the valid objection that
is often made: Should people begin with contemplation, since we always seem to have been taught otherwise? He points out that Lectio Divina is a dynamic
process and that people can in fact start at any stage.
However, perhaps in the light of the West's current
preoccupation with intellectual activity, it may be all
the better to start with simply resting in God through
some practice such as centering prayer. Because
Lectio is a dynamic process, if one starts at the stage
of contemplation, the other stages will also be "filled
in." People will want to know how they got to where
they are and will end up covering the other stages as

well. This has already proven true in practice, especially judging by the experiences of Contemplative Outreach, where many people have experienced just what we are talking about, starting with contemplation and then finding themselves going back to develop the other parts as well:

> The tradition of Lectio Divina has always taught that we can go from one level to another even in the same period of prayer. Every one of the stages is enhanced if we have accessed the final one.[6]

## Chapter 8

# MEDITATION EAST AND WEST

IT IS OFTEN CLAIMED that centering prayer is only a "Christianized" version of Eastern meditation. Is this true? In this section we will look at the influence (if any) of Zen Buddhism and of Transcendental Meditation (TM). One of the great difficulties that emerges when you try to speak about Buddhism or Hinduism in comparison to Christianity is that while Christians like to be able to explain things through theological language, Buddhists deliberately try to avoid this, as they consider it an obstacle to experience. Consequently, there is a great abyss that is very difficult to cross. William Johnston, S.J., who has written extensively on this area, expresses the difficulty in trying to write about Zen and Christianity together:

> The longer I live in Tokyo, the more I become aware of the enormous cultural gap which separates East and West. The way of thinking, the words, the manner of expression of Buddhism and Christianity are so different that anyone who tries to write a theological book about both

is doomed to superficiality and even to failure. For the fact is that Christians and Buddhists talk different theological languages.[1]

As a result, I believe that we are not doing justice to Buddhist concepts in Christian writings, since many of the terms that Buddhists use have completely different meanings in Western culture. This makes dialogue very difficult, but it also means that there is probably far more misunderstanding than people generally realize. However, the purpose of dealing with Zen here is to try to see if and how centering prayer has been "colored" in any way with an Eastern spirituality that could be harmful to Christians.

Keating tells us that in their monastery in Spencer, the monks invited several teachers from the Eastern traditions to offer talks. They also invited a Zen master to come and give them a *sesshin*, or intensive retreat. For several years following, the Zen master led retreats in a nearby retreat house and Keating participated in several of them. Obviously, his teaching made a certain impression on the Trappist monks of Spencer. The monks were also exposed to the teaching of Transcendental Meditation (TM), which is remarkably similar to centering prayer. Again the same question arises: Is centering prayer then just another form of these meditative techniques, or is it something quite different? Here we will make some basic comparisons in order to show that while there are similarities, centering prayer is not in fact a Christianized form of Eastern meditation.

## Zen Buddhism

At the most basic level, Buddhism and Christianity are extremely different. Christianity accepts the one God—the Father, Son, and Holy Spirit—who created all things out of nothing and finally the human person as the high point of creation. Humanity sinned and turned away from God. Through the Incarnation of Christ, humanity was restored to God, but in an even more exalted state than before. Salvation is offered to all humankind through Jesus Christ, who is Lord, as a free gift.[2] Each soul is unique and has been created to enjoy and share in the divine life with God. While God is reflected in creation, just as an artist in his art, God also completely transcends creation. By contrast, although we should note that Buddhism is a very diverse religion, certain branches of Buddhism hold that there is no God and no soul, and that the idea of a God is something humanity invented in order to protect itself:

> Two ideas are psychologically deep-rooted in man: self-protection and self-preservation. For self-protection man has created God, on whom he depends for his own protection, safety and security, just as a child depends on its parent. For self-preservation man has conceived the idea of an immortal Soul or *Atman*, which will live eternally. In his ignorance, weakness, fear, and desire, man needs these two things to console himself. Hence he clings to them deeply and fanatically.[3]

The Buddha's teaching does not support this ignorance.... According to Buddhism, our ideas of God and Soul are false and empty.[4]

Already we can see that we are talking about opposite ends of the spectrum. Pope John Paul II confirms this in *Crossing the Threshold of Hope*:

Among the religions mentioned in the Council document *Nostra Aetate*, it is necessary to pay special attention to *Buddhism*, which from a certain point of view, like Christianity, is a religion of salvation. Nevertheless, it needs to be said right away that the doctrines of salvation in Buddhism and Christianity are opposed.[5]

Buddhism approaches the world with a "negative" enlightenment perspective. It sees the world as fundamentally evil. Our desire for things is what causes us to suffer, so if we can become free from desire, we can also transcend suffering. Therefore, while Buddhism sees suffering as a problem to be overcome, Christianity understands suffering as redemptive. We are redeemed *through* the passion, death, and resurrection of Christ.

The Buddha spoke of "The Four Noble Truths" as the basis of his teaching. They are as follows:

The First Noble truth is *Dukkha*, the nature of life, its suffering, its sorrows and joys, its imperfection and unsatisfactoriness, its impermanence and insubstantiality. With regard to this, our function is to understand it as a fact, clearly and completely (*pariññeyya*).

The Second Noble Truth is the Origin of *Dukkha*, which is desire, "thirst," accompanied by all other passions, defilements and impurities. A mere understanding of this fact is not sufficient. Here our function is to discard it, to eliminate, to destroy and eradicate it (*pahātabba*).

The Third Noble Truth is the Cessation of *Dukkha*, *Nirvāna,* the Absolute Truth, the Ultimate Reality. Here our function is to realize it (*sacchikātabba*).

The Fourth Noble Truth is the Path leading to the realization of *Nirvāna*. A mere knowledge of the Path, however complete, will not do. In this case, our function is to follow it and keep to it (*bhāvetabba*).[6]

So, essentially, the worldviews of Christians and Buddhists are opposed. Christians see the world as fundamentally good,[7] and thus we must work for its improvement and the betterment of society. God meets us in and through the world.

Buddhism also holds that enlightenment, or *nirvana*, is something that is achieved by the individual through his or her own efforts, through the practice of a disciplined lifestyle, which includes meditation and the observance of various principles. Buddhism follows "the middle way," which is neither the way of asceticism, nor the way of self-indulgence, but a balance somewhere in the middle:

We do not free ourselves from evil through the good which comes from God; we liberate ourselves only through detachment from the world, which is bad. The fullness of such a detachment is not union with God, but what is called nirvana, a state of perfect indifference with regard to the world. *To save oneself* means, above all, to free oneself from evil by becoming *indifferent to the world, which is the source of evil*. This is the culmination of the spiritual process.[8]

According to the Buddha, man's emancipation depends on his own realization of Truth, and not on the benevolent grace of a god or any external power as a reward for his obedient good behaviour.[9]

Buddhists (and there are many variations of Buddhism) follow the "Eightfold Path," which leads to enlightenment. The word "Buddha" simply means "enlightened one."

Then more specifically we have Zen Buddhism,[10] which is possibly the most familiar form of Buddhism that has taken root in the West. It has also become very popular. Zen, or more accurately *zazen*, places great emphasis on a well-balanced lifestyle, without which it is not possible to reach enlightenment, and the practice of meditation to help the person reach "one-pointedness." The practice of Zen meditation is considered extremely important and is taught preferably by a Zen master (of which there are now quite a large number in the West, with the result that more people are becoming interested in Zen as it is more easily available). The idea of Zen meditation is to help the individual get rid of the illusions that he or she is an "individual." With practice, enlightenment can be reached, where the practitioner realizes that there is no "self," or "ego," in Zen terminology. The one who meditates begins to realize that all is one and that everything is in flux:

> The aim of Zen training is awakening, and the living of a life that is creative, harmonious, and *alive*. These "goal-less goals," for there really are no goals to attain, no place to *get* to, are brought into being through a process of concentration and absorption. In the sense of purging and freeing the mind from enslavement to fugitive, useless ideas, ideas that bog us down and limit us, Zen meditation, or zazen, might be called "brainwashing."[11]

Already we can see that the ideas of Buddhism are extremely different from those of Christianity. So why the great interest in it? Generally, it seems that some Christians are drawn to Zen because of the sense of a deep spirituality. Many Zen Buddhists lead an admirable lifestyle and show enormous respect for their fellow human beings and the world around them. However, it seems to be the meditation that intrigues people more than anything else and this is where many Christians find it appealing, as so many have lost a sense of deep prayer in the Christian tradition. The East is known for its centuries-old tradition of meditation and meditation techniques. Sadly, the West is not as well known for this dimension of religious practice, although it is certainly there.

Now we come to the actual practice of Zen meditation. The technique is quite similar to what is recommended for centering prayer and indeed for most forms of meditation.[12] One sits in a quiet place where disturbance is unlikely. Preferably the "lotus" or "half-lotus" position is used, which ensures that the spine is straight. This is very important in Zen, as it is believed that this helps to release energy from the base of the spine. One sits with eyes half open but not focused on anything, to prevent sleep and yet not be distracted by what is seen. Then breathing from the diaphragm, one focuses primarily on one's breathing:[13]

> This breathing is indeed the key to both traditional and Christian Zen because, once we are in observance of these conventions, the conscious listening to the sound of our breathing becomes the central continuous deliberate activity during the entire time we are meditating. We strive to make this breathing more and more regular, more deeply from the diaphragm.... As we descend deeper into this centering, the thoughts, desires, and images that our mind naturally generates will diminish to nil.[14]

As with centering prayer, and indeed most forms of meditation, the idea is to reduce the intake of sensible information to a minimum. Then, by using the sacred word in centering prayer or by focusing on the breathing in Zen, thoughts are also reduced to a minimum, so that one can just "be" and, more specifically in Christian meditation "be present to God." However, one of the key differences between the two practices is the intention. The intention with Zen is essentially to purify the mind, so that one can eventually reach enlightenment. With patience, dedication, and good instruction, this can and almost certainly will come about. The practice of centering prayer, on the other hand, does not involve any sense of trying to "achieve" anything. Centering prayer is simply a method to help one be present and open to God. It opens us to God's action within us so that He may bring about purification and ultimately union—if God so wills. Indeed, why would God not want this, since He has created us to be united to him.[15]

M. Basil Pennington reminds us that we cannot think of centering prayer in terms of achievement, success, or having "got there." To approach it this way would be to fall short of the mark. This is also one of the weaknesses of the Western mentality, which is so obsessed with achievement and what one has produced or succeeded in doing. As a result, we Westerners are quick to ask: "How far have I gotten?" or "How far do I have to go?" To ask these questions, although understandable, is to miss the point. What is important about the practice is that we are open to God, that we are giving ourselves completely in this prayer, and holding nothing back from God, not even our thoughts.

Some of the effects of the two practices are also very similar. Keating points out that contrary to the opinion that centering prayer is an isolated "going in on oneself," an escape from the world and its problems, in fact it opens one up to the world and the needs of all humanity more than ever. Since we are continually coming closer to God through this prayer,[16] we are at the same time being more deeply united with all other people who also have their life and being from God. As a result, people tend to become more sensitive to the needs of the people and world around them. They become more concerned to help where they can and to work for justice, etc. This is not the purpose of this kind of prayer, merely one of its effects. Zen seems to have the same effect, but from a different perspective:

> A developed, compassionate, loving person influences people unself-consciously, motivates them, and inspires them to act in similar ways. The whole community benefits. Even just doing zazen in the zendo has a powerful, invisible effect. People find it hard to believe that there can be social usefulness in just sitting and meditating. And yet the truth is that if you purify your mind, if even to a small degree, and transcend ego-attachment, you are at the same time purifying other minds. The effect on other people—on your family, on your circle of acquaintances—grows and grows.[17]

Another similarity between the effects of the two is the dying of the false self and the freeing of the true self. This in turn involves releasing energies that strengthen and literally energize the body for more action. So rather than slowing it down, the practice of meditation revitalizes it:

> When [these abstract notions] are swept from the mind through zazen—the concentrated sitting meditation particular to Zen—our true Mind rises to consciousness in all its beauty and effulgence. Furthermore, through zazen, energies that were formerly squandered in compulsive drives and purposeless actions are preserved and channelled into a unity, and to the degree that the mind attains one-pointedness, it no longer disperses its force in the uncontrolled proliferation

of idle thoughts. The entire nervous system is relaxed and soothed, inner tensions eliminated, and the tone of all organs strengthened.[18]

Keating speaks of something very similar:

The goal of contemplative prayer is not so much the emptiness of thoughts or conversation as the emptiness of self. In contemplative prayer we cease to multiply reflections and acts of the will. A different kind of knowledge rooted in love emerges in which the awareness of God's presence supplants the awareness of our own presence and the inveterate tendency to reflect on ourselves. The experience of God's presence frees us from making ourself or our relationship with God the center of the universe.[19]

It is also interesting that in the above quotation, Kapleau speaks of "energies that were formerly squandered in compulsive drives" now being harmonized or "chanelled into a unity." Keating also speaks of compulsive behavior and the emotional programs for happiness, and how these are healed through the practice of centering prayer. The two are very similar and both writers seem to be speaking of the same phenomenon, although in different language and from a different point of view. The healing of emotional wounds in the unconscious is also mentioned by McCown, as being one of the fruits of Zen practice:

If we do Zen faithfully...even memories of hurts from deep in our childhood, of which were perhaps only barely aware but which still send poisonous tentacles up into our present relationships, can be uncovered and healed.... In short, what we experience in ourselves is a self-rehabilitating human being, perhaps with long-immobilized personal gifts now renewed. From this, then, our own creative energies can emerge unencumbered, with a new freedom.[20]

So both Zen and centering prayer have similar effects. However, the key difference is the intention. Centering prayer and other forms of Christian meditation have the intention of opening the individual more to God, to be disposed to receive him, so that we may be more united with him. Zen stops at self-realization and enlightenment, although it depends what exactly is understood by "enlightenment." Christian mysticism also involves this idea of the purification of the false self, but then continues on to union with God. One is meant to lead to the other. The purification is not intended to be an end itself.

It seems that the influence of Buddhism on Keating's thought helped him to be more open to introducing people to meditation earlier on, as he could see firsthand how people practicing these Eastern forms of meditation were also making progress quickly on their spiritual journey. He himself mentions how the monks were curious about this:

Why were the young disciples of Eastern gurus, Zen roshis, and teachers of TM, who were coming to the abbey in the 1970s for dialogue, experiencing significant spiritual experiences without having gone through the penitential exercises that the Trappist order required?[21]

Keating and his confreres obviously learned a lot from these experiences, yet Keating also clearly points out where we need to be careful concerning the differences between Christian meditation and Eastern methods:

> The Eastern traditions put greater emphasis on what the self can do and hence contain the innate hazard of identifying the true self with God. The Christian tradition, on the other hand, recognizes God present but distinct from the true self. In other words, our uniqueness remains and becomes the vehicle for the divine expression, which was why we were created: to share by grace in the oneness of the Father and the Son.[22]

I will finish with this thought from William Johnston, S. J. He believes that we can certainly learn a lot from Zen, but at the same time we must recognize that we are part of a Christian tradition and so, if anything, it should help us to grow in our faith rather than make us try to take on another faith:

> Returning, then, to the basic question about what Christians can learn from Zen, it seems to me that they can be stimulated into finding and developing something they already possess and have possessed for almost two millennia. I do not think that a Christian (who has real Christian faith) can sit at the feet of a Zen master and obtain enlightenment just as it has been handed down from the time of Bodhidharma. One reason for this is that enlightenment is not an isolated moment but part of the complete

texture of a person's life. It is unthinkable that a Christian enlightenment could be found independently of Holy Scripture, the Mass, and the sacraments. All these go into enlightenment just as sutras go into satori.[23]

## Transcendental Meditation

In 1959 Maharishi Mahesh Yogi arrived in San Francisco and began touring and giving lectures in order to promote what has become known as TM, or Transcendental Meditation. To date, TM has spread all over the world and is practiced by many. What is more, it has enjoyed the backing of a substantial amount of scientific research, indisputably more than any other form of meditation. This has no doubt also contributed to its popularity:

More than 500 research studies have been conducted on Transcendental Meditation by over 300 research scientists in 210 independent universities and research institutions in 33 countries during the past 25 years.[24]

The basic idea behind the practice of TM is now usually spoken or written about in scientific terms. It claims that one of the fundamental forces that underlie nature is what is known as the "unified field":

According to physics the entire universe emerges from the "self-interacting dynamics" of the unified field. And it is the unified field that gives rise to all the laws of nature that govern the entire universe....

The unified field deep within nature is a field of unlimited energy, creativity, and intelligence. The source of thought deep within every individual is also a field of unlimited energy, creativity and intelligence.

Maharishi states: "Modern physics has recently glimpsed the unified field of all the laws of nature. Since ancient times the unified field has been described by Vedic science—a complete science of consciousness—as the field of pure consciousness, the field of infinite energy, creativity, and intelligence underlying man and nature. Through Transcendental Meditation, pure consciousness—the unified field—can be enlivened at the source of thought deep within the mind of every human being.

"This means that we can display the infinite creativity, intelligence, and dynamism of nature in our own life. This is our natural birthright."[25]

TM does not claim to be any kind of religion or spiritual practice, rather just a simple "technique" to enhance our natural well-being. It boasts of being able to reduce stress, improve work performance, increase mental clarity and energy levels, and reduce blood pressure and anxiety levels. Since it does not claim to be any kind of religion, the teachers of TM also insist that not only can anyone practice it, but that those who do invariably find that it helps them in the practice of their own faith. The goal of TM is to help the individual tap into this "unified field" (or the realm of pure consciousness) and by doing this realize one's full potential. TM also claims that this kind of meditation brings peace and is in fact the only thing that will bring about world peace. In other words, it boasts that this is the ultimate answer to world problems that *we* can finally realize. It also promises an end to world suffering and the beginning of utopia for the world:

> Today is the dawn of that great civilization where life will be free from suffering. That unfortunate time is ending when suffering was considered to be an inevitable part of life. That dark period for the human race is coming to an end. The great Vedic wisdom, which declares life to be bliss, is now going to be a common experience in the world.[26]

Obviously for the Christian, there are some problems here. Suffering in the Christian faith is a great mystery, but also one that Christ himself embraced and through which he redeemed humanity. If suffering is finally over (which I seriously doubt), then the sufferings of Christ will seem rather futile and meaningless. Here is another interesting claim:

> The Maharishi Technology of the Unified Field brings the direct experience of the unified field in the state of transcendental consciousness. In this state, consciousness experiences its own self-interacting dynamics, which are the dynamics of the unified field, and an evolutionary impulse is created. Due to the infinite correlation character of the unified field, that impulse of orderliness and coherence instantly radiates in the

environment, harmonizing discordant tendencies. With the enlivenment of the evolutionary power of natural law, everything that is negative—all that opposes evolution—begins to be neutralized.[27]

In some of the other claims that Maharishi makes, there seems to be some extraordinary naivety, where he says that governments should not have to build hospitals, rather they should simply prevent illness! The same goes for war and crime. Having said that, these kinds of statements do not necessarily undermine the good that may come about from the practice of TM. Moreover, TM and its fruits are also presented as something that *we* can do. There is no recognition of a transcendent God, the need for salvation, or responsibility for sin.

In spite of the fact that the promoters of TM—not least Maharishi Mahesh Yogi himself—claim that it is purely a technique with no religious overtones, a little background research shows something else. When Maharishi first came to the United States he presented TM in its original state, which is simply a form of Hindu meditation based on the ancient Vedic science, which is in turn part and parcel of Hinduism. The various mantras that are given to individuals to use are in fact the names of Hindu deities.[28] However, since this did not prove very popular initially, it was later re-presented as a science. Only then did it begin to gain popularity.

The fact that so much research was done on the technique has also no doubt been a great help. However, in its essence, TM is the practice of Hinduism. The mantras that are given to people today are still the names of these Hindu deities.[29] The practice also involves an initiation ritual where the individual is asked to bring a white handkerchief, flowers, and some fruit. He or she is then asked to repeat various phrases that are essentially prayers to Yogi's former teacher and to other deities, to invoke their blessings. However, the one making these prayers is not usually given a translation of them and may not realize the significance of what they are doing. However, while it is claimed that TM is merely a scientific technique, it would seem that it is in fact the practice of Hindu meditation, which is very similar to Zen.

One particular promoter of TM is Fr. Adrian Smith, MAfr, who has written various books and articles on the subject and promotes it as a way to enhance Christian prayer. He claims that it is also a purely natural technique dating back to before Hinduism and rooted in Vedantic science. However, Louis Hughes, O.P., points out that the Vedantic sciences do not predate Hinduism and are in fact the basis for it:

> The context of Transcendental Meditation is constituted by its traditional Hindu initiation ceremony and the fact that the mantra imparted during initiation has for centuries been used in the veneration of one or other Hindu god. From its inception, TM has been taught only within the context of Vedantic Hinduism. As such it needs to be approached with great caution by believing Christians.[30]

The technique itself involves something very similar to that of centering prayer. The person meditating sits comfortably but quietly with eyes closed and gently repeats a mantra given to him or her personally by a TM teacher. There is no difficult concentration or technique needed apart from this. In spite of this, all the books about TM insist that this must be taught individually by a TM teacher and cannot be learned through a book. Needless to mention, you also have to pay a tuition. At face value, it seems to differ little from centering prayer. The mantra helps to quieten the mind and allow the thoughts to go by. In TM it is claimed that this simple technique is the means by which one can tap into the unified field, which is the source of energy underlying all things. Once the meditator begins to harmonize with the unified field, he or she is then enabled to use all the benefits of the powers of nature itself, since the two are from the same source.

From a strictly meditational point of view, centering prayer would seem to be the same thing. One sits quietly but comfortably and gently uses the sacred word to calm the mind and to let go of thoughts. Nevertheless, the motivation and understanding of what follows are quite different. The motivation in centering prayer is primarily to be present to God and to consent to God's action within. It is giving oneself over to his work rather than trying to bring something about by one's own efforts. TM is more of a technique of self-realization.

Perhaps it could be argued that this unified field is an aspect of God and so the meditator is really giving himself over to God's power to transform him. That being said, the focus on TM is very much about what one can do by one's own efforts. Indeed, Mahesh Yogi himself says that it is through the practice of TM and Vedic science that the new and complete man will finally emerge: "World consciousness is going to be more and more purified because of the emergence of this complete science, which is going to evolve a complete man."[31]

Not withstanding the fact that the motivation behind both centering prayer and TM are completely different, there are some interesting similarities, which makes it easy to see how the two could be confused. The following quotation refers to part of what happens from TM:

> TM results in profoundly deep rest, which allows the body to release deeply rooted stresses. During this process, the mind becomes highly alert. The combination of deep rest and alertness is responsible for the body adopting a healthier pattern of behavior.[32]

This is very similar to how Keating describes what happens during centering prayer. He says that in the deep rest of contemplative prayer the emotions are being healed, and we experience this in the form of thoughts coming up from the unconscious. Here is another quotation, this time from Keating, that could be referring to "the unified field" that is spoken of in TM:

> The ontological unconscious, or level of being, contains all the human potentialities for spiritual development that have yet to be activated. These can be differentiated into the natural energies and the energies of grace. In a sense both energies are divine since God is the creator

and sustainer of both. The natural energies go by various names such as life force, dynamic ground, kundalini, cosmic energy. Through them we participate in the creative process through which all things that exist emerge and to which they return.[33]

## WHAT THE CHURCH TEACHES

Although some people are very suspicious of non-Christian religions, often seeing them more than anything else as a possible threat to Christianity, the Magisterium (or teaching body) of the Church teaches that we can learn from them and should be open to them. In regard to some of these Eastern religions, the Church has the following to say:

> The Catholic Church rejects nothing of what is true and holy in these religions. She has a high regard for the manner of life and conduct, the precepts and doctrines, which, although differing in many ways from her own teaching, nevertheless often reflect a ray of that truth which enlightens all men. Yet she proclaims and is in duty bound to proclaim without fail, Christ who is the way, the truth and the life (Jn 1:6). In him, in whom God reconciled all things to himself (2 Cor. 5:18–19), men find the fulness of their religious life.[34]

Just as "the Catholic Church rejects nothing of what is true and holy in these religions," neither should these ways be rejected out of hand simply because they are not Christian. On the contrary, one can take from them what is useful so long as the Christian conception of prayer, its logic and requirements are never obscured.[35]

In 1989, the Congregation for the Doctrine of the Faith issued a letter entitled, *On Certain Aspects of Christian Meditation—Orationis Formas* (quoted above). This letter was in direct response to the many Christians who were, and are, turning to Eastern methods of meditation, such as Zen, Yoga, and TM, and incorporating them into Christian prayer. In trying to distinguish what can be useful for Christians in these forms of prayer, the document states that first we must be clear about what exactly prayer consists of:

> Christian prayer is always determined by the structure of the Christian faith, in which the very truth of God and creature shines forth. For this reason, it is defined, properly speaking, as a personal, intimate and profound dialogue between man and God. It expresses, therefore, the communion of redeemed creatures with the intimate life of the persons of the Trinity. This communion, based on Baptism and the Eucharist, source and summit of the life of the church, implies an attitude of conversion, a flight from "self" to the "you" of God. Thus Christian prayer is at the same time always authentically personal and communitarian. It flees from impersonal techniques or from concentrating on oneself, which can create a kind of rut, imprisoning the person praying in a spiritual privatism which is incapable of a free openness to the transcendental God.[36]

From what we have seen so far, it seems that centering prayer clearly fits into this understanding of prayer. In centering prayer, the focus is on God and on being present and receptive to God. The sacred word is used as a symbol of the individual's consent to God and God's action within us. In this way it cannot be said to be a technique that focuses on self. Through this kind of prayer we are also united with all Christians and indeed all people, who in turn have their source in God. The more deeply we are united to God, the more deeply we are united to others. This is the ecclesial dimension of centering prayer.

Further on, the letter mentions two heresies that can still be found today: Pseudognosticism and Messalianism. Messalianism in particular could easily be mixed up with centering prayer for someone who is not properly familiar with it, and it seems that this is also one of the big temptations for Christians who may attempt to use some Eastern methods of prayer in a Christian context. Messalianism proposed that Christian perfection could be judged by reference to the experience of the divine, especially in prayer. It confused psychological experience in prayer with the grace of the Holy Spirit. The Messalians also understood experiences of abandonment or desolation, as an indication that the Spirit had abandoned the soul. *Orationis Formas* points out that we must be careful not to confuse the grace of the Holy Spirit with psychological experience:

> These false fourth-century charismatics [Messalians] identified the grace of the Holy Spirit with the psychological experience of his presence in the soul. In opposing them, the

fathers insisted on the fact that the soul's union with God in prayer is realized in a mysterious way, and in particular through the sacraments of the church.[37]

In his book *The Mystery of Christ: the Liturgy as Spiritual Experience*, Keating shows how the sacraments are an indispensable part of the Christian life and how the practice of centering prayer can give us a deeper understanding of, and appreciation for, these sacraments. Christians must be very careful not to confuse grace with what is psychological, or vice-versa. The fact is that we can only do a certain amount ourselves. We can dispose ourselves to receiving God's grace as best we can, and we can learn from different techniques that are helpful to prayer and perhaps especially those that help us fine tune our bodies for prayer. This is something at which many in the East seem to be far superior. They are well aware of the importance of the body in prayer and they give it great attention, so that it is best disposed to being as receptive as possible. We can certainly learn from this, while at the same time realizing that ultimately all is grace. We try to cooperate with God's grace as best we can, but we can never be under the illusion that we can somehow force it or reach infused contemplation by our own doing. We can make great efforts, certainly, but then we must wait.

*Orationis Formas* also highlights the danger of trying to "generate" experiences or to put those experiences on the same level as that of God:

Some use eastern methods solely as a psychophysical preparation for a truly Christian contemplation; others go further and, using different techniques, try to generate spiritual experiences similar to those described in the writings of certain Catholic mystics. Still others do not hesitate to place that absolute without image or concepts, which is proper to Buddhist theory, on the same level as the majesty of God revealed in Christ, which towers above finite reality.[38]

This is another error that has been confused with centering prayer. In centering prayer there is no question of trying to "generate" any kind of experience. While there may well be different kinds of experiences these are in no way created, nor are they to be sought after for their own sake. Instead they can be understood as some of the effects of this kind of prayer. Some could mistakenly think that the experience of "deep rest," for example, is something that we can create. However, this is not the case. Instead, given the right disposition and fidelity to the practice, it is likely the practitioner will experience this deep rest. This can be a psychological phenomenon that is experienced in many forms of meditation. The differences are subtle, but important.

In paragraph eighteen of *Orationis Formas*, the Congregation says:

> The seeking of God through prayer has to be preceded and accompanied by an ascetical struggle and a purification from one's own sins and errors, since Jesus has said that only "the pure of heart shall see God" (Mt 5:8).

This brings us back to the question of whether a person should be allowed or encouraged to begin centering prayer without first having tried to live the ascetical life for some time. Does the Congregation's recommendation go against this? I do not believe so. Since the Holy Spirit works in many different ways and adapts to each individual's needs, I think that you cannot decide that introducing someone to a form of prayer such as centering prayer is going "against the rules." Centering prayer may introduce people to the life of prayer in a way that is appealing to them. If they are serious about progressing, they will soon discover that their lives also need to be worked on in other areas. The Holy Spirit will show them this through prayer. While this form of prayer may appear to be something that one normally experiences only after practicing prayer for some time, it is not necessarily so and, as we said earlier, this is not the experience of many who are teaching it. On this point William Johnston makes an interesting observation:

> Discursive meditation of the old style presupposes belief in the existence of God; it was popular in an age of faith when atheism was rare. But this age of faith is no longer with us; and few people are uninfluenced by the death of God talk that has permeated mass media everywhere. Must we, then, resolve people's doubts before we encourage them to pray? I think not. Eastern contemplation of the kind I have outlined can begin as reverence towards a God in whom we believe, but it can also be a search for God who is the great unknown.[39]

"Progress" along the journey of prayer no doubt will not happen apart from the ascetical life and an effort to live as God teaches us. But practicing a way of prayer such as centering prayer may be the very thing that encourages people to do this. This, too, is one of the places where the individual will become quite aware of whether they are doing this purely for their own benefit, or whether it is genuinely prayer and drawing one closer to God. For the Christian, prayer must be focused on Christ, who is the Way:[40]

> The Trinitarian life is manifested in us primarily by our hunger for God. Centering Prayer comes out of the life of God moving within us. Hence it is Trinitarian in its source.

> Its focus is Christological as it helps us to focus more and more on Christ and to deepen our relationship with him. Begun in Lectio Divina ... and other devotions and especially in the sacraments, our relationship with Christ moves to new depths and to new levels of intimacy as we grow in the practice of Centering Prayer.[41]

*Chapter 9*

# Saint Teresa of Avila

St. Teresa of Avila and St. John of the Cross are arguably two of the greatest writers of the Church on the subject of mysticism. Both are mystics and doctors of the Church. Since the time of their writings they have continually been a reference point regarding the stages of prayer and the spiritual life. With this in mind, it would be good to hold the teaching of centering prayer against the light of their wisdom and see how it compares. With Teresa of Avila we will focus more on her teachings on prayer and see how centering prayer fits in with what she has to say. With John of the Cross we will look at his teaching on the inner purification of sense and spirit and how the notion of the healing of the unconscious compares with these. Obviously we cannot give a full treatment of the writings of either saint, so we will only take certain aspects of their works.

St. Teresa of Avila was born on March 28, 1515. She received the name of her grandmother Teresa de Ahumada. As a young girl she was zealous for her faith and at the age of only seven tried to run away with her brother to be martyred for Christ by the Moors. However, in her adolescent years she became less interested in her faith and more interested in tales of chivalry. At sixteen, she was entrusted to the care of the Augustinian nuns of Our Lady of Grace in Avila. During this time the sister in charge of these girls was Doña Maria Briceño, a deeply spiritual lady, who gladly shared her interest and enthusiasm for the spiritual life with the young girls. This rekindled in Teresa the earlier zeal she had experienced. However, it was eventually the *Letters* of St. Jerome that convinced her to give her life to Christ.

On November 2, 1535, at the Carmelite Monastery of the Incarnation, Teresa began her vocation. During the first few years here she experienced bad health, which eventually led her father to take her away for treatment. Sadly, the treatment she received only served to make her worse, leaving her paralyzed for three years. As a result of this time of sickness, her body never properly regained health and she spent most of her life suffering from various ailments. Interestingly enough, she also had great difficulty with prayer for the first eighteen years of her life as a nun, so much so that in her *Life* she wrote that she dreaded the time of prayer in the chapel:

> And very often, for some years, I was more anxious that the hour I had determined to spend in prayer be over than I was to remain there...and so unbearable was the sadness I felt on entering the oratory, that I had to muster up all my courage.[1]

Kieran Kavanaugh mentions that Teresa had almost no instruction of any kind on mental prayer, as the focus of the sisters was on the recitation of the divine office. This practice was largely to keep the public happy—who considered it the sisters' purpose to praise God on their behalf. However, after Teresa's novitiate, her uncle gave her Francisco de Osuna's *Third Spiritual Alphabet*, from which she began to take more of an interest in interior prayer:

> The impact of Osuna's book on Teresa was so forceful that she resolved to spend two hours every day in the prayer of recollection, as was recommended by the author, in addition to the liturgical prayer required by the Carmelite time-table. She considered the hours set aside for this recollection as time for solitude, for being with God. In the beginning, Teresa's practice met with immediate and surprising success. The Lord began to favour her with infused prayer, what she would later term the prayer of quiet and the prayer of union.[2]

Finally, after an unusual experience of regret for her past that Teresa had before an image of the wounded Christ, her prayer life began to change. From then on, Teresa was to experience a new kind of relationship with Jesus, through prayer. It is also from this time on, that Teresa was given some of the extraordinary insights into the stages of prayer that she would later write about.

## Four Ways of Watering a Garden

In the work called *Life*, St. Teresa uses an analogy of four ways of watering a garden to make the flowers grow. The garden is the soul and the different ways of watering it are the various stages in prayer, which help us to grow in the virtues. Initially, a lot of work is involved on our part, but gradually more and more is given over to the Lord, until eventually God does all the work:

> It seems to me the garden can be watered in four ways. You may draw water from a well (which is for us a lot of work). Or you may get it by means of a water wheel and aqueducts in such a way that it is obtained by turning the crank of the water wheel. (I have drawn it this way sometimes—the method involves less work than the other, and you get more water.) Or it may flow from a river or a stream. (The garden is watered much better by this means because the ground is more fully soaked, and there is no need to water so frequently—and much less work for the gardener.) Or the water may be provided by a great deal of rain. (For the Lord waters the garden without any work on our part—and this way is incomparably better than all the others mentioned.)[3]

The beginner in prayer needs to spend a lot of time learning how to be recollected, and how to reflect on scripture and simply to be alone without needing entertainment. This is particularly a problem today, where people have gotten used to a great

deal of entertainment and as a result find it very difficult to be quiet. Teresa says that they also need
to spend time reflecting on the life of Christ and
that this is quite tiring when you are not used to
it. The beginner is the one who has to go and take
water from the well: "This discursive work with the
intellect is what is meant by taking water from the
well."[4] Learning to meditate and reflect is quite an
effort initially and requires a lot of perseverance. If
we persevere the Lord will help us, but there must
also be an effort on our part. Teresa reminds the
reader that the very act of coming to the well pleases
the Lord, even though sometimes we seem to be getting nowhere. Keating similarly mentions that the
very act of being faithful to prayer is all-important.
He speaks of it in terms of coming to the "divine
therapist." We must be prepared to keep coming
back if we wish to make progress, just as you would
with any course of therapy.

For the beginner, sometimes the Lord will give
drops of consolation that can be a great source of
encouragement. However, we should not be looking
for these specifically, as they are not the purpose of
giving ourselves to prayer. The Lord likes to lead people on in prayer without many feelings of sweetness,
to help them grow and realize that they are doing this
out of love for him and not purely out of anything
they can gain. So initially, Teresa tells us we should
not be afraid if we cannot seem to be very quiet and
if it is a real effort to stay on in prayer. Our perseverance will be well rewarded at the right time, as the
Lord knows exactly what we are struggling with and
will help us:

So I return to the advice—and even if I repeat it many times this doesn't matter—that it is very important that no one be distressed or afflicted over dryness or noisy and distracting thoughts.[5]

We should never be put off if we find that our prayer time seems to be nothing but distracting thoughts. The presence or absence of thoughts during prayer is not important, nor is it a measure of progress. All that is necessary is to keep returning to the sacred word and to let the thoughts go. Times of prayer that seem especially distracted with thoughts can be an indication of the unconscious unloading or "processing" thoughts:

When the unloading of the unconscious begins in earnest, many people feel that they are going backwards, that contemplative prayer is just impossible for them because all they experience when they start to pray is an unending flow of distractions. Actually, there are no distractions in contemplative prayer unless you really want to be distracted or if you get up and leave. Hence, it doesn't matter how many thoughts you have. Their number and nature have no affect whatever on the genuineness of your prayer.[6]

Further on in *Life* Teresa points out that the beginner should also take prayer at the right pace; that is, they should not be too eager to go beyond their means. This journey cannot be hurried. She recommends that the beginner keep focused on Christ, especially through discursive meditation (going from one idea to another), as this is essential for growth:

Keeping Christ present is what we of ourselves can do. Whoever would desire to pass beyond this point and raise the spirit to an experience of spiritual consolations that are not given would lose both the one and the other, in my opinion; for these consolations belong to the supernatural. And if the intellect is not active, the soul is left very dry, like a desert. Since this edifice is built entirely on humility, the closer one comes to God the more progress there must be in this virtue; and if there is no progress in humility, everything is going to be ruined.[7]

Humility will always go with real progress in prayer, as the more we practice prayer the more we begin to see ourselves for what we are. Humility is therefore a gift:

The spiritual journey is characterized by the ever-increasing knowledge of our mixed emotions, the dark sides of our personalities, the emotional traumas of early childhood. Nothing is more helpful to reduce pride than the actual experience of self-knowledge. If we are discouraged by it, we have misunderstood its meaning.[8]

Teresa also makes an interesting point at this stage, where she mentions that it is foolish for anyone to try to make their minds go quiet, as we cannot do this ourselves:

In mystical theology, which I began to describe, the intellect ceases to work because God suspends it, as I shall explain afterward if I know how and He gives me His help to do so. Taking it upon oneself to stop and suspend thought is what I mean should not be done; nor should we cease to work with the intellect, because otherwise we would be left like cold simpletons and be doing neither one thing nor the other. When the Lord suspends the intellect and causes it to stop, He Himself gives it that which holds its attention and makes it marvel; and without reflection it understands more in the space of a Creed than we can understand with all our earthly diligence in many years. Trying to keep the soul's faculties busy and thinking you can make them be quiet is foolish.[9]

This point about not trying to make the soul's faculties quiet might be understood as an objection to centering prayer. Teresa says that one should not try "to stop and suspend thought," as this cannot be done. However, in centering prayer one does not try to stop or suspend thought, rather one continually allows the thoughts to flow by so that eventually one is not affected or distracted by them. You are aware of them in the background, but they are no longer a concern:

> The practice of contemplative prayer is not an effort to make the mind a blank, but to move beyond discursive thinking and affective prayer to the level of communing with God, which is a more intimate kind of exchange.[10]

Indeed, our thoughts hardly ever stop and it is not our job to try to stop them, rather just to let them go. With practice this becomes easier and then we begin to experience a deeper silence. Teresa also says that the beginner should always start with discursive reflection and not try to jump ahead too soon:

> [Discursive reflection] is the method of prayer with which all must begin, continue, and finish; and it is a very excellent and safe path until the Lord leads one to other supernatural things.[11]

This brings us back to the question of whether or not one should begin with a form of prayer like centering prayer. According to Teresa's teachings, at first it seems we should not. However, here I would refer again to the wisdom of William Johnston, already quoted in chapter eight, who says that this kind of advice was fine in a time when people generally came from a background where one could presume a certain amount of religious instruction. Today, however, one cannot assume this at all. Should we still have to stick rigidly to a particular system, which even though it has proved very valuable for many could perhaps be departed from if another method that worked well was discovered? If another method such as centering prayer helps people to discover the spiritual life, it would seem naïve to discourage it just because one teaching says otherwise—unless of course it was obviously doing harm. So far, the experience of many who teach it shows that it is in fact very effective. Keating adds this comment:

> Why do we need to know [if someone is called to this kind of prayer or not]?

If, under the prompting of the Spirit, a chronic alcoholic can realize that his life is unmanageable and turn it over to God, why is it so hard to imagine a person, even an "inexperienced" Christian, being moved by the contemplative gifts of wisdom, understanding, and knowledge while praying? It is not that hard for God.[12]

Kieran Kavanaugh suggests that Teresa herself answers the question:

Fortunately, Teresa, indirectly, does answer this doubt. Discussing the first, tedious way of obtaining water for the garden in chapter 12 of her *Life*, in which she is expounding her little treatise on prayer by means of an analogy on four ways of getting water for a garden, she deftly describes what we can do through our own efforts. The soul "can place itself in the presence of Christ." One who remains in his precious company is already advanced, having found therein the key to spiritual progress.[13]

"Placing oneself in the presence of Christ," is also understood as "keeping the eyes of one's soul fixed on Christ" in prayer. In other words, Christ must be the focus, but this doesn't imply that we must be *consciously* thinking of Christ all the time. This is exactly what we do in Christian prayer and in centering prayer through the use of the sacred word, which essentially expresses this very intention. Kavanaugh makes another interesting observation:

If we take the word "mental" to involve the mind alone, we will assuredly misunderstand the reality of mental prayer. In Teresa's thought, both the mind and the heart should be attentive to the one with whom we are in communication. In this realization, Teresa was able to defend mental prayer against those who pressed that the unlettered restrict themselves to their vocal prayers.[14]

Teresa makes another point worth noting here:

There is no stage of prayer so sublime that it isn't necessary to return often to the beginning. Along this path of prayer, self knowledge and the thought of one's sins is the bread with which all palates must be fed no matter how delicate they may be; they cannot be sustained without this bread.[15]

Centering prayer is not meant to replace all other forms of prayer. Rather, it is a certain kind of prayer for a certain time. Those who begin to practice centering prayer usually find before long that they have a desire to return to what might more traditionally be called the earlier stages of prayer, which involve more self-reflection and discursive meditation. The earlier stages are also covered, but not necessarily in the traditional order. Since the grace to pray is itself a gift from the Holy Spirit, perhaps we should not be too quick to make hard and fast rules, outside of which the Spirit does not work.

## Prayer of Simplicity
## or Acquired Recollection

To try to categorize centering prayer theologically is not easy. What is called "the prayer of simplicity," also known as "acquired recollection" by St. Teresa of Avila, seems to most accurately describe centering prayer. Jacques Bossuet (1627–1704) was the first to use this expression. It is sometimes also called "the prayer of simple gaze" or "the presence of God" or "the simple vision of faith." In the seventeenth century, some writers began to call it the prayer of "acquired contemplation," but John of the Cross and Teresa never used that expression:

> The prayer of simplicity was defined by Bossuet as a simple loving gaze upon some divine object, whether on God himself or one of his perfections, on Christ or on one of his mysteries, or on some other Christian truth. It is a form of ascetical prayer that is extremely simplified. The discursus formerly used in meditation has now been transformed into a simple intellectual gaze; the affections that were experienced in affective prayer have been unified into a simple loving attention to God. The prayer is ascetical, meaning that the soul is able to attain to this type of prayer by its own efforts with the help of ordinary grace, but often it is the transition point to mystical prayer.... It is, as it were, the final disposition before the Holy Spirit begins to operate in the soul by means of his gifts. For that reason, one may frequently experience a blending of acquired and infused elements in

the practice of the prayer of simplicity.... Thus, without any shock and almost insensibly, the soul proceeds gently from the ascetical practice of prayer to mystical contemplation.[16]

We will come back to the prayer of recollection in the next section, where Teresa deals with it in greater detail, in relation to the recitation of the Our Father.

## THE PRAYER OF QUIET

Teresa goes on to discuss the "prayer of quiet." In this prayer, the soul experiences a deep rest and great peace. She observes that this is completely a gift from the Lord and not something we can initiate or sustain ourselves:

> The poor little [soul] doesn't understand that since by its own efforts it can do nothing to draw that good to itself, so much less will it be able to keep it for longer than the Lord desires.[17]

It seems that the prayer of quiet is often experienced through centering prayer, although this does not imply that one is able to experience the prayer of quiet by one's own efforts. Instead, through centering prayer the soul is merely disposed to receiving it, which the Lord often grants. Indeed it would be strange that God would draw people to this kind of prayer and then refuse to grant these kind of experiences, as Teresa herself points out. Here is a subtle but important distinction, which is often misunderstood. The temptation is often to think that we can "reach" or "acquire" some of these experiences by our own efforts. It is not us but God's grace that brings this about. This is one of the key differences between Christian prayer and other forms of meditation, where the emphasis of non-Christian meditation is often on what we can achieve by our own efforts:

> For anyone who has experience, it is impossible not to understand soon that this little spark cannot be acquired. Yet, this nature of ours is so eager for delights that it tries everything; but it is quickly left cold because however much it may desire to light the fire and obtain this delight, it doesn't seem to be doing anything else than throwing water on it and killing it.[18]

Prayer is essentially the work of the Spirit. We dispose ourselves to that work, but we cannot force it to happen: "In every kind of prayer the raising of the mind and heart to God can be the work only of the Spirit."[19]

Although they are discussed in quite different terms, it is interesting to see the similarities between the process of thoughts and the letting go of the same, which Keating describes, and Teresa's description of the workings of the intellect, memory, and will. Teresa says that in this kind of prayer the will is united to God, though the intellect can be still running around:

> I have already mentioned that in this first recollection and quiet the soul's faculties do not cease functioning. But the soul is so satisfied with God that as long as the recollection lasts, the quiet and calm are not lost since the will is united

with God even though the two faculties are distracted; in fact, little by little the will brings the intellect and the memory back to recollection.[20]

As the individual begins to experience a "deep rest," the thoughts are still flowing by, but we are no longer distracted by them in the same way. All that need be done at this stage is to remain in the silence and enjoy it. If we try to figure out how we got there, or how we could bring it about again, we are already being led away by the intellect. The temptation is always to try to "possess" the experience, to hold it for longer, or figure out how you got there so you can repeat it again in the future:

> The tendency to reflect is one of the hardest things to handle in contemplative prayer. We want to savor the moment of pure joy, pure experience, pure awareness. We want to reflect on moments of deep peace or union in order to remember how we got there and thus how to get back. But if you can let this temptation go by and return to the sacred word, you will pass to a new level of freedom, a more refined joy.[21]

> Therefore, in these times of quietude, let the soul remain in its repose; let [the learned] put their learning to one side.... Here there is no demand for reasoning but for knowing what as a matter of fact we are and for placing ourselves (with simplicity) in God's presence, for He desires the soul to become ignorant in His presence, as indeed it is.[22]

This "ignorance" that the soul experiences is also what *The Cloud of Unknowing* refers to by the same name. The "closer" we come to God in prayer, the darker it gets, since we cannot know God in himself. We have to enter into this cloud.

While some criticize centering prayer, claiming that it can be an attempt to create these experiences oneself, Teresa also admits that we can in fact produce a certain kind of prayer of quiet ourselves. However, the difference is in its fruits:

> We can discern, in my opinion, whether this quiet comes from the spirit of God or whether we procure it ourselves once God begins to give devotion and we, as I said, want to pass on to the quiet through our own efforts. When we procure the quiet ourselves, it produces no effect, quickly goes away, and leaves behind aridity.[23]

So although it is difficult to know when we are making too much of an effort to produce this kind of quiet ourselves—since this is always going to be a temptation—what is important is that we keep coming to prayer with the intention of growing spiritually and deepening our relationship with the Lord. No doubt the balance will not always be exactly right, or will our intentions for that matter. However, if we are sincere in our efforts, the Spirit will continue to guide us in the right direction, if we are prepared to follow the basic guidelines:

> A solid foundation for the protection of oneself from the tricks and consolations coming from

the devil is to begin with the determination to follow the way of the cross and not desire consolations, since the Lord Himself pointed out this way of perfection saying: *take up your cross and follow me.* He is our model; whoever follows His counsels solely for the sake of pleasing Him has nothing to fear.[24]

Keating puts it this way:

The wisdom of taking the express elevator—the way of pure faith—to the top floor is that it avoids all mystical phenomena that might occur as by-products of the unloading of the unconscious. The way of pure faith is to persevere in contemplative practice without worrying about where we are on the journey, and without comparing ourselves with others or judging others' gifts as better than ours.[25]

The question is also sometimes raised, as to whether one can be deceived by the devil in this kind of prayer of silence. Teresa teaches that we have nothing to fear from the devil when we are in this prayer, as he is powerless over us:

[In this prayer of quiet] the devil can do little harm or none at all if the soul directs to God the delight and sweetness it feels and fixes its thoughts and desires upon Him, as was advised.[26]

In her book *Mysticism: The Nature and Development of Spiritual Consciousness*, Evelyn Underhill makes some interesting observations about the prayer of quiet. Firstly, she points out that all the great mystics consider it a normal state of development of the inner experience. While the prayer of quiet is essentially the work of God, it is also something that we can dispose ourselves to:

> [Meister] Eckhart's view of the primary importance of "Quiet" as essentially *the* introverted state is shared by all those mediaeval mystics who lay stress on the psychological rather than the objective aspect of the spiritual life. They regard it as the necessary preliminary of all contemplation; and describe it as a normal phase of the inner experience, possible of attainment by all those who have sufficiently disciplined themselves in patience, recollection, and humility.[27]

> The true mystic never tries deliberately to enter the orison of quiet: with St. Teresa, he regards it as a supernatural gift, beyond his control, though fed by his will and love. That is to say, where it exists in a healthy form, it appears spontaneously, as a phase in normal development; not as a self-induced condition, a psychic trick.[28]

Recollection, she notes, is essentially a form of training for the interior life. We must be faithful to the practice if we wish to make progress. It is not each individual time of prayer that is important so much as the overall effect it is having on us. The temptation is to give up when one cannot see progress, but the practice is a work of love that requires discipline and dedication:

"God thus rewards the violence which your soul has been doing to itself; and gives to it such a domination over the senses that a sign is enough when it desires to recollect itself, for them to obey and so gather themselves together. At the first call of the will, they come back more and more quickly. At last, after countless exercises of this kind, God disposes them to a state of utter rest and of perfect contemplation." (*Way of Perfection*, ch. 30)

This description makes it clear that "recollection" is a form of spiritual gymnastics; less valuable for itself than for the training which it gives, the powers which it develops.[29]

Underhill also comments on the heresy of "Quietism," which like most heresies contains a certain amount of truth, but not its totality. The teachers of Quietism made the mistake of seeing the prayer of quiet as an end in itself. Instead of recognizing it as a stage of development, they saw it as the goal of the spiritual life. The distinction is vital; and this is where it is very important to have good spiritual direction:

The great teachers of Quietism, having arrived at and experienced the psychological state of "quiet": having known the ineffable peace and certainty, the bliss which follows on its act of complete surrender, its utter and speechless resting in the Absolute Life, believed themselves to have discovered in this half-way house the goal of the mystic quest. Therefore, whilst much of their teaching remains true, as a real description of a real and valid state experienced by almost all contemplatives in the course of their development, the inference which they drew from it, that in this mere blank abiding in the deeps the soul had reached the end of her course, was untrue and bad for life.[30]

## THE WAY OF PERFECTION

Behold, the Lord invites all [to drink this living water through contemplation]. Since He is truth itself, there is no reason to doubt. If this invitation were not a general one, the Lord wouldn't have called us all, and even if He called all, He wouldn't have promised, "I will give you to drink." ... But since He spoke without this condition to all, I hold as certain that all those who do not falter on the way will drink this living water.[31]

Teresa of Avila reminds her readers that the call to contemplation is for everyone. The reason why so many do not get there is because they do not persevere. In *The Way of Perfection*, she deals again with the different stages of prayer. Here I would like to mention some points that she makes concerning "recollection" and "contemplation."

The mystic of Avila tells us that she didn't know how to explain much of what she experienced herself in prayer, but that the Lord then gave her a way of explaining everything. She proposes the slow recitation of the Our Father, as a way for everyone that can lead to contemplation. She emphasizes the importance of vocal and mental prayer here. If one prays without understanding what one is saying, it is useless. Therefore, we must be aware of what we are praying and focus on that. She also mentions that many people have been brought to the highest degrees of contemplation simply by being faithful to vocal prayer:

> To keep you from thinking that little is gained through a perfect recitation of vocal prayer, I tell you that it is very possible that while you are reciting the Our Father or some other vocal prayer, the Lord may raise you to perfect contemplation.[32]

One can begin reciting the Our Father very slowly, even taking a whole hour to pray it. What is important is that you are aware of what you are saying and that you reflect on it. The Lord, if He so wishes, will lead the soul on to the prayer of quiet (or contemplation) if He so desires, and why wouldn't He desire, as she reminds us herself. This way of praying the Our Father very slowly is a way of helping to quieten the senses, which are often a distraction in the work of interior prayer. So by closing one's eyes and being in silence, the faculties are gradually recollected. With practice, this becomes easier, although initially most people find it quite difficult. Once we have been faithful to it for a while, however, we will find that we become recollected much more quickly and easily:

> The intellect is recollected much more quickly with this kind of prayer even though it may be vocal; it is a prayer that brings with it many blessings. This prayer is called "recollection,"

because the soul collects its faculties together and enters within itself to be with its God. And its divine Master comes more quickly to teach it and give it the prayer of quiet than he would through any other method it might use.[33]

This last sentence is interesting. Recollection leads to the prayer of quiet, which is given by the Lord to anyone who gives themselves to this method of prayer, "more quickly ... than he would through any other method." In other words, the effects of this prayer are the same as the effects that come through centering prayer; that is, it disposes the one praying to contemplation, which often follows. Indeed, there are many similarities. In centering prayer, one is using one single word to allow the faculties to be recollected. The will expresses its love of, and desire to be with, the Lord through use of the sacred word. Gradually the mind becomes quieter and often one begins to experience the prayer of quiet. Teresa suggests the very slow recitation of the Our Father, but what is happening is essentially the same:

This alone is what I want to explain: that in order to acquire the habit of easily recollecting our minds and understanding what we are saying, and with whom we are speaking, it is necessary that the exterior senses be recollected and that we give them something with which to be occupied. For indeed we have heaven within ourselves since the Lord of heaven is there.

We must, then, disengage ourselves from everything so as to approach God interiorly and even in the midst of occupations withdraw within ourselves.[34]

Teresa also points out that while the prayer of quiet is certainly from God and we can only wait on it, the prayer of recollection is something that we can bring about ourselves with the normal help of grace:

> ... you must understand that this recollection is not something supernatural, but that it is something we can desire and achieve ourselves with the help of God—for without this help we can do nothing, not even have a good thought. This recollection is not a silence of the faculties; it is an enclosure of the faculties within the soul.[35]

The prayer of the rosary also has a similar effect to that of centering prayer. It is a contemplative prayer and can help one to be recollected and open to the prayer of contemplation. The effect of meditating on the mysteries, or just the continuous repetition of the Hail Marys, can have this same effect of quieting the mind and recollecting the faculties. It is very similar to this way of reciting the Our Father, which Teresa suggests.

Although the prayer of quiet is purely from God and not something we can start or sustain, there are similarities between the experience of this prayer and some of what takes place through centering prayer. When people are practicing centering prayer for a while, many begin to experience some of the effects mentioned by Teresa as being part of the prayer of quiet. This seems to be an indication that centering prayer is disposing one to the prayer of contemplation or quiet. For example, Keating says that people often begin to experience a "deep rest" and while one is still aware of the thought process, one is no longer distracted by it, like traffic in the distance that does not interrupt a conversation with a friend.

"It happens that the soul will be in the greatest quiet and the intellect will be so distracted that it won't seem that the quiet is present in the intellect's house."[36] This line could easily be referring to the thoughts continually flowing in the mind, but no longer disturbing the peace. The will is united to God, but the memory and intellect are still free to "roam about." The following could be an indication of how the use of the "sacred word" can help one to remain undisturbed by the temptation to engage in some of the thoughts that are flowing through the mind: "In this prayer of quiet it seems that [God] wants [the soul] to work a little, although so gently that it almost doesn't feel its effort."[37] The use of the sacred word is meant to be very gentle, and with time it more or less repeats itself, so that there is virtually no effort at all:

When the sacred word drops away, we enter into a no-man's/no woman's land in which the action of the Spirit meets the very simplified activity of renewing our intention by means of the sacred symbol. Then we have contemplation in the strict sense of the word. Until then, the Centering Prayer practice is really "acquired contemplation," a discipline of not dialoguing with the mind, or if the mind keeps thinking, of paying no attention to it.[38]

Kieran Kavanaugh sums up his discussion on meditation and recollection in Teresa's writings as follows:

> From Teresa's teachings, then, we can conclude that mental prayer, the presence to Christ, embraces a wider field than does the prayer of recollection. The method of mental prayer Teresa teaches is the prayer of recollection. Vocal prayer was always to be accompanied by mental prayer, and she urged the practice of recollection in vocal prayer; certainly vocal prayer does not represent a stage of prayer preceding meditation. In contemplation, vocal prayer slows down into silence, and recollection deepens. Discursive meditation was for Teresa, generally, a means to mental prayer and recollection, although the meditation could incorporate some of the elements of the two. In contemplation, meditation reaches its goal and must cease.[39]

## THE INTERIOR CASTLE

At sixty-two years of age Teresa set about writing *The Dwelling Places*, also known as *The Interior Castle*, at the request of her confessor, Fr. Gratian, who was himself an enthusiastic supporter of her reforms. Teresa had already written about various insights she had received in *Life*, but that was now in the over-scrupulous hands of the Inquisition. Therefore, Fr. Gratian suggested she write another book, and she agreed. Teresa now had the advantage of being older and having a clearer understanding of some of the matters about which she had written earlier. However, it was a very difficult time for her to write, because of her poor health and much upheaval in the order. In spite of this, she completed this spiritual masterpiece in a relatively short time. Although she was interrupted for about five months, the actual time given to writing the work was only eight weeks, which is quite extraordinary considering the book's content.

In *The Interior Castle*, Teresa refers to the soul as being like a castle or crystal palace, with many rooms inside. In the center chamber is the King. Each of the seven dwelling places has many rooms. The soul is being invited to the center chamber, but it is a long journey from the outside. In the outermost chambers the light from the King is hardly visible and there are many dangers. As the soul progresses the light gradually becomes stronger. Teresa talks about the beauty of the soul and its capacity for great things. She says that the King in the center chamber is gently calling the soul to come closer. While the soul is extraordinarily beautiful, if it is in serious sin it seems to block out the light within:

> It should be kept in mind here that the fount, the shining sun that is in the center of the soul, does not lose its beauty and splendor; it is always present in the soul, and nothing can take away its loveliness. But if a black cloth is placed over a crystal that is in the sun, obviously the sun's brilliance will have no effect on the crystal, even though the sun is shining on it.[40]

The Holy Trinity is present within us at the center of our being. The more we practice prayer, the closer we come to the center, as the various obstacles that block us from union with God are removed. This is the journey that Teresa is referring to, going through the different dwelling places and being drawn further inward to the innermost chamber. Teresa also mentions that the soul has a great capacity for growth and that we should not prevent it from developing or growing. Part of what is essential for this growth is the humility that comes from self-knowledge. Self-knowledge is part of what comes from the journey of prayer and the purification that accompanies it:

> The soul is capable of much more than we can imagine, and the sun that is in this royal chamber shines in all parts. It is very important for any soul that practices prayer, whether little or much, not to hold itself back and stay in one corner.... Oh, but if it is in the room of self-knowledge! How necessary this room is—see that you understand me—even for those whom the Lord has brought into the very dwelling place where he abides. For never, however exalted the soul may be, is anything else fitting for it; nor could it be even were the soul to so desire.[41]

As Thomas Keating puts it:

> The spiritual journey is characterized by the ever-increasing knowledge of our mixed emotions, the dark sides of our personalities, the emotional traumas of early childhood. Nothing is more helpful to reduce pride than the actual experience of self-knowledge. If we are discouraged by it, we have misunderstood its meaning.[42]

The practice of centering prayer helps us to grow in this self-knowledge and to remain open to the on-going purification that is needed. Indeed the whole journey is really a continual purification, at ever deepening levels of our being.

In the Second Dwelling Places, Teresa speaks of the need to persevere as one begins to live the life of prayer and the need to try to live virtuously, since progress is impossible without this:

> This stage pertains to those who have already begun to practice prayer and have understood how important it is not to stay in the first dwelling places. But they still don't have the determination to remain in this second stage without turning back, for they don't avoid the occasions of sin.[43]

This brings us again to the question of whether one can practice centering prayer without first trying to live a virtuous life and hope to get anywhere. However, as previously discussed, there seems to be no reason why one should not start with centering prayer. Indeed, the practice will soon show the individual what they need to do. So, while the order the practice occurs in may not be as Teresa suggests, the need to try to live virtuously is not ruled out. Here again is another difference between Christian prayer and mere self-realization, the way to which some forms of meditation present us with. The latter may allow one to progress without much care for the virtues, but if it is Christian prayer it simply cannot be done.

Teresa also mentions that the soul should not be too eager for spiritual consolations, as this is not what this kind of prayer is about:

> Even though I've said this at other times, it's so important that I repeat it here: it is that souls shouldn't be thinking about consolations at this beginning stage. It would be a very poor way to start building so precious and great an edifice. If the foundation is on sand, the whole building will fall to the ground.[44]

If spiritual consolations are given, it is a great gift, but they are not the focus. The purpose is to grow closer to the Lord. A very real temptation with centering prayer or any similar practice is to see it purely as a way to reach greater things, or higher consciousness. This certainly may happen, but if this is the focus then the one praying has not understood the practice. The purpose is to give oneself more deeply in prayer and to allow the Lord to work in us.

Teresa also mentions the temptation for people to give up on account of dryness, or when it seems to be impossible to pray as we think we ought to be praying. After a time of practicing centering prayer, the mind usually becomes quieter. But then at times it can become more aggressively filled with thoughts than ever before. However, this is normal and is probably just an indication of the unloading of the unconscious. Teresa also reminds her readers that they should not be put off by many thoughts:

> For the Lord often desires that dryness and bad thoughts afflict and pursue us without our being

able to get rid of them. Sometimes He even per-
mits these reptiles to bite us so that afterward
we may know how to guard ourselves better
and that he may prove whether we are greatly
grieved by having offended Him.[45]

In the Fourth Dwelling Places, Teresa begins to
mention various spiritual delights that the Lord sometimes grants to a soul. She is quick to emphasize that
there is no way that we can produce these ourselves,
no matter how hard we try. Spiritual delights (which
she elsewhere calls "the prayer of quiet") are from
God, whereas consolations begin with us:

> In speaking about what I said I'd mention here
> concerning the difference in prayer between con-
> solations and spiritual delights, the term "con-
> solations," I think, can be given to those expe-
> riences we ourselves acquire through our own
> meditation and petitions to the Lord, those that
> proceed from our own nature.... In sum, joyful
> consolations in prayer have their beginning in
> our own human nature and end in God.

> The spiritual delights begin in God, but human
> nature feels and enjoys them as much as it does
> those I mentioned—and much more.[46]

The focus we need to have is love. The whole work
is one of love and not of effort, except for the obvious
need to be faithful to the practice. If we approach this
kind of prayer with a view only to what we can gain,
we have misunderstood what it is about. This prayer
is about deepening our relationship with and our love

for God. As Thomas Keating writes: "To emphasize a most important point: *Centering Prayer is both a relationship and a method to foster that relationship at the same time.*"[47]

The journey of the soul to the center chamber is usually a life-long experience. The Lord invites the soul to make this journey, which is painful but ever so worthwhile. The story of Jacob's struggle with the angel in Genesis is also understood as an analogy of this struggle of prayer, which results in blessing if one perseveres.[48] Jacob suffered from the struggle, but also left with the angel's blessing. As we move nearer to the King, we are more and more stripped of ourselves, as the false self is put to death. The reason for this is so that we can begin to enjoy full union and full life with God. As we are gradually deprived of all that is familiar to us, we begin to see everything in a new light. The emotional programs for happiness are broken down and we learn to reevaluate much of what we previously held as untouchable. The whole point of this emptying is so that we can be completely united with God: "For it is very certain that in emptying ourselves of all that is creature and detaching ourselves from it for the love of God, the same Lord will fill us with Himself."[49]

## THE FRUITS OF UNION

There is one other aspect of Teresa's writings I would like to touch on briefly here and that is the effect that union has on the soul. While it is true that the Lord draws the soul ever inward to be more and more united to him, the fruits of this union are very important. In an article on St. Teresa as a story theologian, Mary Frohlich presents us with one of the most important fruits of this union:

> Teresa repeatedly emphasizes that the purpose of the spiritual marriage is not rest and delight, but to be joined to the sufferings of Christ and to spend oneself on behalf of souls. She describes the typical condition of such a person as consisting of deep interior peace while enduring extremes of exterior persecution, struggle, and hard work for the sake of the gospel....
>
> The stories [in *Foundations*] reveal to us how Teresa's transformed interior self was united not only with God, but also in a transformative way with the physical, social, cultural, and ecclesial world in which she lived. In other words, the stories both depict and enact the way persons in spiritual marriage gain the capacity to transform their cultural world at its heart.[50]

The purpose of this transformation is not just for the good of the soul, but also for the building up of the Kingdom of God. When we are transformed, we in turn are more effective in our ministry or life, to bring the presence of God to others and preach the Gospel. It is important not to lose sight of this dimension of prayer and where it leads. Otherwise, it could be seen as a purely narcissistic exercise. On the contrary, the practice reaches out to the whole world, enabling us to be more effective than ever as ministers of the Gospel, whether we are lay or religious:

The contemplative journey, of its very nature, calls us forth to act in a fully human way under the inspiration of the gifts of the Spirit. These gifts provide the divine energy of grace not only to accept what is, but also to change what is unjust. The gift of fortitude creates the hunger and thirst for justice. This disposition frees us from the downward pull of regressive tendencies and from the undue influence of cultural conditioning.[51]

Teresa mentions this many times, especially in the Seventh Dwelling Places. She wants to make sure her readers do not just have the impression that if they get to the stage of union all their troubles and sufferings are over. The soul is united to its God in an extraordinary way, but the reason for this is so that it may serve its Lord all the more effectively. The fact that it is at peace enables it to endure trials all the more:

> You may think that as a result [of this union] the soul will be outside itself and so absorbed that it will be unable to be occupied with anything else. On the contrary, the soul is much more occupied than before with everything pertaining to the service of God; and once its duties are over it remains with that enjoyable company. If the soul does not fail God, He will never fail, in my opinion, to make His presence clearly known to it.[52]

Being now all the more deeply united to God, the soul has more energy than before and is able to work all the more effectively. Teresa also mentions that this is surely the source for the unstoppable energy of so many of the saints. Therefore, the contemplative and active dimensions of the Gospel are brought together and serve each other:

> This is what I want us to strive for, my Sisters; and let us desire and be occupied in prayer not for the sake of our enjoyment but so as to have this strength to serve.... Believe me, Martha and Mary must join together in order to show hospitality to the Lord and have Him always rest and not host Him badly by failing to give Him something to eat. How would Mary, always seated at His feet, provide Him with food if her sister did not help her?[53]

The more the contemplative dimension of one's life is developed, the more one is empowered to act. This is one reason why the rediscovery of this kind of prayer is so important in the Church. Not that it has ever completely gone away, but in the last few centuries it certainly has been played down, to the detriment of everyone. Re-introducing people to this contemplative dimension of the Gospel, especially in a simple way that people can relate to, is both a great need and a great service to the Church. We will come back to this point in the last chapter.

## Chapter 10

# SAINT JOHN OF THE CROSS

JUAN DE YEPES, LATER known as John of the Cross, was born in 1542 in a small town called Fontiveros, midway between Madrid and Salamanca. His was a poor family, although his father Gonzalo had come from a wealthy family of silk merchants. However, Gonzalo had been disinherited when he decided to marry Juan's mother, Catalina Alvarez, a girl whose father was a weaver and whose background was poor and humble. Juan's early life was difficult, but at the age of seventeen he enrolled in a Jesuit school, where he began a more serious education.

At age twenty-one Juan entered the Carmelite novitiate, receiving the name Fray John of St. Matthias. In 1567, he was ordained a priest and met with Madre Teresa de Jesús in Medina. At this time he was considering changing to the Carthusians in order to pursue a more solitary life of prayer. However, Teresa convinced him to join her in reforming the order, which he agreed to do. By 1568, Fray Juan and two others began living in the first new monastery, which Teresa had managed to acquire. This was in Duruelo, somewhere between Avila and Salamanca. It wasn't long before others began to join them and St. John became more involved in their formation, especially with spiritual direction. By 1572, John had been moved to Avila to work with the many sisters looking for spiritual direction. John also ended up directing Teresa, although in fact both learned a great deal from each other.

Because of several new monasteries that were set up independently of the superior general's wishes, a series of misunderstandings and accusations followed. Any friar who had accepted a post that was not approved by the superior general, was considered a rebel and could be removed, even by force if necessary. On 2 December 1577, a group of Carmelites and lay people broke into the chaplain's quarters at Avila and captured Fray Juan, taking him to the monastery at Toledo. Here he was first imprisoned in the monastery's jail; however, fearing a rescue attempt, the group later transferred John to a safer place. This room, measuring only six feet by ten, was dark and without air, except for what little managed to enter through a narrow slit high up in the wall. John was imprisoned for a total of nine months. Between the physical conditions and the psychological torture, this imprisonment nearly killed him. Yet during this time he composed some of his most beautiful poetry and the experience would prove to be a life-changing one. Finally, one night in August he managed to loosen the lock on the door and escape. He was able to take refuge with some of Teresa's nuns in Toledo.

While John also suffered severely at the end of his life, through sickness and mistreatment from those who were supposed to be looking after him, these nine months in prison were undoubtedly the most difficult of his life. However, afterward John never complained nor resented those who had imprisoned him. During this "dark night," John had been united to his Beloved and as a result was able to describe it through exquisite poetry, leaving us with some extraordinary insights as to what the journey involves. It is worth noting that this experience of profound spiritual union with God happened during a time of terrible and bewildering suffering for John, and not in comfort in an incense-filled cloister or church. After this experience he was at peace and totally resigned to God's will. He was completely changed.

## THE LIVING FLAME OF LOVE

In his work *The Living Flame of Love*, John has an interesting section on the work of spiritual directors and the damage they can do. More specifically, however, he deals with the transition from meditation to contemplation. In this section (stanza 3, paragraphs 27–67), John digresses from his main discussion, but nonetheless answers some of the objections that also apply to centering prayer.

John points out that the soul needs to be very careful when it is beginning to receive interior blessings from the Lord, especially as it becomes more and more united to its God. There are essentially three pitfalls—or "blind guides," as John calls them—that come in the form of bad spiritual directors, the devil and the soul itself. John speaks at length about the damage that bad spiritual direction can do and often has done. The most basic problem here is a lack of knowledge on the part of the director, who can easily mislead the directee.

First, the director should recognize that it is God who is leading the soul. The task of the spiritual director is to recognize how God is doing it, and to help the directee see how best to follow that path. It is not the director's role to lead the soul along the path that *he or she* wants it to follow. John complains that many directors also do not understand the need to move beyond the stage of discursive meditation, with the result that if they hear that the souls in their care are beginning to leave aside this kind of prayer, they try to convince them that they should not:

> How often is God anointing a contemplative soul with some very delicate unguent of loving knowledge, serene, peaceful, solitary, and far withdrawn from the senses and what is imaginable, as a result of which it cannot meditate or reflect on anything, or enjoy anything heavenly or earthly (since God has engaged it in that lonely idleness and given it the inclination to solitude), when a spiritual director will happen along who, like a blacksmith, knows no more than how to hammer and pound with the faculties.[1]

As a result, not only will the director prevent the soul from going where the Lord is now beginning to draw it, but he or she will in fact be sending it back to what will no longer nourish it. At a certain point, God begins to lead the soul into more silence, relying less on the senses, as the work of the senses is for the most part over. Now God himself wants to work in the soul, and the soul must learn to be still, or "recollected." John also points out that this can happen in some people "after a very short time":

> But when the appetite has been fed somewhat and has become in a certain fashion accustomed to spiritual things and acquired some fortitude and constancy, God begins to wean the soul, as they say, and place it in the state of contemplation. This occurs in some persons after a very short time, especially with religious; in denying the things of the world more quickly, they accommodate their senses and appetites to God and pass on to the spirit in their activity, God thus working in them. This happens when the soul's discursive acts and meditations cease, as well as its initial sensible satisfaction and fervor, and it is unable to practice discursive meditation as before or find any support for the senses. The sensory part is left in dryness because its riches are transferred to the spirit, which does not pertain to the senses.[2]

> Therefore directors should not impose meditation on persons in this state, nor should they oblige them to make acts or strive for satisfaction and fervor. Such activity would place an obstacle in the path of the principal agent who, as I say, is God, who secretly and quietly inserts in the soul loving wisdom and knowledge, without specified acts....[3]

Today we still seem to be suffering from a lack of directors with proper knowledge, who are often suspicious of "silence" or any kind of contemplation. As a result, many souls who are being led to contemplation are not crossing the border, so to speak, as they lack the necessary direction. For so long has the teaching in seminaries been that contemplative prayer is only for those in the cloisters that many priests and religious are easily turned off by the mere mention of the word "contemplation," or anything connected with it. As Thomas Keating puts it:

> Our organization is definitely not a form of lay monastic life. I deliberately rejected that paradigm because I knew as soon as we used the term "monastic," the average citizen would be back into the institutionalized view of contemplation, which is for cloistered people only. Most secular priests have the same concept.... The rank and file were taught that contemplation is only for mystics and saints. In actual fact, contemplation is not the reward of a virtuous life; it is a *necessity* for a virtuous life.[4]

A new education of priests, religious, and the laity is needed, to help people rediscover that contemplative prayer is meant for everyone, that it is a normal part of the spiritual journey, and that it is also possible without being in a monastery. When people get to the stage of no longer being able to practice discursive meditation and feel drawn to spending more time in silence, many will feel unsure of where they are going, especially as the West is much better at "doing" than at "being." This is where the right kind of direction is vital:

When it happens, therefore, that souls are conscious in this manner of being placed in silence and in the state of listening, they should even forget the practice of loving attentiveness I mentioned so as to remain free for what the Lord then desires of them. They should make use of that loving awareness only when they do not feel themselves placed in this solitude or inner idleness or oblivion or spiritual listening. So they may recognize it, it always comes to pass with a certain peace and calm and inward absorption.[5]

The more the air is cleansed of vapors and the quieter and more simple it is, the more the sun illumines and warms it. A person should not bear attachment to anything, neither to the practice of meditation nor to any savor, whether sensory or spiritual, nor to any other apprehensions.[6]

It is interesting that John says here that we should not be attached to anything, not even to the practice of meditation. In the same way the use of the sacred word is not meant to be rigid, but only used when we become aware of thoughts:

In the beginning it is hard to hang on to your intention without continually returning to the sacred word. But this does not mean that you have to keep repeating it.... As you become more comfortable with this prayer, you begin to find yourself beyond the word in a place of interior peace. Then you see that there is a level which is beyond the sacred word.[7]

There will come a time when the word seems to repeat itself and it will hardly be necessary to express it at all. There is great flexibility in this method, unlike some other practices of meditation where you must continually repeat the mantra, regardless of what is going on.

Ironically, the great interest in Zen and other Eastern forms of prayer has contributed greatly to helping people appreciate the need for contemplation and silence. So many have been drawn to different practices of Eastern meditation in recent years that many people are beginning to change their opinion about the need for silent meditation, although it is often only seen as a means of well-being for the individual, at least initially.

John goes on to remind his readers that once people have been led to this stage of contemplation, they should not allow themselves to be drawn back to any kind of discursive meditation, as this would be going backwards:

> Once individuals have begun to enter this simple and idle state of contemplation that comes about when they can no longer meditate, they should not at any time or season engage in meditations or look for support in spiritual savor or satisfaction, but stand upright on their own feet with their spirit completely detached from everything.[8]

The soul is now being led into unknown territory, which is not easy, as our normal inclination is to be in control and to have some kind of sign that we are doing the right thing. But now the Lord is asking the soul to let go and not understand. This is where good direction can make all the difference, as this is often the point where people begin to lose their nerve.

Now the objection may be raised: "But couldn't someone sitting in this silence just be sitting their on their own, thinking that God is acting in them, but in reality doing nothing?" To this, John answers:

> When the soul frees itself of all things and attains to emptiness and dispossession concerning them, which is equivalent to what it can do of itself, it is impossible that God fail to do his part by communicating himself to it, at least silently and secretly. It is more impossible than it would be for the sun not to shine on clear and uncluttered ground.[9]

We are, of course, presuming that the one sitting in the silence does have the intention of being open to God and sees this as a form of prayer and not just some kind of impersonal self-development. This again is the difference between Christian prayer and not. Keating also responds to this objection, first of all by pointing out that people spend several hours a day asleep, apparently doing nothing, and yet we cannot survive without this period of rest. Of course, in this prayer there is in fact a lot happening.

It could also be objected that it must be necessary to make some kind of acts of love every so often toward God. Although the sacred word used in centering prayer does express the intention of being open to God's action, which can also be understood as a loving act of giving oneself to God, St. John says that particular loving acts of the will are unnecessary:

But in the contemplation we are discussing (by which God infuses himself into the soul), particular knowledge as well as acts made by the soul are unnecessary. The reason for this is that God in one act is communicating light and love together, which is loving supernatural knowledge. We can assert that this knowledge is like light that transmits heat, for that light also enkindles love. This knowledge is general and dark to the intellect because it is contemplative knowledge, which is a ray of darkness for the intellect, as St. Dionysius teaches.[10]

So John confirms continually that once the soul has been led to this stage of prayer all it need do is trust in what is happening and allow the Spirit to lead it on into the darkness. Keating is also strong in encouraging people to just stay with the practice, in spite of how it may appear to be going: "The only way to judge this prayer is by its long-range fruits: whether in daily life you enjoy greater peace, humility and charity."[11] If we are following the method, with the right intention of giving ourselves to God and allowing him to work in us, then this will certainly happen. The temptation is to think that we can gauge the progress, but we cannot:

Individuals should take note that even though they do not seem to be making any progress in this quietude or doing anything, they are advancing much faster than if they were treading along on foot, for God is carrying them.[12]

Let us take one more word from John on the value of spending time in this kind of silent prayer, which so many people find incomprehensible. He reminds us that time spent with God in this way is worth far more than our own efforts in the world:

> Let those, then, who are singularly active, who think they can win the world with their preaching and exterior works, observe here that they would profit the Church and please God much more, not to mention the good example they would give, were they to spend at least half of this time with God in prayer, even though they might not have reached a prayer as sublime as this. They would then certainly accomplish more, and with less labor, by one work than they otherwise would by a thousand. For through their prayer they would merit this result, and themselves be spiritually strengthened.[13]

## THE ASCENT OF MOUNT CARMEL

In this section, we look more at John's writings insofar as they deal with the purification through which God leads the soul, in order to bring it closer to himself. *The Ascent of Mount Carmel* and *The Dark Night* are essentially two parts of the same work, though written separately. The first book deals mostly with the night of the senses and *Night* deals with the night of the senses and spirit. While we will take each book individually, they will overlap to some degree.

Earlier, we spoke of the emotional programs for happiness, as Keating describes them, where through a perceived lack of the most basic psychological needs we invest great energy in areas where we believe we will find happiness, or essentially make up for the perceived lack. The reason we do this is that we mistakenly perceive that God is absent:

> Our instinctual needs gradually grew into emotional programs for happiness because in growing up we had no experience of the divine presence within, which is the true security, the deepest affirmation of our basic goodness, and true freedom.[14]

Although we do this unconsciously, it certainly happens. The result is that we search for happiness in the very places that cannot possibly bring satisfaction: through wealth, power, or affection, etc. This can also manifest itself in different forms of addiction. To break the pattern, we must "change the direction in which we are seeking happiness," and turn to the one place where we will find fulfillment; that is, in God. Consequently, through prayer, we begin to reevaluate much of what we learned at an early age, and to discover that these areas will never satisfy us. Instead, by letting go of our desire for them, we are gradually freed from our attachments and enabled to draw closer to God. It is only in God that we will find this fulfillment. Now, this work takes place in the silence of contemplative prayer where the Holy Spirit brings this about. Keating speaks about it in psychological terms, while St. John speaks about it more in spiritual language. Nevertheless, they are speaking about the same thing.

St. John deals with the need to let go of all earthly appetites, since none of these will bring satisfaction, and they are in fact an obstacle to union with God:

> The necessity to pass through this dark night (the mortification of the appetites and denial of pleasure in all things) to attain divine union with God arises from the fact that all of a person's attachments to creatures are pure darkness in God's sight. Clothed in these affections, people are incapable of the enlightenment and dominating fullness of God's pure and simple light; first they must reject them.[15]

In order to free it from these unhealthy attachments, the Lord draws the soul through an inner purification, which opens the way for it to be more deeply united to him. The problem is not so much the things that we are attached to—whether emotional or material—rather it is the attachment in itself:

> Hence, we call this nakedness a night for the soul, for we are not discussing the mere lack of things; this lack will not divest the soul if it craves for all these objects. We are dealing with the denudation of the soul's appetites and gratifications. This is what leaves it free and empty of all things, even though it possesses them. Since the things of the world cannot enter the soul, they are not in themselves an encumbrance or harm to it; rather, it is the will and appetite dwelling within that cause the damage when set on these things.[16]

As you might expect, the Spanish mystic doesn't speak in terms of emotional programs or energy centers, but he is essentially speaking about the same thing. John is speaking about earthly "appetites," that is, the things we are attached to or dependent on. However, this also applies to anything in which we place emotional investment. In fact, the emotional investment is the real problem. Having money or power is not a problem, but being obsessed with them certainly can be. This is the challenge of the Gospel: to be free from our attachment to these things in order to be open to God. Hence, "blessed are the poor in spirit, the kingdom of heaven is theirs" (Mt 5:3). The only one who can free us from these attachments is God, and this seems to happen most effectively when we open ourselves to him in prayer. This is what happens in the darkness of contemplation, according to John. The whole process is a freeing of the soul from all attachments, insofar as they hinder it from union with God:

> The road and ascent to God, then, necessarily demands a habitual effort to renounce and mortify the appetites; the sooner this mortification is achieved, the sooner the soul reaches the top. But until the appetites are eliminated, one will not arrive no matter how much virtue is practiced. For one will be failing to acquire perfect virtue, which lies in keeping the soul empty, naked, and purified of every appetite.[17]

This "renouncing of the appetites," as John calls it, is possible both actively and passively. Actively, we can get used to denying ourselves things or at least moderating the amount we take. This also happens passively during prayer, as the desire for these same satisfactions is gently put to rest as our emotional programs are put in order. Both the active and the passive are important; however, the passive is more so, since it deals with the root of the problem.

The practice of penance has always been understood as a means to grow in holiness. Penance helps people overcome their attachments to unhealthy habits or desires. Doing penance can certainly have different benefits, but the problem is that our attachments are not at a surface level, and so even with the practice of different kinds of penance we may not necessarily rid ourselves of our vices. Indeed, penitential works can even become an end in themselves and a source of spiritual pride:

> The ignorance of some is extremely lamentable; they burden themselves with extraordinary penances and many other exercises, thinking these are sufficient to attain union with divine Wisdom. But such practices are insufficient if these souls do not diligently strive to deny their appetites. If they would attempt to devote only half of that energy to the renunciation of their desires, they would profit more in a month than in years with all these other exercises.[18]

Keating uses a simple story to make this point, which I will paraphrase here. There was a young man, let us call him Matthew, who liked nothing better than to go down to the local bar on a Friday night and have a drinking competition with anyone he could find willing to challenge him. Inevitably he would beat them, and as they collapsed to the floor he would stand up triumphant and soak up the applause of the on-lookers. One day, this young man had a conversion and began to try to live the Gospel. He was so repentant for the way he used to live that he decided to enter a religious order, the strictest one he could find. So he joined the Carthusians and began a new life of prayer and penance.

When Lent came, the severe fasting began and gradually different monks had to be excused from the refectory as they began to fall ill. Toward the end of Lent the last monk apart from Matthew was excused from the fast and left the dining room. As the Easter celebrations began, Matthew found he was the only one left who had been able to keep the fast, and once again he experienced that same triumphant feeling that he used to experience when he beat his friends in drinking competitions. This time he had fasted all the other monks under the table!

The point of the story is that while Matthew might be living a more virtuous way of life on the surface, the unconscious motivations had not changed. Just because we put on a religious garb doesn't mean that the inner person has been renewed. The spiritual journey challenges us to change the unconscious motivations that drive us. Nevertheless, how can we change what is unconscious? This is what happens through the night of the senses that John speaks of. Giving ourselves to contemplation seems to be the most effective way for this to happen, since in this kind of prayer we allow God to do all the work. Because these motivations are unconscious, the Spirit is the only one who can tackle them properly and most effectively. John laments the fact that more people do not take this path, as it is so effective:

> God gives many souls the talent and grace for advancing, and should they desire to make the effort they would arrive at this high state. And so it is sad to see them continue in their lowly method of communion with God because they do not want or know how to advance, or because they receive no direction on breaking away from the methods of beginners.[19]

Centering prayer is one such method that leads us to contemplation, bringing us along the path of this very work:

> Those therefore who value their knowledge and ability as a means of reaching union with the wisdom of God are highly ignorant in God's sight and will be left behind, far away from this wisdom.... Only those who set aside their own knowledge and walk in God's service like unlearned children receive wisdom from God.[20]

John also reminds us that the difficulty in this kind of prayer is the fact that we can no longer be in control. Normally, we want to be in control of what we are doing, but with this prayer we do not know the way and so we have to be prepared to walk in darkness, allowing the Spirit to lead us in a way that we know not. This is perhaps one of the biggest difficulties with contemplative prayer for many souls. Since they cannot see their progress, or the "value" in what they are doing, they frequently give up.

John goes on to speak of how these appetites bind the soul to the things of the earth:

> First these appetites weaken and blind ... then they afflict and torment by chaining that person to the mill of concupiscence, for they are the chains by which a soul is bound.[21]

The difficulty is that the more a person is bound by their appetites, the more difficult it is for them to follow the ways of God, which call for a letting go of these attachments. That is why this purification is quite painful to the soul and we tend to resist it:

> The appetites sap the strength needed for perseverance in the practice of virtue. Because the force of the desire is divided, the appetite becomes weaker than if it were completely fixed on one object.[22]

The more we are purified of our attachments, the easier it becomes to follow the ways of God. However, all this takes time. As long as we continue to act out of our false programs for happiness, we are sending our energy in the very opposite direction to where we will find help. Naturally, we are continually frustrated. Instead, we need to turn around and learn how to let go of these misleading "needs" that are draining us. The practice of the virtues also helps us to overcome our attachments.

One might wonder if there is any point in us trying to do anything in this journey, since this is the work of the Holy Spirit, after all? Here John reminds us that we do have a part to play, by giving ourselves to the practice of the virtues and to prayer:

Since this transformation and union is something that does not fall within the reach of the senses and of human capability, the soul must perfectly and voluntarily empty itself—I mean in its affection and will—of all the earthly and heavenly things it can grasp. It must do this insofar as it can. As for God, who will stop him from accomplishing his desires in the soul that is resigned, annihilated, and despoiled?

But people must empty themselves of all, insofar as they can, so that however many supernatural communications they receive, they will continually live as though denuded of them and in darkness.[23]

John also speaks about the practice of the virtues as being essential to growth. Indeed, if they were not part of the process, we might ask if this work could be centered on God, since the theological virtues are at the core of our practice of the faith:

These virtues ... void the faculties: Faith causes darkness and a void of understanding in the intellect, hope begets an emptiness of possessions in the memory, and charity produces the nakedness and emptiness of affection and joy in all that is not God.

Faith ... affirms what cannot be understood by the intellect.... In relation to our discussion here, this means that faith is the substance of things to be hoped for and that these things are not manifest to the intellect, even though its consent

to them is firm and certain. If they were manifest, there would be no faith.[24]

Our efforts to change and grow are all part of the
practice of the virtues:

> If we are upset by anything we have a problem,
> and we will continue to experience emotional
> turmoil until we change the root of the problem,
> which is the emotional program for happiness in
> the unconscious. The effort to change it is called
> the practice of virtue.[25]

The emotional programs for happiness, which
Keating speaks about, are what John of the Cross calls
the appetites. They have to be laid to rest or "annihilated," as John would say. The journey involves this
inner purification, but it all takes place in ordinary
day-to-day living. What John is talking about is very
concrete, though one would be forgiven for thinking
that it is only something very spiritual, since his style
of writing is largely focused on the spiritual dimension. However, the spiritual and the non-spiritual
aspects of our lives cannot be separated, as though
the two had different and independent existences.
The spiritual aspect of our life is interconnected with
everything we do and is not just for "prayer time."
Marko Ivan Rupnik expresses this beautifully in his
book, *In the Fire of the Burning Bush*:

> Spiritual Gnosticism of whatever type, whether
> psychological or moralistic, is recognized pre-
> cisely in the incapacity to see the connections
> between the various dimensions of the person

and the various facts of life. The spiritual life embraces thoughts, emotions, and physicality. There is no event in daily life, however insignificant, that is excluded, untouched by the life of the spirit.[26]

Spirituality is not a field unto itself. It is an integral part of true dogma. Separated from theology and from theological anthropology—which are like two pillars rising from the same base—spirituality becomes something other than what it is in Christianity, something unable to respond to what it truly is. Whatever is not joined to life, is not rooted in it, cannot serve life.[27]

This is so important if the spiritual life is not to be limited to the few who live "religious" lives, thereby reducing it to something that is only for those who can afford it the time. The spiritual life is part of everyone's life.

St. John also gives a few chapters over to the importance and benefits of keeping the memory still, or in modern language, to the letting go of thoughts. John deals with different kinds of knowledge in the (spiritual) memory, but essentially all his advice on this matter is the same. As long as we keep holding on to ideas or images in the memory, they distract us in various ways or can be a form of deception. John's advice is to try to keep the memory still and empty, insofar as it is possible. Even spiritual thoughts or visions can be a source of distraction and deception. Therefore, the safest thing to do is to be completely detached from them. People are often misled by spiritual experiences as they try to interpret what they mean. John says that this is a waste of time, since the spiritual benefit of any experience of this kind is given at the time it is received. Trying to "understand" it is often where people get confused. So the safest thing to do is always to let them go. In centering prayer, the sacred word helps us let go of whatever comes into our consciousness and not be distracted by it, even if it seems very profound:

> What souls must do in order to live in perfect and pure hope in God is this: As often as distinct ideas, forms, and images occur to them, they should immediately, without resting in them, turn to God with loving affection, in emptiness of everything rememberable.[28]

John also mentions that it is easy to be deceived by the devil with regard to spiritual experiences, which is another reason not to hold on to any ideas during this kind of prayer:

> The second kind of positive harm possible from knowledge in the memory is due to the devil. He has tremendous influence in the soul by this means, for he can add to its knowledge other forms, ideas, and reasonings, and by means of them move it to pride, avarice, anger, envy, and so on, and insert unjust hatred, vain love, and many kinds of delusions.... If the memory is darkened as to all this knowledge and annihilated through oblivion, the door is closed entirely to this kind of diabolical harm and the soul is liberated from these things, and that is a wonderful blessing.[29]

The afflictive emotions can be an aid to us in detecting our false programs for happiness and where we are in need of healing.[30] John of the Cross deals with four emotions in particular:

> So a person may [love God with all his might], we will discuss here purifying the will of all inordinate emotions. These inordinate emotions are the source of unruly appetites, affections, and operations, and the basis for failure to preserve one's strength for God. There are four of these emotions or passions: joy, hope, sorrow, and fear.[31]

> When these emotions go unbridled they are the source of all vices and imperfections, but when they are put in order and calmed they give rise to all the virtues.[32]

*are they leading towards love?*

These emotions can be a great help to us, as they are usually a response to a particular situation. Once they are "ordered" they serve their purpose even more effectively, helping us to be aware of where we are misdirecting too much emotional energy. Contemplative prayer allows these emotions to be purified or properly ordered. We need these emotions to help us in everyday life, so it is not a question of getting rid of them. However, they will best serve us when they are functioning as they were intended. Through the purification of contemplative prayer, we become aware of our false programs for happiness, and we then begin to redirect our energies to their proper end, that is, toward God. The "afflictive emotions" can be reduced to anger, grief, fear, pride, greed, envy, lust, and apathy.[33] St. John doesn't specifically say how the four emotions that he mentions affect us, only that they cause us to direct our interests away from God and so we need to be purified of this. Both John and Keating seem to be referring to the same thing, though again in a different manner. Today, we have the insights of psychology to our advantage, which St. John would not have had in the same way, but it seems that the work that they are both referring to is the same.

Misdirected emotional energy leads us away from God. A concrete example of this might be the businessperson I mentioned earlier with more money than he can ever spend still trying to make more. The money has become his god and is leading him further away from God. Through prayer, he will eventually begin to see the futility of his quest and be freed to move more in the direction of God.

Toward the end of The Ascent of Mount Carmel, John teaches that the purpose of this purification is so that the soul will not only be able to love God more, but in turn be able to serve its neighbor more, just as Teresa of Avila points out. In this way, it cannot be said to be a purely selfish exercise:

> Besides preparing the soul for the love of God and for other virtues, it directly paves the way for humility toward self and general charity toward one's neighbor. By not becoming attached to anyone, despite these apparent and deceptive natural goods, a person remains unencumbered and free to love all rationally and spiritually, which is the way God wants them to be loved.[34]

## ✌ THE DARK NIGHT

> What is really at stake in the spiritual journey to union with God is an ongoing work of purification, a cleansing of all that is repugnant to God's holiness. The purity implied is impossible without personal effort, but this effort, however intense, does not achieve the radical stripping demanded by the union. God's own intervention is necessary through a purifying communication that works passively, beyond the realm of what human effort can achieve. Human effort does little more than dispose one for the divine action.[35]

In this book John deals with the purification of the soul through the active and passive nights of sense and spirit. It is an experience that will often take most of one's life, although for some it may be shorter, depending on the openness of the soul and how the Holy Spirit sees fit to work in it. Since each soul is different, it is impossible to give a hard and fast categorization of how exactly this happens. However, what is clear is that it will generally happen if the soul is so disposed. Here we will look at some of the aspects of this painful purgation. The night of the senses is basically a preparation for the night of the spirit, which is far more intense. The second cannot happen without the first, as the soul would not be able to deal with it, though it may not be particularly obvious which one is happening, and the two may overlap.

In the above quotation, Kieran Kavanaugh points out that for our part we can do little more than dispose ourselves to this work, but disposing ourselves is possible and indeed recommended by John himself:

Yet until a soul is placed by God in the passive purgation of that dark night ... it cannot purify itself completely of these imperfections or others. But people should insofar as possible strive to do their part in purifying and perfecting themselves and thereby merit God's divine cure. In this cure God will heal them of what through their own efforts they were unable to remedy. No matter how much individuals do through their own efforts, they cannot actively purify themselves enough to be disposed in the least degree for the divine union of the perfection of love.[36]

Centering prayer is just such a method that suitably disposes the soul to this work. Although it cannot be said that this purification only happens during the time of contemplative prayer—since it involves every aspect of one's life—yet it seems that much of it does. Since we can only grow a certain amount through discursive meditation, as this is largely our own work, the Spirit draws the soul away from this practice by drying up the satisfaction it found there and then leading it on into the silence:

God desires to withdraw [beginners] from this base manner of loving and lead them on to a higher degree of divine love. And he desires to liberate them from the lowly exercise of the senses and of discursive meditation, by which they go in search of him so inadequately and with so many difficulties, and lead them into the exercise of spirit, in which they become capable of a communion with God that is more abundant and more free of imperfections. God does this after beginners have exercised themselves for a time in the way of virtue and have persevered in meditation and prayer.[37]

Because our souls are so full of sinful tendencies and inadequate spiritual practices, God begins to purge the soul of its weaknesses in order to lead it on to greater things. This, according to John, is an extremely painful experience that involves many trials and can last for several years. The night of the spirit can be an excruciatingly difficult time for the soul, as it is led into total darkness and dryness where God seems to have deserted it. There, it sees only its own misery, believes that even its friends have abandoned it, and is afraid it may have lost God forever.

In order to prepare the soul for this night of the spirit, individuals usually go through various intense trials during the night of the senses. This is often an indication that God plans to lead these souls through the night of the spirit later. John deals with three trials in particular, which we have already dealt with in chapter four.[38] There is a great amount of selfishness rooted in us, which we are largely unaware of, and these three trials are a cleansing of this selfishness:

> God generally sends these storms and trials in this sensory night and purgation to those whom he will afterward put in the other night—although not all pass on to it—so that thus chastised and buffeted, the senses and faculties may gradually be exercised, prepared, and inured for the union with wisdom that will be granted there.[39]

This whole purification involves a relearning of values, and a redirecting of our energies toward God, instead of wastefully investing them in areas that can only frustrate. As we have seen, most people spend their lives putting great energy into habits and projects that will only lead to frustration, since they cannot fulfill the soul, which has been made for nothing less than union with God. Consequently, these "programs" are not only going to frustrate but are actually leading the soul in the wrong direction. As long as the false self remains, union with God will be impossible. Therefore, this night involves the complete death of the false self, in order to allow us to be united to God:

> The stains of the old self still linger in the spirit, although they may not be apparent or perceptible. If these are not wiped away by the use of the soap and strong lye of this purgative night, the spirit will be unable to reach the purity of divine union.[40]

John also points out that this night involves a "reformation and bridling of the appetite." Putting it this way seems to confirm the process as a reordering of our emotional programs, or a reforming of our value system:

> The real purgation of the senses begins with the spirit. Hence the night of the senses we explained should be called a certain reformation and bridling of the appetite rather than a purgation. The reason is that all the imperfections and disorders of the sensory part are rooted in the spirit and from it receive their strength.[41]

The nights of sense and spirit are often understood more in terms of a purgation—in the sense of a "burning away" of what is not good—as opposed to a reordering of our appetites. John describes it as an "undoing" of what the soul has already learned throughout its lifetime. Naturally, since this is taking away from all that is familiar to the soul, it finds the whole process very painful:

> As fire consumes the tarnish and rust of metal, this contemplation annihilates, empties, and consumes all the affections and imperfect habits the soul contracted throughout its life. Since these imperfections are deeply rooted in the substance of the soul, in addition to this poverty, this natural and spiritual emptiness, it usually suffers an oppressive undoing and an inner torment.[42]

One of the more subtle temptations that we may experience in the night of the senses is to see ourselves as something special in God's eyes, in particular if we have received any kind of spiritual gifts. It is not uncommon for people to experience gifts such as healing or preaching, which can be of great benefit to the Church. However, we may over-associate ourselves with the gifts we have received, quietly enjoying the fact that we are "a healer" or "renowned preacher," or whatever it might involve. This is especially worth mentioning today, when a great emphasis is often put on spiritual gifts of different kinds. In the Charismatic Renewal, the experience of various spiritual gifts can often be seen at work. But if there is a lack of sound teaching in these circles, there may be a temptation to get caught up in the importance of the gift, instead of seeing it as a means of building up the Christian community: "Service is the hallmark of one who is sent by God. The true prophet, martyr, spiritual leader, or teacher does not try to dominate others."[43] The purification of the night of sense annihilates any temptations in this area, as people become painfully aware of their own sinfulness and misery before God. This in turn helps them to rely totally on God for all things, allowing him to be the power that works through them:

> The night of spirit reduces such temptations [to see ourselves as something special] to zero because, through its purifying action, we experience ourselves as capable of every evil. Not that we are likely to commit evil deeds, but we feel completely dependent on God in order to avoid personal sin or the habitual hang-ups of the false self that lead to it.[44]

The whole process is a "making space" for God. Once the space is made, God pours into the space and fills us.

## FRUITS OF THE DARK NIGHT

Through the dark night, the soul is being made ready not only for union with God but also so that it can work more effectively in the world. The more it is united to God, the more the soul mediates that presence of God to others in all that it does. Being purified of prejudices and "worldly" ways of thinking, the soul is also able to help others without bias. The soul begins to see everything with the eyes of God:

> Even though this happy night darkens the spirit, it does so only to impart light concerning all things; and even though it humbles individuals and reveals their miseries, it does so only to exalt them; and even though it impoverishes and empties them of all possessions and natural affection, it does so only that they may reach out divinely to the enjoyment of all earthly and heavenly things, with a general freedom of spirit in them all.[45]

There are five fruits in particular that come from this night of the spirit. The first fruit is the purification from the temptation to see ourselves as something special, because of any spiritual gifts we may have received, as mentioned earlier. A second fruit of this night is freedom from the domination of our emotions. Our emotions are meant to serve us and support the decisions of our free will, but until they have been properly ordered they tend to dominate and get in the way of balanced judgments. For example, when someone loses their temper, the anger expressed is often quite out of proportion to the event that has caused them to become angry. When the emotions are properly in order, this no longer happens. Jesus driving the moneychangers from the temple is a good example. Jesus was justifiably angry. He acted on it, and then it was over. He didn't go on obsessing about it for the following two days, as many of us might do:

[This ordering of the emotions] takes place not by repressing or unduly suppressing unwanted emotions by sheer willpower, but by accepting and integrating them into the rational and intuitive parts of our nature. The emotions will then serve and support the decisions of reason and will, which is their natural purpose.[46]

A third fruit of this night is that our idea of God is purified. We may have grown up with all kinds of ideas about God, either from our parents or from a particular group we belonged to. During this night, God may shatter our ideas about who or what God is, but at the same time He will reveal himself to us in a vastly superior way. Our understanding of God usually needs to be changed into something quite different from what we have grown up with, especially if we have come to understand God as some kind of policeman, or judge, waiting to punish us for every wrong move. A huge number of people have grown up with this kind of idea of God, but God wants to help us mature in our faith and relate to Him in a completely different way.

A fourth fruit of this night is the purification of the theological virtues: faith, hope, and love. We may find that we can no longer associate with the same group of people who formerly supported us, even our spiritual director, as our faith is changing. God draws us away from many of the props we used up to this point, giving us no choice but to rely on him more, though without necessarily understanding how to do this. The Bible gives many accounts of people who experienced this, such as Abraham, Moses, Job, and

Our Lady. Their faith was constantly being brought to a deeper level:

> The greatest fruit of the night of spirit is the disposition that is willing to accept God on his own terms. As a result, one allows God to be God without knowing who or what that is.[47]

God "forces" us to depend completely on him and on his mercy, especially as we see more clearly than ever before that we have nothing to boast about. We have become painfully aware of our weaknesses and now God asks us to live with them and accept his unconditional love and mercy in a way that we may not have been doing up to now, because of a false notion of who we are and who God is. As Iain Matthew writes:

> John is himself masterfully aware ("and this is something we are constantly experiencing") of how the roots from the past can tyrannise the emotions; and of how the future can paralyse with worry one's fluidity in the here and now.[48]

So the healing of memory that we experience is not a destroying of impressions that we have; rather it helps us to no longer be dominated by them in a negative way. The purifying of the virtues of faith, hope, and love is healing us of the past and allowing us to move on and no longer be dominated by it. It is also freeing us from fear of the future and making "space" for God to come in. The healing of the emotions involves this same growth of the theological virtues. The emotional wounds are being healed and we are being enabled to move forward toward God, although

with greater freedom than before. However, this transformation can be quite frightening, as we are being led
into a realm that we find completely unfamiliar:

> This night withdraws the spirit from its cus-
> tomary manner of experience to bring it to the
> divine experience that is foreign to every human
> way.... The reason is that the soul is being made
> a stranger to its usual knowledge and experience
> of things, so that, annihilated in this respect, it
> may be informed with the divine, which belongs
> more to the next life than to this.[49]

A fifth fruit of this night is the experience of a
great desire to be rid of all selfishness that still lin-
gers within us, especially insofar as it hinders us from
coming closer to God. The longing now is only for
union with God. Thomas Keating writes:

> Thus, the divine plan is to transform human
> nature into the divine, not by giving it some spe-
> cial role or exceptional powers, but by enabling it
> to live ordinary life with extraordinary love.[50]

John of the Cross speaks of the growth of all the
virtues in this way:

> Another very great benefit for the soul in this
> night is that it exercises all the virtues together.
> In the patience and forbearance practiced in
> these voids and aridities, and through persever-
> ance in its spiritual exercises without consola-
> tion or satisfaction, the soul practices the love
> of God, since it is no longer motivated by the
> attractive and savory gratification it finds in its

work, but only by God. It also practices the virtue of fortitude, because it draws strength from weakness in the difficulties and aversions experienced in its work, and thus becomes strong. Finally, in these aridities the soul practices corporeally and spiritually all the virtues, theological as well as cardinal and moral.[51]

Keating teaches that the purification through the nights of sense and spirit also releases great energy from the unconscious, enabling us to work more effectively:

> The night of sense is doing more than dismantling the false self. In relaxing our compulsions and habitual ways of overreacting, it also releases the energies of the unconscious.[52]

As the virtues are purified and the emotions are being ordered, more energy is channeled in the right direction. This in turn gives the whole person more energy in their life.

In an excellent presentation of the teachings of John of the Cross in a modern context, Iain Matthew confirms this idea and how it enables people to do extraordinary work:

> What the night journey does—where that which comes upon us takes us out of our control—is retrieve our scattered human potential, place it in our hands, and so enable us, at last to employ it in loving. This releases immense power. It may in part account for the extraordinary effectiveness of Jesus and of some holy people.[53]

John of the Cross also refers to this in *Night*:

> [Through the night], God gathers together all the strength, faculties, and appetites of the soul, spiritual and sensory alike, so the energy and power of this whole harmonious composite may be employed in this love. The soul consequently arrives at the true fulfilment of the first commandment which, neither disdaining anything human nor excluding it from this love, states: *You shall love your God with your whole heart, and with your whole mind, and with your whole soul, and with all your strength.*[54]

Thus, we can see that while Keating speaks about the healing of the unconscious, the redirection of our energy toward God and the growth of the virtues, John of the Cross deals with it more in terms of the purification of the virtues, out of which these others flow. The language is different, but the teaching is essentially the same. When God leads the soul through this purification, he puts the house in order, establishes the proper harmony and balance, and thereby makes the soul far more effective in its work as it is no longer wasting energy on what does not give life.

## THE TRANSFORMING UNION

The transforming union, which is the final union with God in this life, is the greatest result of the night of the spirit. The soul is now transformed, purified completely, and allows God to shine through it perfectly, making his presence felt everywhere.

Anthony of Egypt spent over twenty years in the desert secluded in an abandoned fortress doing battle with the "demons." Finally the people came and pulled down the door, which Anthony took as a sign that God wanted him to return and minister to the people. His biographer St. Athanasius tells us that when Anthony came out, he was neither emaciated, nor overweight, but healthy and calm:

> Again the state of his soul was pure for it was neither contracted by grief, nor dissipated by pleasure, nor pervaded by jollity. He was not embarrassed when he saw the crowd, nor was he elated at seeing so many there to receive him. He had himself completely under control, a man guided by reason and stable in his character. He exhorted all to prefer nothing in the world to the love of Christ.[55]

Anthony had been completely purified and was now in a better position to minister to people than ever before. He was now free of prejudice, cultural conditioning, or any of the false self that could get in the way of ministry. The night of spirit brings about this purification of our value system and it orders the emotions in such a way that they can now properly serve us and enable us to minister the love of God to others in a far superior way. Thomas Keating reminds us:

> The Fathers of the Desert had a word for this experience. They called it "apatheia," which is sometimes taken to mean "indifference." It is rather a tremendous concern for everything that

is, but without the emotional involvement characteristic of the false self. We are free to devote
ourselves to the needs of others without becoming unduly absorbed in their emotional pain.
We are present to people at the deepest level
and perceive the presence of Christ suffering in
them. We long to share with them something
of the inner freedom we have been given, but
without anxiety and without trying to change
them or to obtain anything from them. We simply have the divine life as sheer gift and offer it
to anyone who wants it.[56]

The purpose of the nights of sense and spirit is
so that the soul can be completely united with God,
transformed in God, or "divinized." John uses the
analogy of a log being placed in the fire. It first spits
and smokes as its impurities are burned away. Then,
once it is dried out, it slowly begins to glow like the
fire itself. Eventually, it becomes lighter and is hardly
distinct from the fire. The soul is purified in the same
way, and in the end radiates the presence of God
everywhere. It is no longer the "i" of the self, but
the "I" of God that now dwells at the center of the
soul. The trials that it previously went through will
not stop, but they will no longer affect the soul in
the same way. It is now united to God at the deepest
level. While transforming union is comparatively rare,
it is meant to be the norm. This is God's invitation to
all. However, most people do not respond to it with
enough openness. For our part, we need only be open,
since we cannot bring about this work ourselves:

This thrust keeps recurring: sunlight shining, eyes gazing, a mother feeding, water flowing, images of a God who initiates and invades. In this family of images, the emphasis is not on our forging a way, but on our getting out of the way. Progress will be measured, less by ground covered, more by the amount of room God is given to manoeuvre. "Space," "emptiness," are key words; or, as John put it, *nada*.[57]

As we can see from the writings of both Teresa and John, God's plan for us is transformation and union with him. Being open to God allows this to happen. A method of prayer such as centering prayer helps us to have the right disposition and openness for this to take place. After that, all we can do is wait and trust.

*Chapter 11*

# CENTERING PRAYER AND THE NEW AGE

## THE NEW AGE

WITH SO MANY NEW teachings on "spirituality" and prayer available, many people are rightly concerned as to how they can be sure whether something is genuinely Catholic or not. What has become known as the "New Age" movement is having a powerful influence in the West, but it involves such a wide collection of practices that it is often quite difficult to discern what is and is not compatible with Christianity. Various articles and programs have accused centering prayer of being another deception of the New Age, which is subtly leading people away from focusing on Christ and gradually increasing the notion of self-fulfillment and self-realization through different prayer and meditation techniques.

The *New Age* is a term that refers to a large collection of practices and beliefs that have various common elements. Although it is often referred to as a "movement," it is not a movement in the sense of having a particular goal or structure with one purpose. It is a genuine search for meaning and truth in the modern world, but at the same time it can also be reactionary, and tends to exclude the more traditional forms of religion. It is essentially a mixture of Eastern religions, gnosticism, and occult practices. New Agers tend to delight in what is different, unorthodox, and "mystical," in the broadest sense. According to the Vatican's document, *Jesus Christ the Bearer of the Waters of Life*, which deals with the teachings of the New Age and how Christians should respond, some of the practices include the following: acupuncture, biofeedback, chiropractic, kinesiology, homeopathy, iridology, massage and various kinds of "bodywork," meditation and visualization, nutritional therapies, psychic healing, different kinds of herbal medicine, healing by crystals, etc.[1]

Obviously it is not possible to give a proper treatment of the teachings of the New Age here, but some of the more essential aspects include: the idea of a world Mind, or Consciousness; the notion that all things are essentially part of this world Mind; and that through various meditation techniques we can reach higher levels of consciousness and access greater knowledge, becoming fully "realized" and releasing the divine energy within. It is monistic in this sense. It holds that all things are one and we are all small parts of this One. Enlightenment can, therefore, mean coming to recognize that individuality is an illusion. Some New Age teachings suggest that we are divine, that we can heal ourselves, and that there is no need for "formal religion". As *Jesus Christ the Bearer of the Waters of Life* says:

Developing our human potential will put us in touch with our inner divinity, and with those parts of our selves which have been alienated and suppressed. This is revealed above all in Altered States of Consciousness (ASCs), which are induced either by drugs or by various mind-expanding techniques, particularly in the context of "transpersonal psychology."[2]

The New Age tends to be especially antagonistic to Judeo-Christianity, seeing it as patriarchal and domineering. Instead, it proposes a world "religion" or "spirituality." However, this "faith" in itself is quite vague and people can more or less design it to their own requirements or tastes:

> It must never be forgotten that many of the movements which have fed the *New Age* are explicitly anti-Christian. Their stance towards Christianity is not neutral, but neutralising: despite what is often said about openness to all religious standpoints, traditional Christianity is not sincerely regarded as an acceptable alternative.[3]

Care for the environment is also another appealing factor of the New Age for many Christians. However, the New Age's concern for the environment is based on a pantheistic[4] worldview, as opposed to the need to care for it as God's creation.

In spite of the drawbacks to the New Age identities, and there are many, one aspect that many writers on the New Age agree on is that the flourishing of spiritualities called New Age is an indication of the hunger in people for a sense of meaning and purpose—a sign of the spiritual starvation that many people are experiencing, especially in the West, and an attempt to find an answer to fill this void. While many New Age ideas are at variance with many aspects of Christianity, the Church can also learn from them in different ways, as John Saliba points out. Here he is quoting Cardinal Daneels' pastoral letter concerning new religious movements:

> The New Age also offers good things: a sense of universal brotherhood, peace and harmony, raising people's awareness, a commitment to bettering the world, a general mobilization of energies for the sake of good, etc. Nor are all the techniques they advocate bad: yoga and relaxation can have many good effects.[5]

Perhaps the Church also needs to learn from the way the New Age is attracting so many people, drawn by its appeal to the spiritual and equally turned off by the Church's strong emphasis on doctrine and the apparent lack of space given to the spiritual. It appears that the New Age is meeting a need that the Church is neglecting. The rich tradition of the Church certainly has the capacity to satisfy this hunger in people, but it seems that it is currently failing to address this question properly. Louis Hughes, O.P., refers to this in an article reviewing a book on the New Age:

> In the words of Morton Kelsey: "Conventional Christianity, that relies on authority and reason, rather than on human experience, has become unpalatable to many modern Western religious

seekers." Cardinal Daneels acknowledges that there is some validity in the New Age's criticism of the Church "with respect to the lack of lived experience, the fear of mysticism, the endless moral exhortations and the exaggerated insistence on the orthodoxy of doctrine."[6]

In fact the intrigue that people feel with the spiritual is one of the reasons why Keating and his colleagues found themselves wondering if it would be possible to present the Church's rich contemplative tradition in a more modern and "palatable" form. Seeing so many people going to the East in search of "enlightenment" and spiritual nourishment drew their attention to the fact that something needed to be done. To some extent centering prayer is helping to meet this need.

## KEATING'S TEACHINGS AND THE NEW AGE

The reason why I mention these different aspects of New Age teaching is here that some of the language used by Keating is very similar to that used in New Age circles. For example, he speaks of moving to "higher levels of consciousness," the "energies of the unconscious," and "the healing of the unconscious." He also mentions the use of transpersonal psychology, the presence of the Divine within each person, and the dying of the false self. From this point of view, it is easy to see how people are suspicious of centering prayer as another subtle form of New Age teaching. It should be clear now that the teaching on centering prayer is not contrary to Catholic teaching.

While it is true that Keating speaks of the development and healing of the unconscious, he does so in terms of these being effects and not the goals of centering prayer. Nor does he claim that we bring this about through our own doing. In fact, Keating quite clearly points out that the Holy Spirit is the one who brings this work about within us. He also shows that this is one of the key differences between Christianity and non-Christian religions, namely that we cannot bring this about ourselves but must rely completely on grace. By giving ourselves to the regular practice of centering prayer, we open ourselves up to this process, or dispose ourselves in the most receptive way possible.

The following quotation from *Jesus Christ the Bearer of the Water of Life* refers to a New Age understanding of mysticism:

> In order to be converted, a person needs to make use of techniques which lead to the experience of illumination. This transforms a person's consciousness and opens him or her to contact with the divinity, which is understood as the deepest essence of reality.[7]

For people who are not very familiar with the teachings on centering prayer, this quotation might appear to describe what is said about this prayer form. However, while the language used is quite similar, the differences are crucial. It is true that we can make use of a "technique" such as centering prayer through which we are disposed to contemplative prayer. Through contemplative prayer we may eventually experience illumination (in the Christian sense). However, if we do, it is purely God's doing and not ours. The transformation of consciousness is a result of coming closer to God through the spiritual journey; but this also depends on what is understood by "transformation of consciousness." In the Christian understanding, it means a transformed consciousness through the nights of sense and spirit, which indicates a purification of the soul, resulting in a new vision of the world with the eyes of faith. The new perspective on the world is what might be called a purer Christian vision, seeing things with the eyes of Christ. However, this is not understood as something that makes us superior to anyone else. On the contrary, we are more aware than ever of our sinfulness and dependence on God the creator. This dependence on the Almighty allows us to work all the more effectively in the world, to serve all people as our brothers and sisters. It is not a means to dominate or manipulate others, or to gain material goods to our advantage, as some of the New Age teachings encourage.[8]

*Jesus Christ the Bearer of the Water of Life* makes the following comment, which refers more clearly to what is said about centering prayer:

All meditation techniques need to be purged of presumption and pretentiousness. Christian prayer is not an exercise in self-contemplation, stillness and self-emptying, but a dialogue of love, one which "implies an attitude of conversion, a flight from 'self' to the 'You' of God." It leads to an increasingly complete surrender to God's will, whereby we are invited to a deep, genuine solidarity with our brothers and sisters.[9]

To see centering prayer as a form of "self-con-templation" or "self-emptying" is also to misunder-stand it. The "letting go of thoughts" that we speak about is very different from trying to make one's mind go blank. Nor could it be described as a form of self-contemplation, as it is meant to help one rest in God through silence. The problem, as is often the case, is largely a question of how you understand the terms.

The New Age also tends to be esoteric or elitist. Those who manage to acquire the right knowledge—often at quite a price, as a significant hallmark of the New Age is that everything must be paid for—are able to enjoy the new freedom of the "enlightened." Centering prayer, on the other hand, does not come at a (financial) price. Granted various "intensive retreats" have to be paid for, but this is not for the sake of profit. In other words, centering prayer is not a moneymaking business. Many aspects of New Age teaching are quite expensive and are being used to make money.[10]

One of the pitfalls that Keating and other writ-ers on centering prayer stumble into is the deliberate wish to avoid using the more traditional spiritual language, which many people find so off-putting. They decided that using more modern language and giving explanations in terms of psychology rather than just spirituality might be more appealing to people who have a preconceived idea of prayer and the contemplative life as being something only for the "cloisters." From the interest generated in their workshops, it seems they were right. The problem here is that, as a result, it is very easy for such writings to be misunderstood.

## Chapter 12

## MORE OBJECTIONS

WITH SO MUCH CONFUSION today in the whole area of "spirituality," a form of prayer such as centering prayer often causes a good deal of suspicion. Although we have already dealt with several objections, in this chapter we will look more directly at various concerns that have been raised, and try to address them. We will also look at the teachings of the Second Vatican Council and see how centering prayer is a response to what both the Council and John Paul II have called for.

Johnette S. Benkovic is founder and president of Living His Life Abundantly, International, Inc.,[1] which broadcasts programs on radio and television, primarily on EWTN (Eternal Word Television Network) in the United States. Johnette and Fr. Edmund Sylvia, CSC, produce programs on many different aspects of Catholic teaching. They also have produced a series of programs on "The New Age Counterfeit," which address different aspects of New Age teaching. This series also covered centering prayer, claiming that it is another New Age form of prayer under a Christian guise. A version of these programs is also available online in article form.

## "Is Centering Prayer Contemplation?"

This question forms the title of an article written by Johnette S. Benkovic and printed in her book *The New Age Counterfeit*. We will try to address some of the objections given:

> *Benkovic*: One prayer method or technique that is gaining great popularity in prayer communities, parishes, and groups throughout the country is centering prayer. By this term we are referring to that prayer which concentrates on emptying the mind of thought through the repetition of a single word. We are not referring to prayer that centers on Jesus Christ and our relationship with Him.[2]

First, centering prayer is not a method that attempts to empty the mind of thoughts, as we have shown. Rather, it helps the one praying to "let go" of thoughts, until they are no longer a distraction. Sometimes the period of prayer will seem to be very peaceful; at other times, it may be full of thoughts. Either way, what is important is that we are resting in the presence of God in silence and allowing him to do the work. Thomas Keating writes:

> The practice of contemplative prayer is not an effort to make the mind a blank, but to move beyond discursive thinking and affective prayer to the level of communing with God, which is a more intimate kind of exchange.[3]

Second, this prayer does focus on Jesus Christ and our relationship with him. However, it is not expressed in the form of mental reflection on his person, or on particular mysteries of Christ. Instead, the "sacred word" expresses the consent to be with God and to allow God to work in us:

> In Centering Prayer, then, the humanity of Christ is not ignored, as some critics claim, but affirmed in the most positive and profound manner. Centering Prayer presupposes a living faith that the sacred humanity of Jesus contains the fullness of the Godhead. Christ leads us to the Father, but to the Father as *he* knows him.[4]

Here is another criticism leveled by Johnette Benkovic:

> First of all, contemplative prayer is usually the fruit of a long life of prayer. While God can and will give such a favor to whomever He chooses, it seems that He usually gives the favor of contemplative prayer to those who have made progress in living a life of virtue for some time.[5]

This last quotation reflects a common misunderstanding of our time, which has come about because of several factors. In the Middle Ages when theology was becoming more systematized, various categories of prayer were developed. Since there was a great tendency to analyze, those areas of prayer that were more intellectual tended to get more emphasis. As a result the stage of contemplation began to be neglected, until eventually it was hardly spoken of:

With the tendency to analyze that was so characteristic of the late Scholastic Middle Ages, the
spontaneity of the spiritual journey got lost, and
the final stage of Lectio, resting in God—the
purpose of all the other stages—tended to be
left out. One was expected to do spiritual reading and discursive meditation for x number of
years; if one lived to be very old—or maybe on
one's deathbed—one might hope for an experience of contemplation. But in actual fact one
rarely or never expected it and hence did not
take steps to prepare for it.[6]

Also, because of the heresy of Quietism, many
people became very wary of contemplation and mystical experience, and so it tended not to be spoken
of, partly out of fear. Gradually, it became more and
more associated with those who lived religious life,
though even then it was understood as something
reserved for just a few. It was slowly drifting into the
category of an elitist venture.

The *Spiritual Exercises of St. Ignatius of Loyola*,
composed between 1522 and 1526, also played a significant role in how the understanding of contemplative prayer developed. Ignatius proposed three methods of prayer, although the methods proposed for
each of the four "weeks" can be greatly adapted to
the needs and ability of the exercitant. The overall
idea of the *Exercises* is to help the exercitant discern
the will of God in his or her life. The discursive medi-
tations that are proposed in the first week are to be
used according to the three faculties of memory, intellect, and will. The memory is to recall the point for
meditation. The intellect is meant to reflect on what

lessons can be developed from that particular subject. Then the will is meant to lead one to new resolutions based on the insights gained so that the application is practical: it is intended to lead one to reformation of life. Contemplation, as understood in the *Exercises*, is a kind of reflecting on or recreating in the mind a scene from the Gospel, a particular mystery, or doctrine. Thus, the person praying could picture her- or himself in a Gospel scene, imagine how one would respond, etc. This second method of prayer was meant to help one develop "affective prayer."[7] The third method that Ignatius proposed involved applying the five senses, spiritually, to the subject of the meditation. The idea here was to develop the use of the spiritual senses and lead one on to, or at least prepare one for, contemplation (in the Theresian sense). According to Keating, the problem was the application of Ignatius' teaching by the Jesuits themselves. They tended to reduce the *Exercises* to discursive meditation only. In other words it stopped short of the stage of prayer where we just rest in God, in silence:

> In 1574 Everard Mercurian, the Father General of the Jesuits, in a directive to the Spanish province of the Society, forbade the practice of affective prayer and the application of the five senses. This prohibition was repeated in 1578. The spiritual life of a significant portion of the Society of Jesus was thus limited to a single method of prayer, namely, discursive meditation according to the three powers. The predominantly intellectual character of this meditation continued to grow in importance throughout the Society during the course of

the eighteenth and nineteenth centuries. Most manuals of spirituality until well into this century limited instruction to schemas of discursive meditation.[8]

Considering the huge impact the Jesuits had on the education of so many, it is not hard to see how this understanding of prayer began to spread. Many religious congregations also followed Ignatian methods of prayer and spirituality, or adopted the Jesuit *Constitutions*, with the result that this practice of the exclusion of contemplation had a significant effect on spirituality in the West:

> *Benkovic*: Meditation on Scripture or on things of the divine (Christian meditation) usually is the prelude to the contemplative prayer experience. God then moves the prayer into a deeper awareness of His presence and infuses him with His love. Centering prayer does not include meditation on Scripture.[9]

While it is true that centering prayer does not directly include meditation on scripture—that is, during the time of centering itself, since this is a time for silence only—yet Keating speaks about its close link to Lectio Divina, and how the first three stages of Lectio are meant to lead the person praying, to contemplation. The time given to centering prayer is intended to be silent, but this does not imply that scripture is meant to be left out at other times; quite the contrary in fact. Indeed, it is understood that time will be given for meditation on scripture, if not initially then at least after a suitable period, as not all people who begin with centering prayer may be accustomed to using scripture: ·

> *Benkovic*: ...If centering prayer is to lead us to contemplation and if contemplation is the experience of the loving presence of God, how can this occur if we reject His overtures through loving impulses or thoughts of Him?[10]

The writings of St. John of the Cross will quickly answer this question, since John says that while God may give various kinds of mystical grace and experiences, the best and safest thing we can do is to ignore them, since then we won't be distracted by them. John calls the journey of faith "a ray of pure darkness" and we shouldn't be afraid to leave all consolations, visions, feelings, etc., aside. If God wants to communicate something to us, God will, and in whatever way God so desires. John also points out that it is very easy to be misled by spiritual experiences and that we should be very slow to trust them. The safest path is always the path of pure faith. It is also not strictly true to say that in centering prayer we "reject" any loving impulses, or thoughts of God; instead, we try not to cling to them, as otherwise they can become a distraction:

> *Benkovic*: St. Teresa repeatedly opposes the total suppression of discourse and the movement of thought as long as one has not received infused contemplation (*Life*, chap. 12; *The Interior Castle*, fourth mansion, chap. 3; St. John of the Cross, *The Ascent of Mount Carmel*, Bk. II, chap. 15).[11]

We have already dealt with this objection in chapter nine, but let us make one further comment here. St. Teresa says:

> Taking it upon oneself to stop and suspend thought is what I mean should not be done; nor should we cease to work with the intellect, because otherwise we would be left like cold simpletons and be doing neither one thing nor the other.[12]

This seems to be one of the most common misunderstandings regarding centering prayer. As we have shown, it is not an attempt to make the mind go blank or to suspend thought; rather, it is a means to help the individual be silent and no longer distracted by thoughts:

> The primary function of the sacred word is not to push thoughts away or to thin them out. It is rather to express our intention to love God, to be in God's presence, and to submit to the Spirit's action during the time of prayer. It is only when one of the [thoughts] does not simply go by but attracts or repels us that we need to return to our sacred symbol. The reason is simple: when we are attracted to a particular thought, we have begun to lose the purity of our general loving intention to be in God's presence.[13]

We have also seen that St. John of the Cross goes to great lengths to show the damage that can be done when people who are being drawn to prayer in silence are encouraged to return to discursive meditation. The misguided directors who do this are sending the souls backward instead of forward, since the Holy Spirit is leading these souls on to silence, discursive meditation having largely served its purpose:

> *Benkovic*: The author of *The Cloud of Unknowing* states "that techniques and methods are ultimately useless for awakening contemplative love." The Jesus Prayer expresses a complete thought, thereby putting a thought into our mind. It also places the prayer in right relationship with Our Lord as one who is a sinner in need of God's mercy.[14]

While the author of *The Cloud* points to the futility of "techniques" for awakening contemplative love, he is at the same time teaching a "technique," in the same work. So what does he mean by a "technique"? Almost every kind of prayer could be described as a technique,[15] since it involves doing the same thing—such as reciting the rosary—the same way, each time. That is surely a technique, as are many forms of prayer. So, presumably, the author must be referring to the fact that one cannot presume that a technique alone is enough to "awaken contemplative love" or produce mystical experience, etc. From this point of view, centering prayer is no more of a technique than the rosary, insofar as it can "cause" anything to happen. Instead, it disposes one to be more receptive to contemplation.

Benkovic says that the *Jesus Prayer* also makes us aware of our need for God as sinners. Since the "sacred word" used in centering prayer is consenting to God's work in the soul, this would also seem to acknowledge that we need God to work in us, as we are sinners in need of salvation. Otherwise, why would we seek God in the first place, if we were capable of doing all this ourselves without help?

> *Benkovic:* For the major proponents of centering prayer, this is to be a time for the "dismantling of the false self." The false self is the result of all the psychological and emotional baggage we have been carrying with us throughout our lives. Its root, according to centering prayer proponents, is original sin which is defined as "...a way of describing the human condition, which is the universal experience of coming to full reflective self-consciousness without the certitude of personal union with God." For the centering prayer practitioner, regular practice of "contemplative" prayer sets in motion a dynamism of "divine psychotherapy, organically designed for each of us, to empty out our unconscious and free us from the obstacles to the free flow of grace in our minds, emotions, and bodies." As this false self is dismantled, we come to see our true Self, the center of which, so say proponents, is God—"God and our true Self are not separate. Though we are not God, God and our true Self are the same thing."[16]

Benkovic has an understandable objection to Keating's definition of original sin. This is certainly not the traditional way that it is defined. Yet Keating is trying to present the teaching in a more modern language that people can better relate to. The danger, of course, is that the true doctrine can be watered down for the sake of making it more "acceptable" to people. However, I do not believe that his definition of original sin is a problem either, rather a different way of explaining it.

Benkovic also says that Keating claims that the deepest part of ourselves and the divine presence are one and the same thing. This is not true. What Keating says is that at the deepest center of ourselves we will find the divine presence, or the divine indwelling. He doesn't claim that one is the same as the other:

> We might conceive of God as our deepest center and our true self as a circle around it.[17]

> Thus ... whenever a certain amount of emotional pain is evacuated, interior space opens up within us. We are closer to the spiritual level of our being, closer to our true self, and closer to the Source of our being, which lies in our inmost center but is buried under the emotional debris of a lifetime. We are closer to God because through the process of unloading we have evacuated some of the material that was hiding the divine presence.[18]

Keating also refers to a diagram as an aid to describing the movement of centering prayer. At the very center of this diagram is the divine presence. The circle around this shows the true self, but the divine presence is at the center, and the two are separate. If Keating were trying to show that our deepest self and God are one and the same thing, this would also be obvious in the rest of his writings. This is certainly not the case, and all his teachings on centering prayer continually speak of it being a journey to deepening our relationship with the Holy Trinity, who is completely separate from us, although his presence dwells within us. The more deeply purified we become through prayer, the more we are united with God; but this is the work of the Holy Spirit within us and not our doing. Hence, we continually make use of the "sacred word" to reaffirm our consent to God's work within us. The purpose of practicing centering prayer is so that we can be open to this work of removing the obstacles that make us unaware of, or give us a feeling of being distant from, the divine presence at the deepest center of our being:

> Deep rest is not only the result of freedom from attachments or aversions to thoughts, but also the feeling of being accepted and loved by the divine Mystery that we sense within us and that Christian doctrine calls the Divine Indwelling. In other words, our awareness of the divine presence begins to reawaken.[19]

Finally, Benkovic also points out the similarities between centering prayer and TM. She also mentions the fact that many of the proponents of centering prayer were instructed in techniques of Eastern meditation and that they encourage a certain integration of these techniques with Christian prayer. We have already dealt with these comparisons in the section on TM and the influences of Eastern meditation, but here I will just add that certainly this is an area that Christians need to be wary of, especially as many will not be aware of the subtle but important differences between the different religions. Keating is very open in his dealings with Eastern techniques. While this is all right for those who are well versed in their faith, the danger would be in presenting the two as though they were compatible, which they are not, although we can certainly learn from them, as the Church's documents point out.[20]

While this article by Johnette S. Benkovic is well intentioned, it is badly misinformed and the author is not well enough acquainted with the writings of Thomas Keating and others on centering prayer. I hope that our explanation has made this clear.

## "THE DANGER OF CENTERING PRAYER"[21]

While there are quite a number of articles critical of centering prayer,[22] they generally have the same complaints and most of the objections have been covered in the last section on Benkovic. However, we will now address some other objections not mentioned above.

John D. Dreher, the author of "The Danger of Centering Prayer," makes some sweeping criticisms of the practice, such as the following:

> Many people assume centering prayer is compatible with Catholic tradition, but in fact the techniques of centering prayer are neither Christian nor prayer. They are at the level of human faculties and as such are an operation of man, not of God.[23]

We have already shown that the practice of centering prayer is Catholic and certainly is prayer. While the technique itself is of course at the level of human faculties—as are all techniques for prayer, such as the rosary, or the Divine Office—this does not imply that it cannot be prayer at the same time. Because one uses a technique to help one pray, that does not imply that it is therefore not prayer. What *is* important is the intention and the will of the person praying. Two people walking in the country thinking silently as they walk may psychologically be doing the same thing, even using a particular technique to reflect, while one is praying and the other is not. The technique itself is not enough to determine whether someone is praying or not. The difference is that the will and intention of one is to be in communion with God. We have also seen this difference between TM and centering prayer. The techniques of the two are almost identical, but one is directed toward God while the other is not:

> *Dreher*: Centering prayer differs from Christian prayer in that the intent of the technique is to bring the practitioner to the center of his own being. There he is, supposedly, to experience the presence of the God who indwells him. Christian prayer, on the contrary, centers upon God in a relational way, as someone apart from oneself.[24]

In an attempt to explain what happens, Keating says that centering prayer is gradually drawing the practitioner to the center of his or her being. When all the obstacles that prevent us from being fully united to God are finally removed, we experience union with God, who is present in us from our baptism. However, the intention of the technique is not to bring one to the center of one's being, but rather to be present to

God. "Going to the center of one's being" is not the aim of centering prayer, rather—like all Christian prayer—the idea is to help the individual be present or relate to God by resting in silence.

The mistake that many critics make is to think of centering prayer as being a technique that aims at giving the individual some kind of control or power over what happens in his or her spiritual life, as though they could then bring about union with God or inner healing by their own doing. As we have seen, centering prayer merely disposes us to be open to God in a very receptive way; but what happens after that is up to God. The following quotation from the same article highlights this confusion:

> *Dreher*: The confusion of technique over encounter arises from a misunderstanding of the indwelling of God. The fact that God indwells us does not mean that we can capture him by techniques. Nor does it mean that we are identical with him in our deepest self.... We can no more manipulate this indwelling of grace by psychological techniques than we can manipulate our existence.[25]

*Chapter 13*

# PRAYER AND EVERYDAY LIFE

## PRACTICAL APPLICATION

IF PRAYER DOES NOT have a practical application, there is something wrong. Prayer—understood as our relationship with God—should flow into all the other areas of life and enrich them, since the life of God flows into everything and sustains it. If our prayer life only revolves around ourselves, then it is questionable whether it is genuine prayer or not. Centering prayer, if it really leads one to contemplative prayer, must be the same. Since contemplative prayer is the "deepest" kind of prayer—in the sense that it allows us to be most intimately united to God—it should also have the most powerful impact in practical ministry. Men and women who give themselves to the enclosed life of the cloisters, dedicating their whole being to a life of prayer and work for the love of God, have a huge impact on the world because of their prayer. Of course many people do not understand or believe this; however, many of those who profess the Christian faith recognize this hidden treasure that contemplatives bring to the world.

In the document *Consecrated Life in the Third Millennium*, the Congregation points out the value of the witness of this way of life to the world:

> Today's world is expecting to see in consecrated men and women the concrete reflection of Jesus' way of acting, of his love for every person without distinction or qualification. It wants to experience that, with the Apostle Paul, it is possible to say: "I still live my human life, but it is a life of faith in the Son of God who loved *me* and gave himself for *me*" (Gal 2:20).[1]

This hidden treasure, however, is not just reserved to those in the cloisters. On the contrary, all who seriously try to live a life of prayer—both laity and religious—also bring this powerhouse of grace to the world, though usually in a hidden way. The more people take the spiritual journey seriously, allowing the Spirit to lead them along the winding path, the more effective they are in the world, bringing the values of the Gospel to the people around them, albeit indirectly. Even the fact that people dedicate their lives to silent prayer and meditation is in itself a witness to others of something beyond, of something greater than what can be seen.

In *The Essentials of Mysticism*, Evelyn Underhill speaks about the "Christianization" of society. Part of our mission as Christians, is to "Christianize" society, in the sense of allowing it to be touched by the love of God. It is not just about imposing a moral code, rather allowing people to experience the transforming love of God:

... the living Christ is a tincture, not added to life but transmuting life wherever He enters it; and therefore that we must seek to bring under that influence not only the souls of individuals, but the corporate soul too and so effect its transmutation. It is this change, not the imposition of a new moral code, which we should mean by the Christianization of society; for Christian law can only be understood and practiced by Christian souls. Such a Christianization of society involves, ultimately, the complete interpenetration of God and human life; the drenching of life, on all its levels, with the divine charity—its complete irradiation by the spirit of goodness, beauty and love.[2]

This transformation of society cannot, however, come about merely by "doing things," even if they are praiseworthy in themselves, unless they are filled with the love of God: "Though I should give away to the poor all that I possess, and even give up my body to be burned—if I am without love, it will do me no good whatever" (1 Cor 13:3). It also follows that those who do such work, if they are to be effective in the right way, must themselves be filled with the divine energy, the love of God which transforms all things. Therefore, they must be people of prayer, people whose active lives are balanced with an equally serious dedication to the contemplative, to listening to the Spirit, and to being filled, energized, and thus enabled to do the work of the Spirit and not just seeking to achieve their own goals. Underhill continues:

In the *Yearly Meeting Epistle* of the Society of Friends for 1920, the question was asked: How can we gain a new spirit? How can we break loose from our fears and suspicions and from the grip of complacent materialism, and face the issues with new faith in God and humanity? And the answer is: Only by a fresh sense of the presence and character of God. I am convinced that this is the right answer and the key to success in the work which we want to do.[3]

In certain parts of the world, such as Europe and America, where Christianity has seen a decline in recent decades, the renewal that is called for must come from a proper understanding of the message of the Gospel, if it is to be effective and convincing. It is no longer a matter of just proselytizing but showing people that what we believe in has a very rich spiritual depth, that it is not just a collection of moral "have tos," since people are not convinced by this. Continual listening in prayer enables us to keep to the right path, in the right way and at the right pace. As Underhill confirms:

Before we can mend our unreal confusions, we must have a clear vision of the real; and the gaining and holding of such a vision in personal life is one of the main functions of prayer, as in corporate life its holding up is the chief business of institutional religion. Efforts to Christianize our social conduct are foredoomed unless those who undertake them give themselves time to look steadily at Christ.[4]

Keating speaks about the transformation that comes about in those who try to be faithful to the spiritual journey, and the fruits that follow from this. He refers to the two different stages of consciousness: mythic membership consciousness and mental egoic consciousness. According to Ken Wilber's theory that we discussed earlier, humanity is currently at the stage of moving from the former to the latter. The problem with the mythic membership stage is that people tend to over-identify with their culture. The result is that all kinds of authority groups, from governments right down to individuals, perceive *their* way of doing things as being the right (and often the only) way. This leads them to impose their way of doing things on others, regardless of the cost:

> The limitations of mythic membership consciousness, especially its naïve loyalty to the values of a particular cultural or interest group, hinder us from fully responding to the values of the gospel. We bring to personal and social problems the prepackaged values and preconceived ideas that are deeply ingrained in us.[5]

> Mythic membership mindsets lead to serious injustices because they tend to disregard the rights and needs of others.[6]

The outcome of this is intolerance and oppression, one country thinking they have the right to invade another to "liberate" or "enlighten" them, or whatever the excuse may be. Those who have moved to the mental egoic level, on the other hand, are open to dialogue, and recognize the need for tolerance, patience, and the possibility of doing things differently. This is particularly evident in some of the remarkable figures of history, such as Mother Teresa of Calcutta, Gandhi, and many others, who have done extraordinary good in the line of social justice, often because they were no longer prejudiced by race, color, or creed. The Missionaries of Charity,[7] for example, are quite happy to minister to all the poor in need of their help, regardless of their faith, and neither will they try to convert them. In the not too distant past (and to some extent it still exists), many religious groups tried to help those in need, but they also wanted to "win them over." The Gospel teaches us to help people because they are people, and not just because they need to be taught something, even if this also follows. Otherwise it can become another form of dominance, though under the guise of "spreading the Gospel." Thomas Keating writes:

> Those who have reached the mental egoic consciousness perceive the necessity to be persons of dialogue, harmony, cooperation, forgiveness, and compassion. The problems of our time have to be dealt with creatively—from the inner freedom to rethink ethical principles in light of the globalization of world society now taking place.[8]

The significance, therefore, of growing in the direction of mental egoic consciousness, or maturity of spirit, is huge. The more people mature in the spiritual journey, the more effective they are in their ministry. This is because they are no longer dominated by cultural conditioning or disordered emotions.

Is it necessary for this transformation to take place fully before we can minister? Of course not. We can start straight away, just as the first apostles did when they were sent out by Jesus to heal the sick and cast out demons. In spite of their lack of training, the apostles had faith and a desire to serve God, and this was enough. In ministry we are called to recognize the need for grace above anything else, while not neglecting whatever preparation and training is possible: "The failure of our efforts to serve teaches us how to serve: that is, with complete dependence on divine inspiration. This is what changes the world."[9]

Sarah A. Butler makes a similar point and highlights how we need to focus more on participating in God's work, as opposed to just trying to do the work for God:

> In pastoral situations we always pray for God's intervention as though God were blissfully unaware of the crises and required our supplications. However, God is already active in the heart and life of both care-receiver and caregiver long before the faintest whisper of need and longing. Our prayers should not be an alarm for God's attention but a request to participate in God's healing process. Indeed, we function best as pastors when we recognize that we are a part of a process greater than our efforts, which is the healing that God has initiated.[10]

Butler reminds us of the importance of being sensitive to how we can participate in God's work, and not the other way around. One of the fruits of contemplative prayer is this sensitivity, a kind of spiritual intuition that enables us to see how we can partake in God's ministry to his children and their needs. Without this sensitivity, ministry is in danger of imposing its ideas of how the other "should" be.

## The Need for the Experience of Prayer

> If anyone believes that he can practise a new type of Christian living in the Church and can make out a convincing case for it, let him submit it, this devolution of his, to the "discernment of spirits." He will then find that one criterion of the genuineness of his Christian living which is far from unimportant is to test whether in practising it he can preserve the heritage of Christian wisdom and experience in the spirituality of past centuries.[11]

Karl Rahner presents us with some interesting ideas on the Christian of the future—which in fact very much apply to the time we are now in—and how the idea and practice of prayer may change. He points out that while great good has come from various devotions and spiritual practices of the past, they may not serve the Christian of the future in the same way. Because of the way society has changed and is changing, people will not accept religious indoctrination as before. It is as if God now has to prove himself to humanity, rather than the other way around. As a result, people now more than ever want an "experience" of the spiritual.

An interesting phenomenon in Ireland over the last fifteen to twenty years has been the emergence

of a significant number of prayer groups, which have
given many people a sense of a more living faith and
have even led some people back to the practice of their
faith. The same can be said of certain places of pil-
grimage, one of the most striking being Me jugorje,
in Bosnia-Herzegovina. The extraordinary number of
books and articles written on the claimed apparitions
in this place, point to the fact that thousands of people
have rediscovered the experience of prayer, which in
turn has led them back to the sacraments. Regardless
of what may or may not have happened here concerning alleged apparitions, it is undeniable that this one
place alone has helped many people find a new depth
to their faith, but above all through the actual experience of prayer. Other places, such as Taizé, have
served a similar purpose. Rahner writes:

> Now it must be admitted that if we are to have
> the courage to enter upon a direct relationship
> with God in his ineffability, to accept that our
> devotion must, in this sense, be cut down to the
> bare essentials and to accept, furthermore, the
> silent self-bestowal of God as the true mystery
> of our own existence, then we do need to do
> something more than merely to take up a given
> rational attitude to the speculative problems of
> the divine, and to respond in merely doctrinal
> terms to the teaching of Christianity. We do
> need to work out a certain theology of mysti-
> cism, a mysticism that leads to a religious expe-
> rience which indeed many suppose that they
> could never discover in themselves, a theology
> of mysticism which can be imparted in such a

way that each one can become his own teacher of mysticism.[12]

The interest in meditation and all things spiritual, and the hunger for an experience of the divine, are being expressed in terms that we can no longer ignore today, especially in the West. If people do not find help in satisfying this hunger in the Christian Church, they will seek it elsewhere, and many already have.

## The Training of Priests

In *Pastores Dabo Vobis*, speaking on the formation of priests, John Paul II notes how, in order to pass on to the world the "mystery" of the Incarnation, priests must themselves experience this mystery. Otherwise their witness will be ineffective:

> Only if future priests, through a suitable spiritual formation, have become deeply aware and have increasingly experienced this "mystery" will they be able to communicate this amazing and blessed message to others (cf. 1 Jn 1:1–4).[13]

The formation that priests need must include a suitable training in the spiritual life, the life of prayer. Education in the contemplative dimension of the Gospel is also a necessary part of this training. The priesthood—and especially the diocesan priesthood—tends to be very busy with the active ministry. This is important. However, without the balance of the contemplative side, something essential is missing. If it is through the contemplative dimension, the "one thing necessary,"[14] that priests receive their strength, inspiration, and energy to minister, then this is also an aspect that needs to be given greater consideration today. While there will always be plenty of work to be done, the danger is that the work can serve as a way for the minister to feel useful or needed. Unless adequate time is given to listening to the Spirit, priests may be "doing" lots of work but it may not be the work that is actually required or desired. John Paul II affirms this and lived this himself, giving a great deal of his day to prayer:

> Prayer should lead candidates for the priesthood to get to know and have experience of *the genuine meaning of Christian prayer*, as a living and personal meeting with the Father through the only-begotten Son under the action of the Spirit, a dialogue that becomes a sharing in the filial conversation between Jesus and the Father....

> A necessary training in prayer in a context of noise and agitation like that of our society, is an education in the deep human meaning and religious value of *silence*, as the spiritual atmosphere vital for perceiving God's presence and for allowing oneself be won over by it (cf. 1 Kgs 19:11ff).[15]

Trying to find the energy alone to do the work required is a daunting enough task for many priests. A large number in the ministry suffer from "burnout," which amounts to giving too much of oneself without receiving enough first, or at least having a properly balanced lifestyle. Serious cases of burnout can take up to two years to recover from properly. But what is considered a proper "balance" in a modern context often does not give much emphasis to spiritual nourishment. Of course it is mentioned, but the emphasis—in the West at least—tends to be that prayer is something you "fit in," as opposed to an essential aspect of ministry from which the priest gets all his energy, inspiration, and identity. Without a serious life of prayer the priest simply cannot minister properly as an ambassador of Christ. Instead, there is the danger of him being an ambassador of himself. The focus on contemplative prayer is a reminder to the priest of who he is, that he is nothing without the strength of the Spirit and that he is there on behalf of another. Many priests have embarked enthusiastically into very demanding ministries without being adequately equipped for it. Giving proper time to a serious prayer life is an essential part of good ministry. But if this is not part of a priest's training he is not likely to suddenly develop it once he has begun his ministry. The Pope also reminds us that:

> One aspect of the priest's mission, and certainly by no means a secondary aspect, is that he is to be a "teacher of prayer." However, the priest will only be able to train others in this school of Jesus at prayer, if he himself has been trained in it and continues to receive its formation.... Christians expect to find in the priest not only a man who welcomes them, who listens to them gladly and shows a real interest in them, but also and above all *a man who will help them to turn to God*, to rise up to him. And so the priest needs to be trained to have a deep intimacy with God.[16]

One thing I became very aware of in my own seminary formation was that we were often encouraged to have a good prayer life and to give time to "meditation." However, nobody ever told us exactly how we were supposed to "meditate" or what meditation involved. While prayer was certainly encouraged, accurate instruction on the different stages and kinds of prayer was never given. This seems to be a common experience in many seminaries. Yet the priest is expected to be someone who will teach others how to pray. If priests themselves are not familiar and comfortable with prayer and the spiritual life, they are unlikely to be able to teach others. Conversely, if the faithful do not find in their priests people who can give them genuine and informed guidance in the spiritual life, they will look elsewhere for help.

In an article on the experience of introducing centering prayer to a seminary in the United States, Sandra Casey-Martus explains how she came across this same lack of instruction on prayer and the spiritual journey in her (Anglican) seminary. Having already had an interest in centering prayer for several years, she ended up being asked to give a seminar on it in a local parish. Before long, many of the seminarians from her seminary were also asking for help:

> Everyone agreed that seminary prepared us intellectually but that little attention was paid to our spiritual lives. If our spiritual lives were neglected, our physical bodies were completely ignored as either temples of the Holy Spirit or as vehicles of consciousness as Eastern traditions emphasize.... When we were established

in our ministries, we could then turn to the care of our souls.

I accepted this reality, too, but it seemed inconceivable that a seminary student could graduate without being taught anything about the forms and disciplines of prayer—or about methods for teaching *others* to pray![17]

While this experience is referring to an Anglican seminary, the same principle holds true with Catholic seminaries. Indeed, the lack of instruction mentioned seems to be a common problem. Eventually, Casey-Martus was able to introduce a course in this same seminary under the name "The Art and Practice of Christian Prayer." The prayer form she was basing it on was that of centering prayer. While this is by no means the only way of leading people deeper into prayer, it is at the same time a very practical and easily taught one. There is both need and room for similar courses on prayer in Catholic seminaries.

## Charismatic Renewal

Thanks to a revival of Charismatic Renewal,[18] many people have found the experience of prayer and the gifts of the Spirit an exciting new window onto their faith. Thomas Keating writes:

The renewal speaks powerfully to two needs that Catholics experience today with special urgency: the need for prayer, or, more exactly, for the experience of prayer, and the need to feel part of a Christian community.[19]

What is known as the "baptism in the Spirit" seems to be the key initiation experience of most people in renewal. Through this experience many have had a profound—and sometimes life-changing—new awareness of the love of God or the person of Jesus. Participants usually enjoy a renewed interest in their faith, in the teachings of the Church, and in the sacraments. Keating also points out that "while baptism in the Spirit does not establish an advanced state of spiritual development, it is a manifest call to contemplative prayer."[20] Praying in "tongues" and the prayerful reading of the scriptures usually lead people to a greater desire for silence. After a time, many of these new converts find dryness in prayer and often become discontent with their prayer groups. This is where proper teaching can help people to understand that they are probably being led into the night of sense, which is a stage of growth and not a dying of their faith, as they may perceive it to be:

> They must be encouraged to see this period of pervasive dryness as a necessary stage in the growth of the risen life of Christ within them. In the model developed in Centering Prayer, these periods of dryness are explained as part of the purification of the unconscious, without which our initial experience of conversion suffers the same fate as the seed that falls on rocky ground described by Jesus in the parable of the sower. Another way of envisioning these times of dryness is as a more intimate sharing in the Paschal mystery.[21]

> The Charismatic Renewal needs spiritual guides
> who are thoroughly qualified through knowl-
> edge and personal experience of contemplative
> prayer to distinguish what is essential from what
> is accidental in the spiritual path.[22]

While more lay people than before are learning
about the spiritual journey, priests are expected to
have this kind of knowledge, but often do not. Since
priests are sometimes not adequately equipped to help
people who come looking for a deeper experience
of prayer or to understand such an experience, it is
understandable that so many people end up going to
Eastern gurus, who can and do offer instruction in
meditation techniques of all kinds. In the Christian
Church we have a very rich contemplative tradition,
but the current problem seems to be in passing it on.
Thomas Keating notes:

> A new formulation of the principles of the spiri-
> tual journey for Christians is urgently needed
> today that will be faithful to the tradition but
> expressed in contemporary language and under-
> standing.... A new formulation should take thor-
> ough account of contemporary developments
> in theological and scriptural studies and of the
> insights of psychology and sociology, especially
> those that bear directly on human development
> and consequently on the spiritual life. In devel-
> oping the method and conceptual background
> of Centering Prayer, I have attempted to address
> some of these urgent needs.[23]

## A Word on Ecumenism

As Christians we are constantly searching for new tools to help us reach out to our brothers and sisters of different Christian denominations and of other creeds altogether. Because of the nature of centering prayer it can be practiced by anyone, Christian or non-Christian. Clearly it is initially a Christian prayer and for most people it will be. However, for people who are searching for God and not sure where to look, there is no reason why they cannot start with centering prayer. If this practice leads them to an experience of the spiritual, it will probably also get them asking questions. This, of course, is where proper guidance is essential. But between different Christian communities it can also be a useful tool for strengthening relationships and encouraging dialogue, based on the common experience of Christians from diverse backgrounds:

> Until spiritual leadership becomes a reality in Christian circles, many will continue to look to other religious traditions for the spiritual experience they are not finding in their own churches. If there were a widespread renewal of the preaching and practice of the contemplative dimension of the Gospel, the reunion of the Christian churches would become a real possibility, dialogue with the other world religions would have a firm basis in spiritual experience, and the religions of the world would bear a clearer witness to the human values they hold in common.[24]

Many groups who practice meditation have already discovered the ecumenical aspect of this kind of prayer, as it does not pose a threat to those who have a different understanding of God. Instead, it tends to focus more on the spiritual experience of God through prayer and provides a basis from which dialogue can begin. This is not suggesting that centering prayer is *the* way forward for interfaith dialogue; however, it certainly is a realistic possibility for those open to dialogue with others from a different faith background.

*Chapter 14*

# THE QUESTION OF HEALING

HAVING EXPLORED THE BACKGROUND and development of centering prayer, let us now look again at the question of healing. We speak of the healing of the unconscious through the practice of centering prayer. Over a long period—although it is impossible to say exactly how long, since it varies from person to person—the unconscious is gradually healed of emotional wounds. This is essentially because, when we regularly rest in deep prayer, we are in the most secure environment for this to take place; that is, the loving presence of God. In the security of this presence we begin to let our unconscious guard down and the emotions are gradually healed or "unloaded." This is experienced in the form of thoughts coming to our consciousness.

In this kind of prayer we do not have to do anything except gently repeat the sacred word as often as we feel is necessary, in order to express our consent to God's healing presence. The experience of many who practice this kind of prayer is that thoughts from different times or experiences in their lives come to con-

sciousness seemingly out of the blue. Some are interesting and some are painful. Keating says that this
is an indication of various emotions that are being
brought to the surface of our consciousness in order
to be healed. The fact that they are often completely
unrelated to anything going on in the person's life at
that time is an indication of this. That is to say, they
are not just the normal thoughts related to whatever
the person is doing or involved in around that time.
The one praying has to do no more than let these
thoughts go. They are being processed or released
from the unconscious. As this happens, the whole person is slowly being renewed and healed at the deepest
level. But how can we know if this is true?

## The Spiritual Aspect of Healing

First, it should be said that it is virtually impossible to "prove" scientifically that healing is taking
place, since we are talking about the emotions and
the unconscious, which are not measurable or quantifiable. What we can do, however, is to see how the
teaching bears up in comparison to teachings in psychology, and to the writings of the spiritual masters
such as Teresa of Avila and John of the Cross. As we
have seen with Teresa and John, both speak about the
soul's journey into God as a kind of purification. It
involves many trials experienced in day-to-day life, all
of which are molding the soul into something more
whole, more integrated, and more beautiful. As the
soul comes closer to God, the purgation becomes
more intense and this is experienced as more painful.

However, this is a necessary stage that the soul must go through if it wants to come close to God.

Teresa speaks of this procedure in terms of the different mansions, while John speaks of the nights of sense and spirit. What they are referring to is the same process that Keating speaks of, although it is expressed in different terms. If growing closer to God means growing in holiness, then presumably this must also mean becoming more integrated as a person. Those who have advanced along the spiritual journey are more in harmony with themselves. Why? Because they have been healed, to a greater or lesser extent, emotionally. As a result they are more at peace, they are better able to minister to people or just work with others without prejudice, since their prejudices have largely been put to rest. They begin to see things more with the eyes of faith and to recognize God in the people and world around them. This is often the experience described by those who have come through the dark night of the soul. The world around them is transformed, because they have been transformed. Suddenly God is everywhere. This is what the spiritual journey is about: the integration of the person, body, mind, and spirit as he or she comes closer to God. The more we become ourselves, the more we give glory to God. Thomas Merton puts it this way:

> A tree gives glory to God first of all by being a tree. For in being what God means it to be, it is imitating an idea which is in God and which is not distinct from the essence of God, and therefore a tree imitates God by being a tree.

The more a tree is like itself, the more it is like
Him.[1]

John of the Cross' own experience after his imprisonment ordeal was that he had greater energy, greater
compassion, and apparently less prejudice. Even as he
was dying, he was patient and forgiving of the man
who was mistreating him in his illness. This eventually led to the man's conversion. He begged John to
forgive him before he died.

A more modern example is that of Cardinal Văn
Thuận of Vietnam, who spent thirteen years in prison,
nine of which were in solitary confinement. He experienced unimaginable suffering, and yet it brought
him closer to God. After he was released from prison
he was noted for his compassion and love of the people around him. According to his biographer, André
Nguyễn Văn Châu, Cardinal Văn Thuận never spoke ill
of his persecutors. When he did have to speak about
them, he usually excused them because of their own
weakness or circumstances:

> As far as possible he always tried to show his
> guards and Communist officials at their best; he
> stressed their humanity and compassion rather
> than their indifference or cruelty. Even when
> he had to reveal the brutality of the guards
> and Communist officials, Thuan excused their
> behavior, which he believed was not the fruit of
> personal evil, but mechanical obedience to an
> indifferent and cruel bureaucracy.[2]

For Văn Thuận—just as for many others—an inner
transformation had taken place. They were different,

remade in Christ, even if through a most painful experience. The more we grow in holiness, the more we give glory to God, since we begin to blossom as human beings, reflecting better the image of God in which we were created. Humanity's sinfulness, or dis-integration, is the opposite of what was intended in God's creation. Therefore, the gradual reintegration through healing in every area is a growth in holiness, a step in the direction of God. The process is referred to as purification by John and Teresa, and as a healing of the unconscious by Keating.

While both are pointing to the same thing—that is, a deeper union with God—there is another impor-tant distinction to make here. While emotional heal-ing can be part of the journey to a deeper union with God, this union does not necessarily follow, since many people can be healed emotionally without it bringing them any closer to God. However, in the way that Keating speaks about it, healing is under-stood to be a part of the spiritual journey leading the soul closer to God, since the whole process takes place in the context of prayer. Now let us take a look at what seems to be very similar in psychology.

## THE PSYCHOLOGICAL ASPECT OF HEALING

A psychological explanation of sickness and heal-ing also confirms what happens on the spiritual jour-ney. One writer in particular who deals with this inner healing in both a psychological and spiritual way is M. Scott Peck. Peck is a psychiatrist, but he also understands that the psychological and spiritual are closely linked and cannot really be separated. Peck

speaks first of all about the development of consciousness as a process that is ever going forward. It cannot
go backward. This is symbolized by the sword bear-
ing cherubim at the gates of Eden, to prevent anyone
from re-entering if they so wished.[3] In other words,
we cannot go back to the blissful state of Eden, which
symbolizes our unconscious self, since we are now
self-conscious:

> We come then to yet another great truth (among
> others) that this rich story [in Genesis] teaches
> us: We cannot go back to Eden…. We can only
> go forward through the desert into deeper and
> ever-deeper levels of consciousness for our
> salvation.

> This is such an important truth because an
> enormous amount of psychospiritual disease—
> including the abuse of drugs—arises out of the
> attempt to get back to Eden.[4]

Dr. Peck also holds that the account of the
Garden of Eden represents humanity in its innocence. The Fall was, among other things, a step
in the development of consciousness. As he rightly
points out, one of the first effects of the Fall was
that Adam and Eve became aware of their own
nakedness and wanted to be covered. They were
now self-conscious. This also brought with it the
feeling of being more alone, or the realization of
being separate and vulnerable: they were afraid.
Keating also claims that the fundamental pathology
that the human race is suffering from is this feeling
of being alone without God:

Contemplative prayer is addressed to the human situation just as it is. It is designed to heal the consequences of the human condition, which is basically the privation of the divine presence. Everyone suffers from this disease. If we accept the fact that we are suffering from a serious pathology, we possess a point of departure for the spiritual journey. The pathology is simply this: we have come to full reflective self-consciousness without the experience of intimacy with God. Because that crucial reassurance is missing, our fragile egos desperately seek other means of shoring up our weaknesses and defending ourselves from the pain of alienation from God and other people. Contemplative prayer is the divine remedy for this illness.[5]

Peck also confirms that for the first several months of life, a baby—as far as psychology can tell—is not conscious of itself as a separate being. He or she seems to see him- or herself as an extension of the mother. However, in normal development, at about nine months, the baby suddenly becomes afraid of strangers. In other words, the infant is suddenly aware of itself as a separate being and a very vulnerable one. Therefore, the child runs and buries him- or herself in the mother's lap as soon as a stranger comes. Fear of the unknown has developed. At a cocktail party people enjoy a few drinks, which often help them to relax. They become less "self-conscious" and find it easier to talk to others. Peck says that this is an attempt to return to Eden. Nevertheless, this blissful state cannot last for long, and the long-term consequences of trying to stay this way are dangerous. Instead, we need to recognize that our ability to feel pain is a healthy thing, since it is a sign of healing:

> Pain is a signal of disease, not the disease itself. Indeed, it is primarily a disease-preventing mechanism. Without it we would all quickly become crippled. So a second moral is that we need to experience pain for our healing and health.[6]

Physicians, Peck says, recognize that pain is the sign of a healthy system addressing its problems. This applies not only to the individual but also to systems like the family, the Church, and every kind of organization. If an organization, say for example a car manufacturing company, fails to address its own shortcomings and goes on foolishly investing money when the market is actually in decline, it will soon go bankrupt. If, on the other hand, it recognizes that there is a slump in the economy and bravely cuts back on production, including letting go of some of its staff, it may survive. In other words, if it properly addresses its problems and faces the "pain" of having to cut back, it may still be in business the following year. The same can also be said of the individual. If someone develops a cancer, but continues to ignore it, he or she may eventually die. But if they have surgery, even though it may be painful and risky, and they bravely address the problem by removing the diseased part of the body, they may survive. The pain is an indication of a healthy system.

This idea also applies to the emotions. Emotional pain is not necessarily a bad thing; rather it is a sign that there are issues that need to be addressed. It is often more dangerous when someone obviously in need of help refuses to admit there is anything wrong. Feelings that are buried are buried alive and will resurface one way or the other:

> People will anesthetize themselves to deal with their emotional pain—either with drugs or, more commonly, through a variety of psychological tricks called "defense mechanisms." While sometimes necessary—even life-saving—these defense mechanisms are more often employed in an unhealthy fashion to limit consciousness so as to ward off existential, "legitimate" suffering. When used this way they are the cause of psychospiritual disease. As self-imposed limitations of consciousness they prevent the person from moving forward through the desert and becoming all that she or he can be. Conversely, psychotherapy—the healing of the psyche—is a process of relinquishing these defenses so as to directly face the painful issues of life....

> So the further you proceed through the desert, the more conscious you become, the more healthy and "saved" and civil you are, the more it will hurt.[7]

Peck here makes an interesting point. He says that "self-imposed limitations of consciousness prevent the person from moving forward." Refusing to address a problem prevents growth. Human beings are geniuses at blocking out what is too painful to face. In the twelve-step program of Alcoholics Anonymous, it is well known that the biggest obstacle to recovery is usually getting the individual to admit that he or she

has an alcohol—or whatever addiction—problem.
Once people admit to themselves that there is a real
problem, only then can they begin to do something
about it. Our ability to suppress what is too painful to
face is amazing, but it also serves as a survival mechanism. Issues that are too painful to face are unconsciously suppressed in order for the individual to be
able to continue with ordinary living. However, they
will eventually take their toll and if they are not dealt
with at some stage they will probably manifest themselves in an unhealthy way.[8]

In order to "move forward through the desert"
we will eventually have to face up to these problems,
wounds, and diseases. Once they begin to come to
consciousness they can be dealt with, whether this
happens with the help of psychotherapy, or some
other method. Of course, this can be very painful
and understandably people are reluctant to face the
pain. We generally prefer to tranquilize it with alcohol, drugs, work, or another substitute. This rising to
the surface of the emotions is exactly what happens
through centering prayer, though of course it is not a
goal of centering prayer but rather one of its fruits.

As a relationship of trust is established with a
psychotherapist, the patient will gradually become
more comfortable with disclosing his or her problems.
What happens through prayer is very similar. As the
one praying enters into the deep rest of contemplative prayer, he or she is more easily able to release
the emotions that are in need of healing, even though
this happens unconsciously. This is the work of the
Holy Spirit, of course, who is a kind of divine psychotherapist helping us to heal at ever-deeper levels. The

longer we stay at this practice the deeper the healing that takes place, as the Spirit draws us further and further into God.

Emotional healing is just as real as any other kind of healing. It is believed that the process of addiction is, among other things, largely because of emotional illness. The addiction is a coping mechanism. Healing of the emotions often goes a long way toward the healing of the addiction. If the healing of the emotions is an essential part of growing as a person, of coming closer to meeting our full healthy selves, then this is also part of the spiritual journey. The journey that brings us closer to God is the same journey that involves us becoming more integrated, more whole. Peck reminds his readers that the very word "salvation" comes from the word to heal:

> Becoming the most that we can is also the definition of *salvation*. The term literally means "healing." As we apply "salve" to our skin to heal it, so we can learn to apply the principles of mental health in our lives to heal, to make us whole, to save our souls, individually and collectively.[9]

Salvation is all about becoming the people that God wants us to be, that is, humanity at its most beautiful. As St. Irenaeus says: "Man fully alive is the glory of God."

At this stage I hope that the pattern is becoming clear. All of these writers, whether in spiritual or psychological terms, are talking about the same process. It is the spiritual journey that leads us to God, the voyage that leads us to greater wholeness. Now some may argue that just because people are apparently becoming more integrated or healed emotionally doesn't mean that they are any closer to God. While that may be true if we understand "coming closer to God" in a strictly religious sense—i.e., in a way that shows someone has suddenly developed in their faith, or is more seriously practicing their religion. In a broader sense, however, God is working in all people no matter what religion they do or do not practice. Since all people are God's creation, it must follow that God is interested in the well-being of all his children, whether or not they appear to recognize him: "I have come so that they may have life and have it to the full" (Jn 10:10). Helping us to realize our full potential as human beings is part of the spiritual journey.

In the Christian Church we recognize that God works through medicine and technology as much as through the spiritual. God makes use of any and every means to communicate and deepen his relationship with his children. It is, therefore, no surprise that God also heals his people through contemplative prayer, just as through many other means: "If you, then, evil though you are, know how to give your children what is good, how much more will your Father in heaven give good things to those who ask him!" (Mt 7:11).

# Conclusion

CENTERING PRAYER IS PRIMARILY a form of prayer, and the purpose of this prayer—like all forms of Christian prayer—is to help the person praying to grow closer to, and deepen one's relationship with, God. If healing does take place, it is secondary and while it is certainly not the "goal" of centering prayer it is one of its effects. The spiritual journey, which is bringing us ever deeper into God, involves an ongoing purification of the soul. This can also be understood as a kind of healing that takes place, bringing the soul to greater integration and wholeness. In its turn, this helps one to be more effective in ministry and life in general, since the process is gradually overcoming prejudice and cultural conditioning.

In spite of the many criticisms to the contrary, we have seen that centering prayer is not something new—as Keating readily admits; rather, it is a re-presentation of the centuries-old practice of Christian contemplation. It is deeply rooted in the scriptures. We have seen from the writings of St. Teresa of Avila that the method of prayer itself falls somewhere between discursive meditation and acquired contemplation, and is probably most accurately categorized as the latter. Here is a "technique" that helps the one praying to be as receptive as possible, open to the possibility of the Holy Spirit drawing them further into the silence of contemplation. This contemplation is not something that we produce, but it is something we can be better disposed to.

We have also seen that the practice of centering prayer—which is almost identical to what is described in *The Cloud of Unknowing*—can also be traced back to the teachings of the Desert Fathers, in particular to John Cassian, John Climacus, and Evagrius Ponticus, who also describe a means of growing in prayer through the repetition of a single word or phrase, helping one to move beyond thoughts, insofar as this is possible—since God is not to be found in thoughts or ideas but is completely beyond them. And so, if we want to draw closer to the all-knowing God, we must be prepared to enter into the cloud of unknowing, by the darkness of pure faith, as John of the Cross puts it. The teaching of centering prayer is, therefore, well founded in Christian tradition.

While Keating's main teaching on centering prayer does not go against the teaching of the Magisterium, some of the ideas that he associates with it are not so orthodox, such as the evolution of consciousness and the explanation of original sin. Having said that, I do not believe that these ideas take from the teaching itself; however, I think they are not the most helpful and could certainly use some clarification.

Perhaps the question that is still most debated in this area is whether people can or should be introduced to centering prayer before they have already had much experience in a life of prayer and trying to live the Gospel. One school of thought sides for the more traditional arguments, held by St. Teresa and St. John, that this kind of prayer should not be introduced to people until they are well established in prayer themselves. The other side of this argument holds that that was fine in the time of Teresa and John, where the culture was predominantly religious, but that different forms of prayer are more suitable to different times. The time we are now living in—at least in the West—can no longer be described as predominantly religious. Today, people of many different cultures and creeds are living side by side, which is opening people up to new ideas. Thousands do not claim faith in any particular religion. Does that mean that they should be excluded from an introduction to Christianity through a means such as centering prayer, simply because the traditional rules say otherwise? If through such a practice they manage to discover first an interest in what is spiritual and then perhaps are drawn more in the direction of Christianity proper, can this not be used as a vehicle to help them discover or rediscover faith?

According to traditional theology, this may appear to be doing things backwards, but God is well known for writing backwards at times. The early Christians were continually discovering new aspects of their faith, and the Spirit helped them to constantly redefine the boundaries, such as whether the gentiles could become Christian, the question of circumcision, and the place of the law, etc. While being careful not to stray from the teaching of the Church, there is no reason why we cannot experiment today with what will and will not work, to try to meet the needs of so many who are spiritually starving.

As humanity's search for God goes on, God continues to reveal Himself to His people in different ways, helping us to discover the infinite richness of the Godhead. Among other things, the Incarnation made it possible for humanity to relate to God in a more concrete way, even as to another person. Today we often hear the call to "give us something new," as though in some way God had not already given us everything in His Son. Instead, it is a question of humanity rediscovering the treasures we already possess. I believe that centering prayer is one of the many ways that God is helping His people to rediscover some of the great riches that we have been given, to enrich our life, to draw us deeper into Himself. I would even say that centering prayer is a gift of the Holy Spirit to the Church at this time, meeting some of the deeply felt needs of God's people.

# NOTES

## INTRODUCTION

1. IWG, p. 162.

## CHAPTER 1: THE BEGINNINGS OF CENTERING PRAYER

1. Anne A. Simpkinson, "Resting in God," www.center-ingprayer.com/resting.htm.
2. ITL, p. 2.
3. Thomas Merton, *Contemplative Prayer* (New York: Doubleday, 1996), p. 107.
4. Keating defines the emotional programs for happiness as, "the growth of the instinctual needs of survival/security, affection/esteem, and power/control into centers of motivation, around which our thoughts, feelings and behavior gravitate." ITL, p. 145.
5. Thomas Merton, *Seeds of Contemplation* (London: Burns and Oates, 1960), p. 9.
6. *Ibid.*, pp. 11–13.
7. *Ibid.*, p. 11.
8. *Ibid.*
9. We speak here about the unconscious, as opposed to the subconscious, since the person is completely unaware of these things. The *Concise Oxford Dictionary* defines unconscious as "that part of the mind which is inacces-

sible to the conscious mind, but which affects behaviour, emotions etc." It defines "subconscious" as, "the part of the mind which is not fully conscious but influences actions etc." According to *A Student's Dictionary of Psychology*, "the most important use of the term [unconscious] is in psychoanalytic theory as a reference to mental activity which is not available to consciousness because it concerns material which is too threatening to the ego to be recognised directly. Freud believed that the unconscious has its own way of working... which is different to that of the conscious mind. For example, there is no awareness of time in the unconscious, so all threats are felt as if they were still present, even if the source of the threat disappeared years ago." This would also help to explain why we react so strongly when we feel that our happiness is in some way being compromised. Unconsciously, not only has our perceived deprivation never gone away, but it is still present to us.

10. Thomas Merton, *The New Man*, as quoted by M. Basil Pennington in *True Self, False Self* (New York: Crossroads, 2000), pp. 89–91.

11. ITL, p. 10.

12. *Ibid.*, p. 26.

13. The *Catechism of the Catholic Church* says the following with regard to original sin and its effects: "Scripture portrays the tragic consequences of this first disobedience. Adam and Eve immediately lose the grace of original holiness. They become afraid of the God of whom they have conceived a distorted image—that of a God jealous of his prerogatives. The harmony in which they had found themselves, thanks to original justice, is now destroyed: the control of the soul's spiritual faculties over the body is shattered; the union of man and woman becomes subject to tensions, their relations henceforth marked by lust and domination. Harmony with creation is broken: visible creation has become

alien and hostile to man. Because of man, creation is now subject 'to its bondage to decay'. Finally, the consequence explicitly foretold for this disobedience will come true: man will 'return to the ground,' for out of it he was taken. Death makes its entrance into human history." CCC, #399–400.

14. Benedict Groeschel, *Healing the Original Wound* (Cincinnati: Saint Anthony Messenger Press & Franciscan Communications, 1993).

15. ITL, p. 59.

16. Keating defines the false self as: "the self developed in our own likeness rather than in the likeness of God; the self-image developed to cope with the emotional trauma of early childhood. It seeks happiness in satisfying the instinctual needs of survival/security, affection/esteem, and power/control, and bases its self-worth on cultural or group identification." IWG, p. 163.

17. Merton, *Seeds of Contemplation* (London: Burns and Oates, 1960), p. 15.

18. Ann A. Terruwe, MD, and Conrad W. Baars MD, *Psychic Wholeness and Healing: Using All the Powers of the Human Psyche* (New York: Alba House, 1981), p. 191.

19. ITL, pp. 22–3.

20. Assagioli, *Psychosynthesis*, www.synthesiscenter.org/articles/0110.pdf.

## CHAPTER 2: GROWING IN CONSCIOUSNESS

1. For a more developed account of this theory, see Ken Wilber, *Up from Eden* (Boulder: Shambhala, 1983).

2. ITL, p. 27.

3. I am not suggesting that this is how consciousness necessarily developed, since this theory would also seem to suggest that human beings evolved from a more primitive species, which is contrary to Catholic teaching.

However, it does present an interesting model that helps to explain much of what we experience today with regard to consciousness.

4. ITL, p. 27.
5. Wilber, *op. cit.*, p. 26.
6. *Ibid.*, p. 107.
7. *Ibid.*, p. 105.
8. ITL, p. 32.
9. *Ibid.*, p. 33.
10. *Ibid.*, p. 36.
11. Wilber, *op. cit.*, p. 171.
12. ITL, p. 42.
13. *Ibid.*, p. 31.
14. *Ibid.*, pp. 40–41.
15. ITL, p. 59.
16. Wilber, *op. cit.*, p. 305.
17. CCC, #387.
18. *Ibid.*, #397.

## Chapter 3: Centering Prayer and Contemplative Prayer

1. This can be further distinguished as "infused contemplation," which is purely from God, as opposed to "acquired contemplation," which is as far as the individual can progress in prayer through a method such as centering prayer. This is discussed further in chapter 4 in the writings of St. Teresa of Avila.

2. Not everyone may agree with Keating's interpretation of the word μετανοειτε, which is a spiritual rather than exegetical one. However, for the purpose of what he is discussing, namely the challenge to address unconscious motivation, it makes good sense. Neither does it go against the more strict interpretation of the word μετανοεω, which, according to the *Greek–English Lexicon of the New Testament and other Early Christian*

*Literature*, can be translated as change one's mind; feel remorse, repent, be converted, "as a prerequisite for experiencing the Reign of God in the preaching of John the Baptist and Jesus," p. 640.

3. IWG, p. 11.

4. *Ibid.*, p. 79.

5. M. Basil Pennington, *Centering Prayer* (New York: Image Books, 2001), p. 106.

6. Francis Kelly Nemeck, Marie Theresa Coombs, Hermit, *Contemplation* (Dublin: Dominican Publications, 1982), p. 57.

7. While a completely quiet space is obviously ideal, this kind of prayer can be practiced with a surprising amount of noise in the background. So long as the sounds are not too distracting it is not an obstacle. I have often been able to give time to this kind of prayer on such places as trains, planes, and in airports, etc.

8. For the purposes of explaining centering prayer, Keating defines a thought as "any perception that appears on the inner screen of consciousness. This could be an emotion, an image, a memory, a plan, a noise from outside, a feeling of peace, or even a spiritual communication. In other words, anything whatsoever that registers on the inner screen of consciousness is a 'thought,' " OM, p. 35.

9. OM, pp. 34–35.

10. *Ibid.*, p. 113.

11. ITL, p. 3.

12. While we use the term "goal" or "purpose" in regard to centering prayer, this can be misleading. To approach the prayer with the idea of trying to achieve something is really to miss the point. In this kind of prayer we are simply being present to God. We are not trying to do anything, only be there and not do anything. So it would be a mistake to talk about "trying" to make it work or how far we have or haven't gotten. Centering

prayer is simply about giving ourselves totally to God, keeping nothing for ourselves, not even our thoughts. In this prayer we give ourselves totally to God, without even allowing the eye of the false self to act. This "eye" always wants to assess how we are doing. In this prayer, all is for God. While we speak about the dismantling of the false self, it would also be a mistake to think of this in terms of one of the purposes of the prayer. Rather, it is one of the fruits.

13. Cf. Jn 10:10.
14. IWG, p. 136.
15. Merton, *Thomas Merton, Monk*, as quoted by M. Basil Pennington in *Daily We Touch Him* (Kansas: Sheed and Ward, 1997), p. 51.
16. ITL, p. 20.
17. This story is borrowed from Keating. See ITL, p. 20.
18. *Ibid.*, p. 25.
19. *Ibid.*, p. 27.
20. Anne Wilson Schaef, *When Society Becomes an Addict* (San Francisco: Harper and Row, 1987), p. 29.
21. *Ibid.*, p. 91.
22. Keating has taken the following theory of the four consents from John S. Dunne's *Time and Myth* (New York: Doubleday, 1973).
23. ITL, p. 44.
24. *Ibid.*, p. 45.
25. *Ibid.*, p. 46.
26. *Ibid.*, p. 47.
27. *Ibid.*
28. *Ibid.*, p. 48.

## CHAPTER 4: THE NIGHT OF SENSE AND SPIRIT

1.  Francis Kelly Nemeck, Marie Theresa Coombs, Hermit, *The Way of Spiritual Direction*, (Delaware: Micheal Glazier, 1985), p. 27.

2.  The most important characteristic of our personal conversion is that God directly effects it. The fundamental option, the radical decision and the unconditional commitment that are part and parcel of this conversion experience constitute our personal response to his initiative. We convert because we are converted. We turn because God turns us irrevocably to himself. We change because we are changed. Yes, it is my conversion, but in the sense that "I live now, no longer I, but Christ lives in me" (Ga 2:20). Francis Kelly Nemeck and Marie Theresa Coombs, *The Spiritual Journey* (Wilmington, DE: Michael Glazier, 1988), p. 140.

3.  *Ibid.*, p. 104.

4.  For a more detailed account of the "night of sense" see ASCENT.

5.  IWG, p. 93.

6.  NIGHT, 1.14.2.

7.  ITL, p. 73.

8.  NIGHT, 1.14.3.

9.  ITL, pp. 74–75.

10. Cf. Gen 12:1.

11. ITL, p. 75.

12. *Ibid.*, p. 76.

13. *Ibid.*, p. 85.

14. Gerald G. May makes an interesting point regarding "higher" or "altered" states of consciousness: "Awareness is the aspect of consciousness that is noticed, recognized, appreciated, or otherwise sensed by a given person. Although consciousness may have pervasive, constant, even eternal qualities, awareness is subject to a wide range of variability. Sometimes, as in much

of sleep, it is absent altogether. . . . Thus the popular parlance that speaks of "raising consciousness," "altering consciousness," or "expanding consciousness" is actually referring to manipulations of awareness—that part of consciousness that is experienced—rather than consciousness in its entirety. Awareness can indeed be expanded; this is what happens when one begins to appreciate more and more of the awesome qualities of consciousness. And awareness can also be limited or restricted. This is called "paying attention." Gerald G. May, *Will and Spirit* (San Francisco: HarperCollins, 1987), p. 46.

15. ITL, p. 78.
16. *Ibid.*, p. 82.
17. *Ibid.*, p. 92.
18. *Ibid.*, p. 93.
19. *Ibid.*, p. 92.
20. *Ibid.*, pp. 93–94.
21. *Ibid.*, p. 97.
22. *Ibid.*
23. *Ibid.*, p. 98.
24. *Ibid.*
25. *Ibid.*, p. 99.
26. *Ibid.*
27. Cf. Mt 21:12–13.
28. ITL, p. 111.
29. *Ibid.*, p. 130.

## CHAPTER 5: THE INFLUENCE OF THE DESERT FATHERS

1. The Edict of Milan was a circular to provincial governors issued in Bithynia by the Emperor Licinius. In accordance with an agreement made with Constantine at Milan, it allowed freedom of worship for all people including Christians and also included the restitution of

much of the confiscated property since the persecutions in 303. See *Oxford Dictionary of the Christian Church*.

2. Laura Swan, "Paradox in the Monastery: Lessons from Two Ammas," Review for Religious, 63.2 (2004), p. 163.

3. William Meninger, "Contemplative Prayer: Many are Called," Review for Religious, 38 (1979), p. 334.

4. Kenneth C. Russell, "John Cassian on Asceticism," Review for Religious, 56.2 (1997), p. 163.

5. *Ibid.*, p. 164.

6. PR, p lxxxi. Today we can substitute "the emotions" for what was then referred to as the passions.

7. Apatheia is a difficult word to translate. It seems to mean an inner calm, a type of indifference where one's inner peace is no longer disturbed by what is going on outside. It represents a certain state of perfection which the soul has reached. "The proof of apatheia is had when the spirit begins to see its own light, when it remains in a state of tranquility in the presence of the images it has during sleep and when it maintains its calm as it beholds the affairs of life" (*Ibid.*, pp. 33–34). For a further explanation of this term see PR, pp. lxxxii–lxxxv.

8. PR, p. 36.

9. *Ibid.*, p. 58.

10. Cf. *Ibid.*, p. 48. See also chapters on Prayer, #106–111 and especially #109.

11. *Ibid.*, p. 57.

12. *Ibid.*, pp. 16–17.

13. *Ibid.*, p. 62.

14. *Ibid.*, p. 25.

15. It is important to mention here that we are not suggesting that we will reach a point where our minds will be completely "blank," as this is virtually impossible. What we are saying is that we will reach a stage where we are no longer affected by the thoughts. They are passing by in the background, as it were, but we are no longer dis-

turbed by them. This is a bit like having a conversation with someone on the street. Initially we are aware of the traffic, but very quickly it fades into the background.

16.  PR, p. 65.

17.  *Ibid.*, p. 66.

18.  *Ibid.*

19.  *Ibid.*, p. 75.

20.  *Ibid.*, pp. 75–76.

21.  Thomas Keating, *The Better Part* (New York: Continuum, 2002), p. 70.

22.  C, p. 39.

23.  *Ibid.*, p. 41.

24.  *Ibid.*, pp. 101–102.

25.  *Ibid.*, p. 132.

26.  ITL, p. 133.

27.  C, p. 110.

28.  *Ibid.*, p. 101.

29.  Thelma Hall, *Too Deep for Words* (New York: Paulist Press, 1988), p. 29.

30.  LD, pp. 275–276.

31.  *Ibid.*, p. 184.

32.  *Ibid.*, p. 178.

33.  *Ibid.*, p. 200.

34.  *Ibid.*, pp. 269–270.

35.  *Ibid.*, p. 50.

36.  *Ibid.*, p. 262.

37.  Cf. Lk 10:38–42.

## CHAPTER 6: THE CLOUD OF UNKNOWING

1.  Cf. Lk 10:38–42.

2.  Cf. Lk 7:36–50

3.  CLOUD, p. 48.

4.  *Ibid.*, p. 56.

5.  *Ibid.*

6.  *Ibid.*, p. 83.

7. IWG, pp. 127–128.
8. CLOUD, p. 92.
9. M. Basil Pennington, "Centering Prayer: Refining the Rules," Review for Religious, 45 (1986), p. 387.
10. CLOUD, p. 50.
11. *Ibid.*, p. 137.
12. *Ibid.*, p. 138.

## CHAPTER 7: LECTIO DIVINA

1. IWG, p. 51.
2. Thelma Hall, *Too Deep for Words* (New York: Paulist Press, 1988), pp. 28–29.
3. *Ibid.*, p. 48.
4. IWG, p. 119.
5. *Ibid.*, p. 122.
6. *Ibid.*, p. 125.

## CHAPTER 8: MEDITATION EAST AND WEST

1. William Johnston, *The Inner Eye of Love* (London: 1981), p. 16, quoted in John Ball, "Christian Spirituality and other Traditions," The Way, 3 (1985), pp. 218–19.
2. Cf. Rm 3:23–26.
3. Walpola Rahula, *What the Buddha Taught* (New York: Grove Press, 1974), p. 51.
4. *Ibid.*, p. 52.
5. John Paul II, *Crossing the Threshold of Hope* (London: Jonathan Cape, 1994), pp. 84–85.
6. Rahula, *op. cit.*, p. 50.
7. Cf. Gen 1:31.
8. John Paul II, *op. cit.*, p. 86.
9. Rahula, *op. cit.*, p. 2.
10. Zen is a branch of Mahayana Buddhism that arose in China. The word *zen* comes from the Chinese *chan*,

which comes from *dhyana*, the Sanskrit term for meditation. Zen developed from its Chinese roots to flourish in Korea, Vietnam, and Japan as well. See Roshi Philip Kapleau, Polly Young-Eisendrath and Rafe Martin (eds), *Awakening to Zen: The Teachings of Roshi Philip Kapleau* (Boston, MA: Shambhala, 2001), p. 74.

11.  *Ibid.*, p. 23.

12.  Robert Ornstein gives an interesting account of the various techniques and effects of meditation, from a psychological point of view in, Claudio Naranjo and Robert E. Ornstein, *On the Psychology of Meditation* (New York: Viking Press, 1971), pp. 142–169. Since many of the effects are common to various forms of meditation, it raises interesting questions as to what is "spiritual" and what is purely psychological.

13.  For a more complete description of the method see, Robert McCown, "Christian Zen-cum-Ignatian Meditation," Review for Religious, 52 (1993), pp. 509–511.

14.  *Ibid.*

15.  Cf. Jn 17:21.

16.  It would probably be more accurate to say, "that the union between the soul and God is being purified, since the obstacles to that union are gradually being removed." However, for simplicity's sake we will say that we are "coming closer" to God.

17.  Young-Eisendrath and Martin (eds), *op. cit.*, p. 94.

18.  *Ibid.*, p. 24.

19.  IWG, p. 41.

20.  McCown, *op. cit.*, pp. 512–513.

21.  IWG, p. 13.

22.  *Ibid.*, p. 126.

23.  William Johnston, "Zen and Christian Contemplation," Review for Religious, 29 (1970), p. 703.

24.  Robert Roth, *Maharishi Mahesh Yogi's Transcendental Meditation*, Revised edition (New York: Primus, 1994), p. 179.

25. *Ibid.*, p. 32–33.
26. Maharishi Mahesh Yogi, *Life Supported by Natural Law* (Iowa: Maharishi International University Press, 1988), p. 37.
27. *Ibid.*, p. 3.
28. Cf. www.trancenet.org/dmbroch.shtml for a list of the mantras normally given to initiates. In spite of the secrecy surrounding the giving of the mantra, which beginners are told they must never share, these mantras are given purely on the basis of the age of individuals. While the impression is given that there must be thousands of these "secret" mantras, there are in fact probably no more than 16.
29. For a critical analyses of the background to TM, see the article by Louis Hughes, O.P., "Is Transcendental Meditation (TM) a Religion?" Spirituality, 16 (1998), pp. 52–57.
30. *Ibid.*, p. 56.
31. Maharishi Mahesh Yogi, *Life Supported by Natural Law* (Iowa: Maharishi International University Press, 1988), p. 37.
32. Cf. www.incandescentpress.com/srm/meditation.htm
33. IWG, p. 92.
34. Nostra Aetate, 2.
35. OF, 16.
36. *Ibid.*, 3.
37. *Ibid.*, 9.
38. *Ibid.*, 12.
39. William Johnston, "Oriental Mysticism and Christian Prayer," Review for Religious, 29 (1970), p. 274.
40. Cf. Jn 14:6.
41. IWG, p. 32.

## Chapter 9: St. Teresa of Avila

1. LIFE, 8.7.

2.  Kieran Kavanaugh, "How to Pray: From the Life and Teachings of Saint Teresa," Kevin Culligan and Regis Jordan (eds.), *Carmel and Contemplation: Transforming Human Consciousness*, Carmelite Studies VIII (Washington, DC: ICS Publications), pp. 117–118.

3.  LIFE, 11.7.

4.  *Ibid.*, 11.10.

5.  *Ibid.*, 11.17.

6.  OM, p. 95.

7.  LIFE, 12.4.

8.  ITL, p. 67.

9.  LIFE, 12.5.

10. IWG, p. 40.

11. LIFE, 13.12.

12. IWG, pp. 122–123.

13. Kavanaugh, *op. cit.*, p. 125.

14. *Ibid.*, p. 127.

15. LIFE, 13.15.

16. Jordan Aumann, *Spiritual Theology* (London: Sheed and Ward, 1980), p. 327.

17. LIFE, 15.1.

18. *Ibid.*, 15.4.

19. OM, p. 14.

20. LIFE, 15.1.

21. OM, pp. 112–113.

22. LIFE, 15.8.

23. *Ibid.*, 15.9.

24. *Ibid.*, 15.13.

25. ITL, p. 118.

26. LIFE, 15.10.

27. Evelyn Underhill, *Mysticism* (Oxford: Oneworld Publications, 1993), p. 319.

28. *Ibid.*, p. 323.

29. *Ibid.*, p. 316.

30. *Ibid.*, p. 323–324.

31. WP, 19.15.

32.  *Ibid.*, 25.1.
33.  *Ibid.*, 28.4.
34.  *Ibid.*, 29.5.
35.  *Ibid.*, 29.4.
36.  *Ibid.*, 31.8.
37.  *Ibid.*, 31.10.
38.  IWG, p. 123.
39.  Kavanaugh, *op. cit.*, p. 131.
40.  IC, 1.2.3.
41.  *Ibid.*, 1.2.8.
42.  ITL, p. 67.
43.  IC, 2.1.2.
44.  *Ibid.*, 2.1.7.
45.  *Ibid.*, 2.1.8.
46.  *Ibid.*, 4.1.4.
47.  IWG, p. 122.
48.  Cf. Gen 32:23–33.
49.  IC, 7.2.7.
50.  Mary Frohlich, "Teresa: Story Theologian and Transformer of Culture," Review for Religious, 61.1 (2002), p. 9.
51.  ITL, p. 125.
52.  IC, 7.1.8.
53.  *Ibid.*, 7.4.12.

## CHAPTER 10: ST. JOHN OF THE CROSS

1.  LF, 3.43.
2.  *Ibid.*, 3.32.
3.  *Ibid.*, 3.33.
4.  IWG, p. 118.
5.  LF, 3.35.
6.  *Ibid.*, 3.34.
7.  OM, p. 48.
8.  LF, 3.36.
9.  *Ibid.*, 3.46.

10.    *Ibid.*, 3.49.

11.    OM, p. 114.

12.    LF, 3.67.

13.    St. John of the Cross, *The Spiritual Canticle*, 29.3.

14.    ITL, p. 44.

15.    ASCENT, 1.4.1.

16.    *Ibid.*, 1.3.4.

17.    *Ibid.*, 1.5.6.

18.    *Ibid.*, 1.8.4.

19.    *Ibid.*, Prologue 3.

20.    *Ibid.*, 1.4.5.

21.    *Ibid.*, 1.7.2.

22.    *Ibid.*, 1.10.1.

23.    *Ibid.*, 2.4.2.

24.    *Ibid.*, 2.6.2.

25.    ITL, p. 24.

26.    Marko Ivan Rupnik, Susan Dawson Vásquez (trans.), *In the Fire of the Burning Bush: An Initiation to the Spiritual Life*, (Cambridge: Wm. B. Eerdmans, 2004), p. 26.

27.    *Ibid.*, p. 30.

28.    ASCENT, 3.15.1.

29.    *Ibid.*, 3.4.1.

30.    See "The Afflictive Emotions," in chapter 3.

31.    ASCENT, 3.16.2.

32.    *Ibid.*, 3.16.5.

33.    See ITL, p. 20.

34.    ASCENT, 3.23.1.

35.    Kieran Kavanaugh, "Introduction to The Dark Night," in LF, p. 355.

36.    NIGHT, 1.3.3.

37.    *Ibid.*, 1.8.3.

38.    See "The Night of Sense and Spirit," in chapter 4.

39.    NIGHT, 1.14.4.

40.    *Ibid.*, 2.2.1.

41.    *Ibid.*, 2.3.1.

42.  *Ibid.*, 2.6.5.

43.  ITL, p. 96.

44.  *Ibid.*, p. 96.

45.  NIGHT, 2.9.1.

46.  ITL, pp. 97–98.

47.  *Ibid.*, p. 99.

48.  Iain Matthew, *The Impact of God* (London: Hodder & Stoughton, 1995), p. 106.

49.  NIGHT, 2.9.5.

50.  ITL, p. 99.

51.  NIGHT, 1.13.5.

52.  ITL, p. 85.

53.  Matthew, *op. cit.*, pp. 63–64.

54.  NIGHT, 2.11.4.

55.  Robert Gregg (trans.), *Athanasius: Life of Anthony* (Mahwah, N.J.: Paulist Press, 1988), no. 14, 32, as quoted in ITL, p. 83.

56.  ITL, p. 101–102.

57.  Matthew, *op. cit.*, p. 37.

## Chapter 11: Centering Prayer and the New Age

1.  Cf. BWL 2.2.3.

2.  *Ibid.*, 2.2.3.

3.  *Ibid.*, 6.1.

4.  Pantheism implies that God is to be found in all things, but not apart from them. The Christian faith believes that God can certainly be recognized in his creation since He is the author of creation, but at the same time God completely transcends his creation.

5.  John A. Saliba, "A Christian Response to the New Age," *The Way*, 3 (1993), p. 228.

6.  Louis Hughes, "Responding to New Age Thinking," *Doctrine and Life*, 49.9 (1999), p. 408.

7.  BWL, 3.4.

8. Cf. *Ibid.*, 2.5.
9. *Ibid.*, 3.4.
10. For example, the teachers of TM insist that it can only be passed on by someone who is trained in the practice, and any course on TM has to be paid for.

## CHAPTER 12: MORE OBJECTIONS

1. For more information see www.lhla.org/contact.htm
2. Johnette S. Benkovic, *The New Age Counterfeit* (Goleta, CA: Queenship Publishing, 1993), p. 24.
3. IWG, p. 40.
4. *Ibid.*, pp. 36–37.
5. Benkovic, *loc. cit.*, p. 24.
6. IWG, pp. 53–54.
7. Affective prayer is where one makes personal responses of love to God in one's own way, without particular formulae. For example, having reflected on the parable of the prodigal son, one might be tempted to spontaneously thank God for his mercy for oneself or others.
8. OM, pp. 22–23.
9. Benkovic, *op. cit.*
10. *Ibid.*, p. 25.
11. *Ibid.*
12. LIFE, 12.5
13. IWG, p. 68.
14. Benkovic, *loc. cit.*, p. 26.
15. *The Concise Oxford Dictionary* defines a technique as; 1) mechanical skill in an art; 2) a means of achieving one's purpose, especially skillfully; 3) a manner of artistic execution in music, painting, etc.
16. Benkovic, *op. cit.*
17. IWG, p. 80.
18. *Ibid.*, p. 81.
19. *Ibid.*, p. 78.
20. Cf. What the Church Teaches, chapter 8.

21. John D. Dreher, "The Danger of Centering Prayer," www.catholicculture.org/docs/doc_view.cfm?recnum=234

22. Two other articles critical on centering prayer are: Dan DeCelles, "Centering Prayer Meets the Vatican," www.dotm.org/decelles-1.htm; "Catholic Meditation or Occult Meditation? A Critique of M. Basil Pennington's article, Centering Prayer, taken from The Contemplative Prayer Online Magazine," www.ourladyswarriors.org/dissent/centerprayer.htm. In this author's opinion, most of the criticisms made in these articles are not well founded and are based more on a lack of understanding of what centering prayer is about, than anything else. There are in fact a far greater number of articles available which are much better researched, and tend to be more in favor of the practice, though of course that doesn't imply that they are right.

23. Dreher, "The Danger of Centering prayer," p. 1. (Please note that the page numbers given here refer to the article once it has been printed by computer, as there are no page numbers in the article on-line).

24. *Ibid.*

25. *Ibid.*, p. 2.

## Chapter 13: Prayer and Everyday Life

1. CL, p. 2.

2. Evelyn Underhill, *The Essentials of Mysticism* (Oxford: Oneworld Publications, 1999), pp. 140–141.

3. *Ibid.*, p. 146.

4. *Ibid.*, p. 147.

5. ITL, p. 121.

6. *Ibid.*, p. 123.

7. The Missionaries of Charity is the order established by Saint Teresa of Calcutta. They live and work among the poorest of the poor. It is currently the fastest growing order in the world.

8. ITL, p. 125.

9. *Ibid.*, p. 129.

10. Sarah A. Butler, "Pastoral Care with Centering Prayer," Gustave Reininger (ed.), *Centering Prayer in Daily Life and Ministry*, (New York: Continuum, 1998), p. 92.

11. Karl Rahner, "Christian Living Formerly and Today," *Theological Investigations 7* (London: Darton, Longmann & Todd, 1966), p. 7.

12. *Ibid.*, p. 14.

13. PDV, 46.

14. Cf. Lk 10:42.

15. PDV, 47.

16. *Ibid.*, 47.

17. Sandra Casey-Martus, "Priestly Spiritual Formation with Centering Prayer," Reininger (ed.), *op. cit.*, p. 112.

18. Charismatic Renewal is a movement within the Church where people have experienced the gifts of the Spirit as described in Acts of the Apostles.

19. IWG, p. 138.

20. *Ibid.*, p. 142.

21. *Ibid.*, p. 143.

22. *Ibid.*, p. 145.

23. *Ibid.*, pp. 140–141.

24. OM, p. 3

## CHAPTER 14: THE QUESTION OF HEALING

1. Thomas Merton, *Seeds of Contemplation* (London: Burns and Oates, 1960), p. 9.

2. André Nguyễn Văn Châu, *The Miracle of Hope: Political Prisoner, Prophet of Peace: Life of Francis Xavier Nguyễn Văn Thuận* (Boston: Pauline, 2003), p. 262.

3. Cf. Gen 3:24.

4. M. Scott Peck, *A World Waiting to be Born* (London: Rider, 1993), p. 16.

5.  ITL, p. 130.
6.  Peck, *op. cit.*, p. 11.
7.  *Ibid.*, p. 17.
8.  For several examples of this kind of suppression and their effects, see Ann A. Terruwe, MD, and Conrad W. Baars MD, *Psychic Wholeness and Healing: Using All the Powers of the Human Psyche* (New York: Alba House, 1981), pp. 76–85.
9.  Peck, *op. cit.*, p. 12.

# Select Bibliography

## Articles

Burrows, Ruth, "Growth in Prayer," *The Way*, 4 (1983), pp. 255–263.

——. "Catholic Meditation or Occult Meditation? A Critique of M. Basil Pennington's article, 'Centering Prayer,' taken from the *Contemplative Prayer Online Magazine*" (www.ourladyswarriors.org/dissent/centerprayer.htm)

Dreher, John D., "The Danger of Centering Prayer" (www.catholicculture.org/docs/doc_view.cfm?recnum=234)

DeCelles, Dan, "Centering Prayer Meets the Vatican" (www.catholicculture.org/docs/doc_view.cfm?recnum=6892)

Dunne, Kathy, "The Still Point: Contemplation," *Review for Religious*, 58.1 (1999), pp. 61–67.

Hughes, Louis, "Is Transcendental Meditation (TM) a Religion?" *Spirituality*, 16 (1998), pp. 52–57.

——. "Responding to New Age Thinking," *Doctrine and Life* 49.9 (1999): pp. 405–410.

——. "From the Buddha to Jesus Christ," *Spirituality*, 45 (2002), pp. 369–372.

——. Independent Research on the Transcendental Meditation Technique (www.trancenet.org/dmbroch.shtml)

Johnstone, Brian V., "Keeping a Balance: Contemplation and Christian Meditation," *Review for Religious*, 63.2 (2004), pp. 118–133.

Johnston, William, "Dialogue with Zen," *Concilium*, 9.5 (1969), pp. 65–69.

Mancuso, Theresa, "The Urban hermit: Monastic Life in the City," *Review for Religious*, 55.2 (1996), pp. 133–142

McCaffrey, Eugene, "A Woman for All Ages: Teresa of Avila," *Spirituality*, 32 (2000), pp. 284–287.

McCown, Robert, "Christian Zen-cum-Ignatian Meditation," *Review for Religious*, 52.4 (1993), pp. 507–518.

Meninger, William, "Contemplative Prayer: Many are Called," *Review for Religious*, 38 (1979), pp. 334–339.

Mohammed, Ovey N., "Yoga, Christian Prayer and Zen," *Review for Religious*, 53.4 (1994), pp. 507–523.

Murray, Paul, "What is Contemplative Prayer?" (1), *Spirituality*, 31 (2000), pp. 217–222.

——. "Contemplation and Human Weakness" (2), *Spirituality*, 32 (2000), pp. 297–300.

——. "Reclaiming the Contemplative: Preachers at Prayer," *Spirituality*, 17 (1998), pp. 100–105.

Pennington, M. Basil, "Centering Prayer: Prayer of Quiet," *Review for Religious*, 35 (1976), pp. 651–662.

——. "Progress In Centering Prayer," *Review for Religious*, 38 (1979), pp. 833–838.

——. "Thomas Merton and Centering Prayer," *Review for Religious*, 45 (1986), pp. 119–129.

——. "Centering Prayer: Refining the Rules," *Review for Religious*, 45 (1986), pp. 386–393.

Russell, Kenneth C., "A Medieval Dynamic Understanding of Meditation," *Review for Religious*, 41 (1982), pp. 411–418.

——. "Pray Always: John Cassian on Distractions," *Review for Religious*, 53.2 (1994), pp. 263–272.

——. John Cassian on Asceticism," *Review for Religious*, 56.2 (1997), pp. 156–168.

Saliba, John A., "A Christian Response to the New Age," *The Way*, 3 (1993), pp. 222–232.

Shimizu, Bonnie J., *et al*, "Questions About Centering Prayer," (www.innerexplorations.com/chmystext/cm1.htm)

Swan, Laura, "Paradox in the Monastery: Lessons from Two Ammas," *Review for Religious*, 63.2 (2004), pp. 158–168.

———. "What is the Transcendental Meditation Technique?" (www.incandescentpress.com/srm/meditation.htm)

Woods, Richard, "What is New Age Spirituality?" *The Way*, 3 (1993), pp. 176–187.

## BOOKS

Abhishiktānanda, *Prayer*, Delhi: ISPCK, 2001.

Andrew, Brother, *What I Met Along the Way*, Hampton Vic.: Hampton Marian Centre, 1987.

Athanasius, Robert C. Cregg (trans.), *The Life of Anthony and the Letter to Marcellinus*, Mahwah, NJ: Paulist, 1980.

Baer, Randall N., *Inside the New Age Nightmare*, Lafayette, LA: Huntington House, 1989.

Benkovic, Johnnette S., *The New Age Counterfeit*, Goleta, CA: Queenship Publishing, 1993.

Burrows, Ruth, *Guidelines for Mystical Prayer*, London: Sheed and Ward, 1976.

Cassian, John, Colm Luibheid (trans.), *Conferences*, The Classics of Western Spirituality, New York: Paulist Press, 1985.

Climacus, John, Colm Luibheid and Norman Russell (trans.), *The Ladder of Divine Ascent*, The Classics of Western Spirituality, Mahwah, NJ: Paulist Press, 1982.

Congregation for the Doctrine of the Faith, *Letter to the Bishops of the Church on Some Aspects of Christian Meditation—Orationis Formas*, Boston, MA: Pauline, 1998.

Dubay, Thomas, *Fire Within: St. Teresa of Avila, St. John of the Cross, and the Gospel—on Prayer*, San Francisco: Ignatius, 1989.

Frankl, Viktor E., *Man's Search for Meaning*, New York: Pocket Books, 1984.

Giardini, Fabio, *Pray Without Ceasing: Toward a Systematic Psychotheology of Christian Prayerlife*, Rome: Millenium Romae Editrice, 1998.

Hall, Thelma, *Too Deep for Words: Rediscovering Lectio Divina*, New York: Paulist Press, 1988.

John Paul II, *Apostolic Letter, Novo Millennio Ineunte*, Rome: Libreria Editrice Vaticana, 2001.

——. Jenny and Martha McPhee (trans.), *Crossing the Threshold of Hope*, London: Jonathan Cape, 1994.

——. *Post-Synodal Apostolic Exhortation of the Holy Father: Consecrated Life—Vita Consecrata*, Boston, MA: Pauline, 1996.

Johnston, William, *Being in Love: The Practice of Christian Prayer*, London: Fount, 1988.

—— (ed.), *The Cloud of Unknowing and the Book of Privy Counseling*, New York: Doubleday, 1996.

Kapleau, Roshi Philip, Polly Young-Eisendrath and Rafe Martin (eds.), *Awakening to Zen: The Teachings of Roshi Philip Kapleau*, Boston, MA: Shambhala, 2001.

Keating, Thomas, *Crisis of Faith, Crisis of Love*, Third revised ed., New York: Continuum, 1995.

——. *The Human Condition*, New York: Paulist, 1999.

——. *Fruits and Gifts of the Spirit*, New York: Lantern Books, 2000.

——. *Invitation to Love: The Way of Christian Contemplation*, New York: Continuum, 2000.

——. *Open Mind Open Heart: The Contemplative Dimension of the Gospel*, New York: Continuum, 2000.

——. *Intimacy with God*, New York: Crossroad, 2002.

——. *The Better Part: Stages of Contemplative Living*, New York: Continuum, 2002.

——. *et al*, *The Divine Indwelling: Centering Prayer and its Development*, New York: Lantern Books, 2001.

Main, John, *Essential Writings*, New York: Orbis Books, 2002.

——. *Christian Meditation: The Gethsemani Talks*, Tucson, AZ: Medio Media, 1999.

Matthew, Iain, *The Impact of God: Soundings from St. John of the Cross*, London: Hodder & Stoughton, 1995.

May, Gerald G., *Will and Spirit: A Contemplative Psychology*, San Francisco: HarperCollins, 1987.

——. *Addiction and Grace*, San Francisco: Harper and Row, 1988.

Meninger, William A., *The Loving Search for God: Contemplative Prayer and the Cloud of Unknowing*, New York: Continuum, 2003.

Merton, Thomas, *The Last of the Fathers: Saint Bernard of Clairvaux and the Encyclical Letter, Doctor Mellifluus*, London: Hollis and Carter, 1954.

——. *Seeds of Contemplation*, London: Burns and Oates, 1960.

——. *Contemplative Prayer*, New York: Doubleday, 1996.

Naranjo, Claudio and Robert E. Ornstein, *On the Psychology of Meditation*, New York: Viking Press, 1971.

Nemeck, Francis Kelly, Marie Theresa Coombs, *Contemplation*, Dublin: Dominican Publications, 1982.

——. *The Way of Spiritual Direction*, Delaware: Michael Glazier, 1985.

——. *The Spiritual Journey: Critical Thresholds and Stages of Adult Spiritual Genesis*, Wilmington, Delaware: Michael Glazier, 1988.

Ó Madagáin, Murchadh, *Thérèse of Lisieux: Through Love and Suffering*, London: St. Paul's, 2003.

Peck, M. Scott, *The Road Less Travelled: A New Psychology of Love, Traditional Values and Spiritual Growth*, London: Ryder, 2003.

——. *A World Waiting to be Born: The Search for Civility*, London: Rider, 1993.

Pennington, Basil, *Centering Prayer: Renewing an Ancient Christian Prayer Form*, New York: Image Books, 2001.

———. *Daily We Touch Him: Practical Religious Experiences*, Kansas: Sheed and Ward, 1997.

———. *True Self, False Self*, New York: Crossroad, 2000.

Ponticus, Evagrius, John Eudes Bamberger (trans.), *The Praktikos and Chapters on Prayer*, Cistercian Studies Series 4, Michigan: Cistercian Publications, 1981.

Pontifical Council for Culture, Pontifical Council for Inter-religious Dialogue, *Jesus Christ the Bearer of the Water of Life: A Christian Reflection on the "New Age"*, (www.vatican.va/roman_curia/pontifical_councils/interelg/documents/rc_pc_interelg_doc_20030203_newage_en.html)

Pseudo-Dionysius, Colm Luibheid (trans.), *Pseudo-Dionysius: The Complete Works*, Classics of Western Spirituality, New York: Paulist Press, 1987.

Rahula, Walpola, *What The Buddha Taught*, New York: Grove Press, 1974.

Roth, Robert, *Maharishi Mahesh Yogi's Transcendental Meditation*, Revised ed., New York: Primus, 1994.

Reininger, Gustave (ed.), *Centering Prayer in Daily Life and Ministry*, New York: Continuum, 1998.

Schaef, Anne Wilson, *When Society Becomes an Addict*, San Francisco: Harper and Row, 1987.

St. John of the Cross, *The Collected Works of*, Kieran Kavanagh, and Otilio Rodriguez (trans.), Revised ed., Washington, DC: Institute of Carmelite Studies, 1991.

St. Teresa of Avila, *The Collected Works of*, translated by Kieran Kavanagh, and Otilio Rodriguez, Revised ed., Vols. 1 (1987) & 2 (1980), Washington, DC: Institute of Carmelite Studies.

Terruwe, Ann A., MD, and Conrad W. Baars, MD, *Psychic Wholeness and Healing: Using All the Powers of the Human Psyche*, New York: Alba House, 1981.

Underhill, Evelyn, *The Essentials of Mysticism and Other Essays*, Oxford: Oneworld Publications, 1999.

——. *Mysticism: The Nature and Development of Spiritual Consciousness*, Oxford: Oneworld Publications, 1993.

Wilber, Ken, *Up From Eden: A Transpersonal View of Human Evolution*, Wheaton, IL: Quest Books, 1996.

gerente
genio
gorra
mor(c)ielago
cigarra
detergente
cielo
siguiente